Drayton Nabers Jr.

THE CASE FOR CHARACTER

Looking at Character
from a Biblical Perspective

DRAYTON NABERS, JR.

THE CASE FOR CHARACTER
ISBN: 0-9702138-5-9
Copyright © 2006 by
Drayton Nabers, Jr.
3300 Dell Road
Birmingham, AL 35223

Published by
Christian Publishing Services
P. O. Box 701434
Tulsa, OK 74170

Text Design: Lisa Simpson

Printed in the United States of America

Endorsements

The Case for Character is a must read. The most critical need in our society is real character development. This book gives a great biblical analysis of the building blocks and the means needed for strong character and excellent illustrations of their implementation in daily living.

> Dr. Frank M. Barker, Jr.
> Briarwood Presbyterian Church
> Birmingham, Alabama

In *The Case for Character* Drayton Nabers has done a service for the church. From his vast judicial and business experience and deep faith he has spoken clearly and distinctly about the character issue in a way that is desperately needed in our day. This was personally helpful to me and has given me a valuable resource for my preaching and teaching on character.

This book will become "must" reading for my staff and lay leaders and gifts to my close pastor friends.

> Dr. Travis Coleman, Jr.
> First Baptist Church
> Prattville, Alabama

My friend Drayton Nabers is one of the most mature laymen I know. He has written this book from experience and from depth of research. I have always admired and appreciated Drayton and his work. He practices the character and virtues he writes about.

> Chuck Colson
> Founder and Chairman
> Prison Fellowship
> Lansdowne, Virginia

If you want to be a better person you need to read this book. The subject of character in the recent past has become both an image and a political issue with character guidelines summed up in slick slogans and ear-catching sound bites. While Drayton Nabers' book will give you some quotes for your next speech on character, it goes far beyond that. Drayton addresses the issue of character from a biblical perspective, but with a keen awareness of the historical philosophical framework discussed in Western culture. Rather than just focusing on behavior, Nabers goes back to the issue of the will.

This is a needed book for the Christian community. Frequently we hear and read reports that state the only difference between the Christian faith community and secular community is what they do at 11:00 a.m. on Sunday morning. Nabers' work provides a very solid blueprint on how to build and enhance character, but this is far from a self-help book that will help the reader have the appearance of character. The book provides a solid foundation for learning about the dimensions of character and how to teach it to future generations.

Nabers' life experiences add great validity to this book. He does not write as an academician, but as a man who has a proven track record as an attorney, business executive, and the Chief Justice of the State Supreme Court. This could easily be required reading for all business, law, and political science graduate students.

The chapter on the relationship between faith and character alone is more than worth the price of the book. Nabers is able to subtly avoid the historical contradictions between faith and works and show the required interconnectedness of faith, character, and behavior. In addition, the chapter on courage addresses a much-needed dimension in our culture while avoiding the oft-quoted courage clichés that keep us from examining the real issue.

You need to buy this book, read this book, teach this book, and live it because it is founded on solid biblical teaching.

Dr. Gary D. Fenton
Dawson Family of Faith
Dawson Memorial Baptist Church
Birmingham, Alabama

The Case for Character is a timely treasure. Nabers writes as a scholar with the heart of a shepherd. His insight not only discusses the problems associated with the lack of character in our land today, but also offers hope in how we might reestablish character and reclaim our heritage.

This book is refreshing, offering both hope and help for the reader's soul and the wounded soul of this great land.

Pastor Rick Hagans
Founder/President
Harvest Evangelism, Inc.
Auburn, Alabama

Drayton Nabers' book on character is badly needed in our world today. The book reminds us of the sacredness of that integral part of ourselves. The stories and points of this book are sure to make its readers think about their character or lack thereof.

Rev. Charles H. Hale, Jr.
Senior Pastor
Spanish Fort United Methodist Church

The Case for Character is a mother lode of wise, practical, well-illustrated, biblical principles which, if followed, would profoundly impact our generation. Best of all, it provides clear-minded teaching that anyone can apply. This new book will be extraordinarily helpful for me in equipping the people of our church and in training young leaders in character development.

Pastor Chris Hodges
Church of the Highlands
Birmingham, Alabama

The Case for Character is an extraordinary book and a joy to read. Drayton has poured into his lovely book both his authoritative moral and legal knowledge and his deeply felt trust in and commitment to his Lord Jesus Christ; he also has displayed the subtle connections between personal morality and public life. His book overflows with reflections on virtue, with stories from a wide range of literature and from his own experience, and with practical wisdom about life. In reading his book we are effectively listening in on a conversation of a Christian with his soul, in much the way we are when we are reading Augustine's *Confessions* or Bunyan's *Pilgrim's Progress*, and it is a bracing and enriching experience.

> Dr. Fisher Humphreys
> Beeson Divinity School
> Samford University
> Birmingham, Alabama

Drayton Nabers has produced a very readable, refreshing reminder of the balance between God's grace and men's responsibility in the crucial area of character development. This book will prove to be helpful to anyone who desires to live a life of excellence and effectiveness. It should be a good study guide for parents and teachers who desire to lead their youth to adopt a biblical worldview.

> Dr. Jimmy E. Jackson, Senior Pastor
> Whitesburg Baptist Church
> Huntsville, Alabama

For many years now, as I have watched the life of Drayton Nabers, I have seen a man whose life exemplified what a Christian should be. But just as powerful as the example of his life, this book impacted me to the very core of my being. My initial reaction after finishing this book was to quietly walk into my study and humble my heart before God and with tears in my eyes, pray, "Oh God, do Your work of grace so complete in me that my life is marked by the principles found in this powerful book."

John A. Loper, Jr., Senior Pastor
Garywood Assembly of God
Hueytown, Alabama   .
Assistant Superintendent
Alabama District Council of the
Assemblies of God

This work by Drayton Nabers is much needed in this modern day in which we live. In the midst of a culture that in many ways is characterized by situation ethics, corporate greed, and moral compromise—this is a clarion call to challenge us and help us understand *character* within a biblical context. This volume stimulated my thinking, challenged my faith, and warmed my heart; and I enthusiastically recommend it to you.

Dr. George H. Mathison, Senior Minister
Auburn United Methodist Church
Auburn, Alabama

Drayton Nabers writes clearly and boldly on the topic of character, which is desperately needed in public and private life today. His writing comes out of the wealth of his own experience, based on a biblical perspective. He gives specific applications of how biblical character can be applied in all aspects of life. He is very transparent in his own successes and failures, which offer hope to all of us to move forward in strengthening our own characters. This is an excellent book. It can make a real difference in our lives and in our families, businesses, and governments. I highly recommend it.

Dr. John Ed Mathison, Senior Minister
Frazer Memorial United Methodist Church
Montgomery, Alabama

Clearly and compellingly written, Drayton Nabers' book explains the virtues necessary to the development of godly character. His use of Scripture, history, and anecdote illustrates how a holy life is achieved and how communities and nations are transformed. This book is a ***must read*** for anyone in pursuit of righteousness who recognizes the necessity of grace. It is also for those whose faith is vague but who suspect that they are not fully the people they can be. The author points all readers to how internal change can occur and how dramatic the outward effects may be. His challenge is for people in every season of life.

Norman H. McCrummen III, Ph.D.
Senior Pastor
Spring Hill Presbyterian Church
Mobile, Alabama

The Apostle Paul encourages us to "walk in a manner worthy of the Lord, fully pleasing to him, bearing fruit in every good work...." (Colossians 1:10) This book will help all sincere followers of Christ realize the secret of walking in a manner worthy of the Lord and enable them to bear fruit in every good work. Our character is the evidence of our walk with the Lord. This is not a book about self-reformation but it is a balanced work describing God's grace and our responsibility. This book differs from most that I have read on character because of the author's emphasis on the grace of God in the believer's life. Nabers challenges us to evaluate life in terms of our purpose, our principles that we live by, and our ultimate source of power. This is an excellent work that I believe God will use to enable us to please Him in all respects.

Rev. Keith Pugh, Pastor
First Baptist Church
Sylacauga, Alabama

Drayton Nabers has provided for us an important and crucial work that calls us to the development of character by the grace of God and for the glory of God, to *know* who we are in Christ, to *be* who we are in Christ, and to *live* according to those glorious truths. In a day in which people declare "perception is reality," this book will call us to bring the reality of substance into life beginning with a heart relationship *with* Christ and a renewed mind *for* Christ. It is my privilege to recommend it as well as purposely enjoy it and use it.

Pastor Harry Reeder III
Briarwood Presbyterian Church
Birmingham, Alabama

Drayton Nabers has written a masterpiece that opens the eye and touches the heart. It is a thought-provoking, heart exposing, stimulating, yet encouraging road map to practical righteousness. He does not just skim through the fruit, but he gets to the root. This book produces "longing" and "loving." It will cause a longing to have more of Christ's character and your love will increase as you understand what Jesus has made available for you. Parts of it you will read and parts of it will read you. But if you take and heed, it will result in the sweet nectar of character flowing from your being.

Pastor Kyle Searcy
Fresh Anointing International Church
Montgomery, Alabama

Drayton Nabers' *The Case For Character* restores an often misused and misunderstood term to its rightful place in Christian ethics. Pointing to the dance between God's plan and our participation in that plan, this book is a good primer for all who would be called disciples of Jesus. I love this book!

Richmond Webster, Rector
Saint Luke's Episcopal Church
Birmingham, Alabama

The Case for Character is a masterpiece – a treasury of practical wisdom! Drayton Nabers has provided a powerful, instructive, and provocative work which effectively addresses a massive need in our culture. We live in a world of characters who lack character. Nabers has effectively crafted a balanced look at character's definition, development, and practical implementation into all regions of daily life.

Nabers provides a compelling call for character that rings true because of the authenticity of Nabers' walk with Christ. Drayton is a brilliant scholar yet practical follower of Jesus Christ. His private world and public service have been fashioned and fueled by his deep and personal relationship with God. His faith in Christ is the centerpiece of His worldview and the compelling motivation for his attitudes and actions.

Drayton's keen insights in *The Case for Character* are inspirational and applicable. His clear call makes complete sense – *"Our purpose is to glorify God which demands that we develop strong character in God's grace – having virtues engraved on us – so that we can become trees that bear sweet fruit for God's glory."*

This is also a practical book, well-designed for teaching and small group study. Though there is a logical progression from beginning to end, each chapter is essentially self-contained. And each chapter is full of fresh insight into basic issues of Christian character. Remarkably, the book will speak to disciples across a broad spectrum of maturity from those who are taking their first steps to those who are advanced. The book is likewise cross-denominational. All serious believers will be fed by the themes developed by Nabers.

America's corporate landscape is littered with the financial wreckage of giant companies that were toppled due to a lack of the indispensable ingredient of character. *The Case for Character* is a timely and timeless treasure. Absorbing and applying Nabers' call for character will not only prevent catastrophic personal and corporate losses, but it will add exhilarating joy and fulfillment to your journey.

Jesus said, *"You will know them by their fruits."* The fruits of Drayton Nabers' pen, personal character, and public service provide an inspiring and instructive model. I highly recommend learning and living the invaluable lessons of *The Case for Character.*

Dr. Jay Wolf, Pastor
First Baptist Church
Montgomery, Alabama

Dedication

To my wife, Fairfax, a precious gift from God to me.

Blessed is the man who trusts in the LORD,
whose trust is the LORD.
He is like a tree planted by water,
that sends out its roots by the stream,
and does not fear when heat comes,
for its leaves remain green,
and is not anxious in the year of drought,
for it does not cease to bear fruit.

—Jeremiah 17:7-8

By this my Father is glorified, that you bear much fruit and
so prove to be my disciples.

—John 15:8

Contents

Preface

"Character counts" is an understatement. Character is crucially important for an abundant life. The purpose of this book is both to deepen our understanding of this fundamental truth and to discuss how we grow strong in character.

Our happiness depends on character. So does the peace of our souls. Our success in family and business depends upon our character. The strength of our nation's government and its economy rests on good character. In fact, character is the single most important building block for quality of life in any individual, company, team, or nation.

Most importantly for the Christian believer, bringing glory to God and being a worthy steward of His gifts depend on character. Beyond conversion, the development of biblical character should be the first priority of the Christian. Christians are called by God "to be conformed to the image of his Son" (Romans 8:29-30). Being so conformed is a process of character formation: It is putting on the character of Christ.

As important as character is, we have, by and large, lost our understanding of character and the ability to talk about it except in vague terms. There are two primary reasons for this.

First, as Stephen Covey tells us, at about the end of the First World War we shifted our main concern about fulfillment in life from a character-based ethic to a personality-based ethic.[1] A character-based ethic, Covey explains, is based on the belief that a full life derives from deep-seated habits that must be developed for good character to be forged. This process takes time (what Covey calls the "law of the harvest" because a farmer can do little to speed up the growth of a crop). According to Covey the personality ethic, on the other hand, teaches that success relates primarily to attitude, techniques, and image and that we can change our personalities almost instantly to develop successful relationships in family and business.

It is easy for the personality ethic to creep into our thoughts. In America we want quick solutions and easy answers. We are in a hurry. We want to achieve success *now*. We want techniques that turn our life around instantly. Such thought is all too welcome in our churches and in our hearts as we face life's obstacles. The problem is, there are no quick solutions or easy answers.

A second reason that character has not been a focus in the Christian church is that in our tradition a character ethic has been seen as being opposed to the doctrine of grace. It is said that character relates to self-development rather than to grace, which is perceived as the power through which God transforms man apart from human effort. The character ethic, it is feared, stands for a concept of self-mastery that is at tension with the Christian ethic of self-denial.[2] For this reason Christian literature, especially on the Protestant side, has shied away from exploration of character.

The tension perceived between God's role and ours in developing good character has long been with us. The thesis of this book is that God's grace and our efforts to develop godly character are not in opposition but instead work together. Grace works through character, which we, in grace, have a responsibility to develop. I find this theme solidly within the Christian tradition and biblically sound.

We need to recenter the character ethic in American life, in our churches, in our families, in our schools, and in ourselves. This book is an effort to help us understand what recentering character means, in biblical terms. At the very least, I hope it opens a dialogue among those such as I who seek to serve God and others in ordinary callings in business, hourly work, the professions, family, and community.

Part one of this book is about the building blocks of character—purpose, principle, and power. In it we will seek to understand what character really is, namely a bundle of character traits (virtues or vices) that have grown and strengthened in us over time. We will see how character should be shaped in terms of the ultimate purpose in our life, the moral precepts that are to guide us, and the grace by which God empowers us.

Part two is about the eight character traits (virtues) at the core of a life that glorifies God: humility, faith, hope, wisdom, courage, self-control, justice, and love. We will explore the tight interrelationship among these virtues and also a sequence that must begin with humility and must end with love. As we discuss the character traits, we will seek to understand how in God's grace they can grow in each of us.

In part three the discussion turns to a more practical level to show how character relates to government, business, and leadership. We will see how we cannot be free spiritually, politically, morally, or economically without strong character. It is my hope to show that biblical virtues lead to a more successful and abundant life in the everyday world of work and family than does any other combination of character traits.

In the conclusion I discuss briefly why our nation finds it so difficult to arrive at a solution to the challenges we all see in forging stronger character. The simple answer is that there is no top-down solution to our character dilemma. Character is a matter that is developed in each of us, one by one, from the inside out.

This book is written from the perspective of the Christian faith. I am aware that this might be off-putting—even offensive—to some, but it is the only book that is in me to write. I have little to add on the subject apart from this point of view. For those who may find it inappropriate, I apologize.[3]

By no means do I think that Christians have a monopoly on strong character. I have known many who do not hold to the Christian faith who are more generous, courageous, humble, and loving than I.

The subject of this book is very important. I would not be truthful if I did not say that at times I have felt inadequate for the task.

Many have helped me along the way.

The periodical *First Things* has been a cornucopia of fresh insights on character from a biblical perspective, and to its editor in chief, Richard John Neuhaus, I am particularly indebted.

I thank all those who have discussed character in clear, nonacademic ways, especially Chuck Colson, Dallas Willard, Michael Novak, Os Guinness, Stephen Covey, and Scott Peck.

Of those who have gone before us, C. S. Lewis and Oswald Chambers have contributed greatly to my understanding of character from a biblical perspective.

I was allowed to teach a course at Beeson Divinity School on this subject, maturing my thinking immensely. To the students in that course who taught me more than I taught them, I offer thanks.

To Eric Stanford, who helped with editing, I am enormously grateful. He was a stimulating sounding board as I sought to sharpen my thought and analysis. By no means is he responsible for any of the ideas, much less the errors and weaknesses, in the book. You can rest assured that where ideas may be faulty or not well presented, he tried to help but was rebuffed by me. If you find the text clearly written, he deserves the credit.

To my wife, Fairfax, who put up with my absence from her in fact or in thought all too long as I wrote this book, I express both thanks and apologies. She has been a source of sound advice, wisdom, and love for me for more than two-thirds of my life.

Finally, if this book has not been inspired by the Holy Spirit, everything about it is lost. I have tried to be faithful to His direction and prompting. As for whatever may be found worthy in this book, to God alone be the glory.

Part 1

The Foundation of Character

We are his workmanship, created in Christ Jesus for good works, which God prepared beforehand, that we should walk in them.

—Ephesians 2:10

Introduction to Part 1

The United States is a land full of people of strong character. Our moral capital is abundant as God blesses this country. We saw strong character in the "greatest generation"—for example, in their reconstruction of Japan and the Marshall Plan. This virtue came to the fore again after September 11, 2001, and we see it today in our efforts to establish a beachhead of freedom in Iraq. I see it in the morning on the way to work before dawn; the road is teeming with eighteen-wheelers and pick-ups, all transporting productive people who are already at work serving others.

Several decades ago, Russell Kirk, one of the keenest observers of America in the second half of the twentieth century, wrote that the "regeneration of spirit and character" should be our nation's primary concern.[1] At first blush many of us would not rate regeneration of character as our highest priority. We might rank economics, health, or education concerns higher. But when we think about it, perhaps we would conclude that Kirk is right about character, even today.

Despite the deep reserve of moral capital in our nation, we worry, and rightly so, that this reserve is diminishing. We know that the breakdown of the traditional family is a primary cause. We deplore the negative influence of rock stars and Hollywood flimsies. We lament the lack of discipline in our schools and the rising tide of drug abuse and gambling.

We know we have a character problem in this country. We see it in the suburbs and in the inner city. We find it in the boardrooms and in our families. We've seen it in the casinos, on the Internet, and in the popular songs. It's there in our prisons. We've even seen it in sports. If we look at statistics on accounting scandals, tax fraud, gambling, pornography, abortions, unwed mothering, teenage pregnancies, and the like, it is easy to become alarmed.

Though our concern about character is often expressed in a national scope, and almost always we talk about the problems others have, this book is not about "them." It is about "us," or even better, "me." It is too easy to leave responsibility for the character challenge with others and forget that "It's me, it's me, O Lord, standing in the need of prayer." This book is for those, especially its author, who need to better understand our own characters and how in God's grace and through our faith they can be strengthened. Only as we as individuals grow in character can our national character be restored.

In order to understand what character really is, where do we begin? Alasdair MacIntyre has told us that we have lost our understanding of what character is all about.[2] Those who came before my generation delved deeply into the subject. They learned about virtue and studied the great figures of our history in terms of character. Those in my generation and later, however, were not taught much about character in school. We have even lost the vocabulary of character.

Thus, we have lost touch with a subject that has a rich and noble tradition. We need to recover that tradition, understanding what the Bible, and sound thinkers outside the Bible, teach about character. We need to be able to formulate a view of character for ourselves.

Part one of this book attempts to do just that. It offers a biblical framework for character that we can apply in our daily life.

1

Why Character Counts

Theologian Dietrich Bonhoeffer, an opponent of National Socialism in his native Germany, moved to the United States in the summer of 1939 when he was offered a teaching position in New York. But he quickly grew uncomfortable with this choice to move. "I have come to the conclusion that I made a mistake in coming to America," he said. "I shall have no right to take part in the restoration of Christian life in Germany after the war unless I share the trials of this time with my people."[1]

He returned to Germany to support the Confessing (anti-Nazi) Church in Germany, participate in the resistance movement, and even conspire in a plot to assassinate Hitler. He was arrested in 1943 and after a lengthy incarceration was finally hanged in the concentration camp at Flossenbürg on April 9, 1945, only days before the end of the war in Europe. The SS doctor who witnessed Bonhoeffer's death later recalled, "I have hardly ever seen a man die so entirely submissive to the will of God."[2]

What made Bonhoeffer leave safety in America and return to a place where he knew he might suffer grim consequences? In a word, character. This was a man who knew what God wanted of him and was willing to do it, even if his friends and every instinct of self-preservation were crying out for him to do otherwise, to hunker down, to play it safe.

At one point Bonhoeffer said of his fellow German Christians during that dark time in human history, "We have been silent witnesses of evil deeds; we have been drenched by many storms; we have learnt the arts of equivocation and pretence; experience has made us suspicious of others and kept us from being truthful and open; intolerable conflicts have worn us down and even made us cynical. Are we still of any use?"[3] That final question must make us ask of ourselves, are *we* of any use? Do *we* have the character to do what is right, regardless of risk, cost, or ridicule? It's all about character.

Let's begin by establishing what exactly it is that we are talking about.

What Is Character?

The Oxford English Dictionary defines *character* as "a distinctive mark impressed, engraved, or otherwise formed." When we talk about character, then, we are referring to traits that lie deep within us, engraved in our hearts and souls through practice as an artisan engraves a design in silver or stone.

Because character is engraved in us, it has a permanence about it. Not only does character count, but also we can count on character. Because character is predictable, each day millions of decisions are based upon it. Résumés, credit reports, college transcripts, and sports statistics tell us how a person has performed in the past, and we make decisions assuming an individual will continue to behave in the same way in the future.

That assumption is usually correct. A person who has been honest for years can in general be trusted to be honest tomorrow. It is as if honesty has been engraved into him. By the same token, we expect that a person who has lied in the past will continue to lie in the future.

The permanent, engraved nature of character is well illustrated by President Eisenhower. Biographer Stephen Ambrose made this observation of Ike as he moved from military leadership to politics: "By 1952, the year Eisenhower entered politics at age sixty-two, his character … was set in concrete. It included qualities of love, honesty, faithfulness, responsibility, modesty, generosity, duty and leadership, along with a hatred of war. These were bedrock."[4]

Character is bedrock. And it is about the kind of people we become over time, as a sapling grows into a magnificent tree.

Healthy Trees

More than twenty-five hundred years ago, the ancient Greeks were the first culture to study character. Interestingly, their word for character was "ethics." In today's world, when we think about ethics, we tend to focus on the "goodness" or "rightness" of particular actions—whether abortion should be legal, whether stem cell research should be allowed, whether a particular war is just. But the Greeks came at things from the other direction. For them, the key to good action was good character. They focused their efforts not so much on determining what was good as on becoming good people. Why? Because they knew that a good person—one with good character engraved in his or her soul—would likely do good.

This was also Jesus' message. We see it, for example, when He taught, "Every healthy tree bears good fruit, but the diseased tree bears bad fruit. A healthy tree cannot bear bad fruit, nor can a diseased tree bear good fruit. Every tree that does not bear good fruit is cut down and thrown into the fire. Thus you will recognize them by their fruits" (Matthew 7:17-20).

The study of character is really the study of how to mature into a "healthy tree," or a person who naturally inclines to do the right thing. And this depends on virtue—an internal orientation that frees us to be good people.

Good Habits

Virtue is a word that was out of favor for years. However, since around 1990 (and aided in 1993 with the publication of Bill Bennett's *The Book of Virtues*) it has been more frequently used. But what is a virtue? The concept of virtue has several dimensions.

First, virtues are sources of strength and energy. The word *virtue* comes from the same Latin root as does *virility*. A virtue has moral power in the same way that a virile man is powerful.

Second, the traditional meaning of virtue has always been "excellence"—not excellence in a vacuum, but always excellence in relation to a purpose. Fish, for instance, are made to swim. Thus, virtue in a fish relates to the characteristics of the fish that make it an excellent swimmer. For those of us seeking moral excellence, virtues allow us to be excellent as we seek to fulfill all the purposes in our lives—as mothers and fathers, husbands and wives, church members, employees, professionals, athletes, citizens, or friends.

Finally, virtues are good habits. Habits are deep-seated patterns of thought and action that we develop through practice. Put another way, habits are strengths for good or evil that are "engraved" in us.

President Ronald Reagan gave an eloquent summary of how character develops and displays itself in our lives.

> The character that takes command in moments of crucial choices has already been determined. It has been determined by a thousand other choices made earlier in seemingly unimportant moments. It has been determined by all those "little" choices of years past—by all those times when the voice of conscience was at war with the voice of temptation, whispering a lie that "it doesn't really matter." It has been determined by all the day-to-day decisions made when life seemed easy and crises seemed far away, the decisions that, piece by piece, bit by bit, developed *habits* of discipline or of laziness; *habits* of self-sacrifice or self-indulgence; *habits* of duty and honor and integrity—or dishonor and shame.[5]

President Reagan was passing on the wisdom of the ages. Crises reveal our character, and the character revealed is the product of habits developed through the years, good and bad, as we have moved through life.

This short poem—one that may be familiar to you—puts it another way.

Sow a thought, reap an action.
Sow an action, reap a habit.
Sow a habit, reap a character.
Sow a character, reap a destiny.

Little actions matter, and matter a lot, because of what they lead to.

It is this last aspect of virtue as a pattern of good habits that we will emphasize in this book, for deliberately developed good habits have the power to change our lives in wonderful ways.

A Habit and a Joy

We don't much like the word *habit* these days. Our "liberated" culture tells us that spontaneity, innovation, and creativity, not habit, are the keys to a full life. We associate habit with being regimented or programmed, and we would rather think of ourselves as free. But good habits—that is, virtues—are friends, not enemies, of freedom. Virtues are strong and liberating, freeing us to be all we can be.

Oxford professor C. S. Lewis described character, virtue, and habit in terms of a tennis player:

> There is a difference between doing some particular just or temperate action and being a just or temperate man. Someone who is not a good tennis player may now and then make a good shot. What you mean by a good player is the man whose eye and muscles and nerves have been so trained by making innumerable good shots that they can now be relied on. They have a certain tone or quality which is there even when he is not playing, just as a mathematician's mind has a certain habit and outlook which is there even when he is not doing mathematics. In the same way a man who perseveres in doing just actions gets in the end a certain quality of character.

Now it is that quality rather than the particular actions which we mean when we talk of "virtue."[6]

Virtue is a character strength leading to excellence that comes through training and repetition. In this light, acquiring good habits, far from constricting us, is essential to freeing us to achieve excellence in whatever is truly important to us.

Now let's move from tennis to golf.

As I write, Vijay Singh is one of the best golfers in the world. In 2004, Singh won nearly twice as much money as the player who finished second on the PGA tour. And who works hardest on the practice tee? Vijay Singh. All those hours of practice have helped Singh internalize—engrave, if you will—the patterns of thought and action that make him a winner. Those hours of practice haven't deprived Singh of freedom. Far from it. Instead, they have freed him to be the best.

There's something going on in this example besides mere repetition. First, there's a payoff for practice. Singh wins tournaments. More importantly, there is internal reward for a job well done. Singh loves the feeling of doing his best on the course. (Any amateur golfer can understand the feeling.)

A habit, in its most profound meaning, is more than pure repetition. In order for the internalization that converts a behavior pattern into a habit to occur, repeating the pattern must feel good inside. Somehow it must feed the soul. A virtue is an internalized habit that does something satisfying for us inside, for when it does not, it becomes drudgery, performed only because it is ordered or necessary. Virtues give us a sense of internal joy, and thus the habit that sustains them is rewarding.[7]

Now that we have a better understanding of what a virtue is, what are the key virtues, and how many are there?

Virtues and Vices

Many qualities and characteristics have been described as virtues by one or another writer. For example, Bennett's *Book of Virtues* lists ten virtues. An anthology on virtue by Scott Peck lists ninety.

This book, primarily in part two, will focus on eight virtues. Four of them—wisdom, justice, courage, and self-control—have been known through the ages as the "cardinal" virtues. The word *cardinal* originally meant "hinge." For believers, these four virtues join the four Christian virtues of humility, faith, hope, and love to open the door to a full, robust life that is lived to God's honor.

Meanwhile, we cannot forget the shadow side to virtues: their opposites, the vices. These are internal orientations that constrict and enslave us, preventing us from developing the sort of character God would like us to have. An old adage says it well: "The chains of habit are too light to feel before they become too heavy to break." Just as a vise in a tool shop provides a tight grip to hold objects in place, so vices hold us in bondage, spiritually and morally.

A good character is simply a cluster of virtues; a bad one, a cluster of vices. The truth is that we all have both virtues and vices. As Paul teaches, the Christian life is a process of "taking off" the bad habits (he calls these the "old self with its practices") and "putting on" the good ones—that is, "the new self, created to be like God in true righteousness and holiness" (Ephesians 4:24 NIV; See also Colossians 3:9).

Doing and Being

If virtues are good habits growing from practice, it is clear that what we do repeatedly is a key to the development of our characters. What we do relates powerfully to who we become. As J. C. Ryle says, "God has wisely ordained that our well-being and well-doing are tied together."[8]

A child is initially disobedient because he is born that way. If through discipline and training the disobedience is resisted and the habits of obedience are taught and instilled in the child, the child becomes obedient. If not, the disobedience becomes a habit and a vice and the resulting pattern of conduct greatly influences who the child is. Likewise, becoming an Eagle Scout or doing a four-year stint in the Marines develops good habits, or virtues, that deeply influence who we are.

Here we must be careful. We all know being (who we are inside) is more fundamental than doing (what we do). We agree with the old adage that we sin because we are sinners, not vice versa. Character is all about becoming a tree that produces good fruit—becoming a human *being* who naturally inclines to do the right thing. Thus the focus of character is first on being. But what we do has profound influence on who we are. Habits, good or bad, are powerful, so the study of character also focuses on doing.

For character, being and doing are like two blades of a pair of scissors. Who we are determines what we do, and what we do strongly affects who we are. Still, we would agree with Oswald Chambers, who says, "The only thing that exceeds right-*doing* is right-*being*."[9]

We can get the doing and being right if we will see character in its proper context.

The Character Framework

In his popular *Mere Christianity*, C. S. Lewis has given us an illustration to understand morality and character's place within it. Imagine a fleet of ships, he says. How do they sail without getting lost or bumping into one another?

The ships need three things. First, if their voyage is to be successful, they need a specific *destination*. Second, the ships must have *rules* for their formation and for their roles in the fleet's mission. Third, the ships must have *internal systems*—

sails or engines, mechanical, electrical, and navigational equipment, rudders, and so on.[10]

What is true for a fleet of ships, Lewis tells us, is true for people. Our "destination" is our *purpose* in life, given to us by God. Our "rules" are biblical *principles*, showing us how to live, believe, and make choices in daily life. Our "internal systems" are our habits of doing what is right—our *character*, in short.

All this is fine as far as it goes, but I would add one element to Lewis's analogy. Along with a destination, rules, and internal systems, a fleet of ships also needs a source of *power*. For the ships, this power comes from wind in the sails or fuel for the engines to propel the fleet on its way. In terms of character, our source of power is the Holy Spirit or God's grace. We cannot be people of strong character merely by trying hard; we become people of character who live by God's rules and fulfill God's ultimate purpose for our lives only if we have God's grace in us by His Spirit.

We can put this all together in a triangle diagram. The three P's—purpose, principles, and power—are located at the points of the triangle. They guide, shape, and strengthen the virtues that form our character—the center of it all.

The Character Triangle

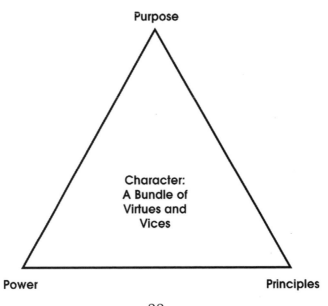

Purpose

Character:
A Bundle of
Virtues and
Vices

Power

Principles

As we discuss the elements of this triangle in the pages ahead, we will notice that for us as believers our purpose, the principles to guide us, and the power to get us there all come from God. Character formation—developing the internal systems (virtues) so we become a good tree bearing good fruit— is the joint work of God and ourselves. It is the part of the character context where we have responsibility through faith. We will also see that without character formed around biblical virtues, God's purpose, principles, and power risk being forfeited.[11]

In chapter two, we will be looking at the purpose dimension of the character framework. In chapter three, we will move on to the principles and power aspects. In it all, we will be learning how to become the people God wants us to be, engraved with the behavior patterns that in His goodness He chose for us from before the foundation of the world.

Character Questions

1. In your view, what is character and what significance does it have in your life?

2. Do you agree with the idea that we can ingrain character in our lives through habit? Why or why not?

3. What specific character issues for your own life do you think you ought to keep in mind as you read this book?

2

Our Ultimate Purpose

For many years I worshiped in the same church with Julia, a fine Christian woman so wracked by arthritis that she is confined to a stretcher and in pain most of the time. The only way she can get to church is for her friends to carry her in. *What a shame,* we might think. *The woman is so dependent.* But if we think that way, we would be wrong.

Julia is a great pray-er. Apart from a pure heart and a joyful spirit, her ability to pray is perhaps her primary gift. But I can tell you that for those of us who know her, it is a tremendous comfort when we get a chance to tell Julia of the concerns on our hearts. For we know that a great saint will be interceding earnestly and powerfully on our behalf.

As an example of how Julia's prayers "availeth much," consider her prayers for a young woman named Julie. This woman was advised by her obstetrician that the baby she was carrying in her womb had died. After all the medical testing, the doctor confirmed that the baby had no heartbeat, wrote "miscarriage" on her chart, and scheduled Julie for a D&C the following week to remove the fetus. When Julia, our pray-er, was asked to pray over the situation, she answered that the Lord was telling her that Julie's baby was not dead and that the family should join her in interceding for a heartbeat. Reminded of the diagnosis, Julia stated, "Why, doctors make mistakes, but the Great Physician makes no mistakes." A few days later, when Julie reported for her D&C, the baby inexplicably had a strong heartbeat. The doctor proclaimed it a "medical miracle." Julie just praised the Lord and thanked Julia.

Due to her physical condition, Julia may not have a lot to offer physically, but what she has, she uses to the glory of God and the building of His kingdom. I believe she brings as much joy to God as does the most mesmerizing preacher, the most talented worship musician, or the most erudite Bible scholar. And she shows us that nothing is limiting us from glorifying God in our lives except we ourselves.

Building a Christian character, as we learned in the previous chapter, takes three things: heading toward the right purpose, living by biblical principles, and drawing on the power of God. In this chapter we will be focusing on the first part, our ultimate purpose in life. We might have many purposes in life, but we need to make sure that the number-one purpose remains number one, or else we will become sidetracked. Julia is fulfilling her ultimate purpose.

In Pursuit of Purpose

When Vince Lombardi became head coach of the Green Bay Packers in 1969, his purpose was to build a football team that would win championships. He put his goal this way: "To be the New York Yankees of football. World champions, every day, year-round. Admired everywhere."[1]

All worthwhile endeavors begin with a lofty purpose. Your life has one, as does mine.

Serious people throughout the ages have studied the question of what the purpose of mankind is. Two ancient peoples, the Greeks and the Hebrews, gave this question considerable thought, and their answers provide us with helpful insights.

The ancient Greeks in the main believed mankind's primary purpose is to attain long-term happiness. To them, happiness meant satisfaction and peace over the course of a lifetime. Thus, the Greeks believed a person should first think about what would make him happy in the most important endeavors of his life—marriage, career, parenting, faith—and then develop virtues that would allow him to attain those goals.

This long-term focus can be useful. Stephen Covey refers to this approach as "beginning with the end in mind." To illustrate what this means in practice, Covey gives us an uncomfortable thought assignment: envisioning our own funeral. He asks us to imagine the eulogies that a relative, a fellow church member, a business colleague, and someone from our community would deliver.[2]

What kind of person do we want such speakers to describe? What sort of life do we want them to say we led? The answers to these questions can help us define the kind of life we want to live, the end to which our life should point.

In many ways, this approach is a sound way to think about our time on earth. It causes us to take a long view of the important things in life and for most of us it will result in a noble vision for our lives. And that vision should guide us to develop those virtues that empower us to live toward that vision.

But there's a problem with this approach: Its reference point is us. It's a self-centered way to think about life. It concentrates on what others think of us. And any approach that does not reach beyond us to the eternal is flawed.

The ancient Jewish nation considered the question of life's ultimate purpose, and their answer was far more profound than that of the Greeks. Why? Because it pointed beyond self to God.

The Old Testament contains several summaries of life's ultimate purpose for the children of Israel. One states, "Israel, what does the LORD your God require of you, but to fear the LORD your God, to walk in all his ways, to love him, to serve the LORD your God with all your heart and with all your soul, and to keep the commandments and statutes of the LORD?" (Deuteronomy 10:12-13).

The primary purpose in life for the Israelites was righteousness—loving and serving God by obeying His law. This goes well beyond the self-focused approach of the Greeks' concept of happiness. It doesn't ask us whether we would be satisfied with an appraisal of our life at its end; rather, it asks whether God is satisfied with our lives now.

The Christian concept of life's ultimate purpose is based solidly upon the Hebrew approach.

The Chief End of Man

What is the ultimate purpose of the Christian life? If we were at a seminar and divided into small groups to consider this question, we would likely arrive at several different answers. But to my mind, the best answer is found in the Westminster Catechism, which the Puritans gave us some 360 years ago.

The Westminster Catechism gets straight to the fundamental character issue in its first question: "What is the chief end of man?" The catechism's reply? "Man's chief end is to glorify God, and to enjoy him for ever."

When I first considered this answer, I was uncomfortable with it. Why didn't the catechism speak of love of God or love of neighbor? Why didn't it mention faith or Christlikeness?

But as I pondered the issue, I became convinced that the Puritans had it right. I began to see that the whole of biblical revelation, from God's acts of creation in Genesis to the wedding supper of the Lamb in Revelation, is about the glory of God and our blessed hope through Jesus Christ to enjoy Him forever.[3] I was helped to this conclusion by some prayers I had adopted.

For some time, my regular prayers relating to everyday affairs had included three based upon Scripture: 1 Peter 4:10-11, Hebrews 13:20-21, and Ephesians 3:14-21.[4] I had memorized the meat of these teachings but not their endings. One day I noticed that the ending of each pointed to the glory of God forever.

- "... in order that in everything God may be glorified through Jesus Christ. To him belong the glory and dominion forever and ever. Amen" (1 Peter 4:11).

- "...through Jesus Christ, to whom be glory for ever" (Hebrews 13:21 NIV).

- "to him be glory in the church and in Jesus Christ throughout all generations, for ever and ever. Amen" (Ephesians 3:21 NIV).

This language is all-inclusive, referring to all things, everywhere, and for all time. As I used these passages for prayer relating to the mundane affairs of daily living, focusing for the first time on their endings was an epiphany for me. Everything I do was to relate to God's glory.

I was past age forty when God finally got my attention. But understanding our ultimate purpose is critically important. If we don't get the ultimate purpose right, nothing else in our life will fall into place. It's like buttoning a sweater. If the first button is off, every other one will be as well.

It is easy for us as Christians to lose sight of the ultimate question. And as we do, we err in thinking about what constitutes a morally good life. Our ultimate purpose needs to be a part of daily consciousness and it needs to relate to everything we do and every significant decision we make.

How do we glorify God?

We glorify God principally by bearing fruit in good works.

Fruit Bearing

The importance of the fruit of good works is a recurrent theme in Scripture. In fact, the first commission in Scripture is to "be fruitful and multiply" (Genesis 1:22). In the writings of Isaiah, the nation of Israel is compared to a vineyard planted to produce good grapes (Isaiah 5:1-7). The theme that we are to produce good fruit was introduced in the New Testament by John the Baptist when he preached, "Every tree ... that does not bear good fruit is cut down and thrown into the fire" (Matthew 3:10). But Jesus had the most to say about fruit bearing.

One day Jesus walked by a fig tree bearing no fruit and cursed it: "May no fruit ever come from you again!" (Matthew 21:19). Later, echoing John the Baptist, Jesus concludes His parable of the tenants by telling the Pharisees that "the kingdom of God will be taken away from you and given to a people producing its fruits" (v. 43).

In Luke we find the parable of the barren fig tree, whose owner wants the plant cut down. The vinedresser appeals for an extra year to fertilize the tree so that it might produce fruit. The owner consents but adds, "Then if it should bear fruit next year, well and good; but if not, you can cut it down" (Luke 13:9).

The night before He was crucified, Jesus taught, "This is to my Father's glory, that you bear much fruit, showing your-selves to be my disciples ... I chose you and appointed you to go and bear fruit—fruit that will last" (John 15:8,16 NIV).

In simple terms, Jesus was telling the disciples (and us) how to glorify God. We are to bear fruit—not a little fruit but "much fruit." And not just perishable fruit but fruit of the eternal sort—"fruit that will last." This is not just some inci-dental part of the Christian life; according to Christ, it is the task for which He chose us.

Bruce Wilkinson, author of *Secrets of the Vine,* says the Bible uses the term "fruit" as a synonym for the phrase "good works." Practically speaking, Wilkinson says, "fruit represents good works—a thought, attitude, or action of ours that God values because it glorifies Him. *The fruit from your life is how God receives His due honor on earth.*"[5]

Wilkinson drives the point home. "Jesus loved to convey the deepest truths with simple, earthy examples. In His last message before His death, He wanted you and me to compre-hend with our whole being that He has left us on this planet for one compelling reason—it has everything to do with fruit."[6]

It's important to realize that Jesus was a production-oriented vineyard owner. He cared immensely about both what we do and how we do it. Though He concentrated on our hearts, He was also concerned with our actions. (Remember, being and doing are two blades of a single pair of scissors—see chapter one.)

Clearly, we need to pay attention to our spiritual fruit bearing if we want to fulfill our ultimate purpose of glorifying God. And that means doing good works which flow from being a good tree.

Created for Good Works

The Scriptures do not always rely upon the metaphor of fruit bearing; they also come out and plainly state that we are to glorify God through good works. As Jesus says in His Sermon on the Mount, "Let your light shine before others, so that they may see your good works and give glory to your Father who is in heaven" (Matthew 5:16).

The apostle Paul emphasized the importance of good works as much as did his Lord. In his letter to Titus, Paul says that Jesus gave Himself on the cross to redeem us and "to purify for himself a people of his own possession who are zealous for good works" (Titus 2:14). In 2 Corinthians 9:8 Paul states that God's grace abounds to us so that we may "abound in every good work." He wrote that we are God's "workmanship, created in Christ Jesus for good works" (Ephesians 2:10). He prayed that the Colossians would "[bear] fruit in every good work" (Colossians 1:10) and counsels Timothy that a central purpose of all Scripture is that "the man of God may be ... equipped for every good work" (2 Timothy 3:17).

Years ago, Benjamin Franklin—a theist but not a Christian—wrote to a Christian friend,

> The Faith you mention has doubtless its use in the World. I do not desire to see it diminished, nor would I endeavor to lessen it in any Man. But I wish it were more productive of Good Works than I have generally seen it: I mean real good Works, Works of Kindness, Charity, Mercy, and Publick Spirit; not Holiday-keeping, Sermon-Reading or Hearing, performing Church Ceremonies, or making long Prayers, fill'd with Flatteries and Compliments,

despis'd even by wise Men, and much less capable of pleasing the Deity. The Worship of God is a Duty, the hearing and reading of Sermons may be useful; but if Men rest in Hearing and Praying, as too many do, it is as if a Tree should value itself on being water'd and putting forth Leaves, tho' it never produc'd any Fruit.[7]

It's a fair criticism for our time as well as for Franklin's. We must do more than just talk Christian; we must do good works that make a difference in the real world. As the Puritans said, "The soul of religion is the practice of it."

The "End" of the Christian Life

Today's evangelical believers place great emphasis upon conversion, the "new birth" in Christ. And well we should. After all, the new birth is where eternal life begins, and without it we can neither glorify God nor enjoy Him. But we should never forget that making new converts is only the first half of Jesus' Great Commission—we are not only to baptize converts but also to make disciples and teach them to obey Christ (Matthew 28:18-20).

The new birth is not the purpose, or "end," of the Christian life. Like any birth, it is only the beginning.

Jonathan Edwards, who preached in Massachusetts during the Great Awakening of the eighteenth century, carefully studied what marked the true Christian. He rejected many characteristics: fervor in worship, the "right" talk, biblical knowledge, regular prayer, frequent church attendance, and so on. All of these, he says, were too easily "put on." Edwards concluded that the signature mark of the true Christian was fruit expressed in good works.

Looking at the new birth in relation to the "end," or purpose, of Christian life, Edwards wrote, "The new birth, which is the work of God in grace, is directly related to the fruit of good works, *for good works are the end to which the whole work of new birth is intended.* All is calculated in this great change in the soul so as to directly tend to good works. Yea, the fruit of good works is the very end of redemption in Christ."[8]

Edwards, a good Puritan, was intimately familiar with the Westminster Catechism and the doctrine of new birth. He thought in terms of the "end" of things and knew well that good works were the "end" of new life in Christ—indeed the ultimate purpose of redemption itself.

Yet, lest we think that such thoughts are antiquated and don't belong in our modern Christian thought (as if any biblical truth could be antiquated), Bruce Wilkinson tells us the same thing in 2001. "Fruit is your only permanent deposit in heaven. Real fruit always lasts! And it's the main earthly reason you were saved."[9]

The new birth is a profoundly life-changing experience. "The old has passed away; behold, the new has come" (2 Corinthians 5:17). Lives are turned around. Blind eyes are opened. New life is implanted. Desires are transformed. A glorious new way of understanding our lives and their purpose is given to us. Though a new foundation has been established, character qualities engraved deep within our souls, good and bad, remain, and the lifetime ahead is a matter of putting on the character of Christ by grace through faith.

The Taste of the Fruit

The owner of any vineyard cares about the quantity of the grapes. A good crop—a pleasing and satisfying crop—is a big crop. But taste is more important. What good is a plentiful crop if the fruit is tasteless or bitter?

In biblical terms, the taste of the fruit relates to *how* we perform good works. If what we do is not done in love, or with patience and in humility, it makes no difference how much fruit is produced. None of it will bring glory to God.

Paul provided the Bible's simplest and most vivid teaching on the importance of how we produce fruit. We can have faith sufficient to move mountains; we can give away all that we have; we can deliver our bodies to be burned as martyrs; we can understand all mysteries and have all knowledge—but if our works are not done in love, our actions are worthless (1 Corinthians 13:1-3).

We do well to remember the old saying, "God loveth the adverbs," referring to those "–ly" words that describe how something is done. We can take the categories of the fruit of the Spirit outlined in Galatians 5:22-23 and convert them to adverbs—thus, we are to bear fruit *lovingly, joyfully, peacefully,* and so forth. We can do the same with the description of love in 1 Corinthians 13:4-7: we should bear fruit *patiently, kindly,* and the rest. These adverbs provide a list describing the kingdom's market of sweet fruit.

If we are to glorify God in *what* we do, our characters need to be shaped and our hearts filled with the Holy Spirit so that *how* we do it also honors Him. Grantland Rice, the great sports writer who also composed practical spiritual poetry, says that "when the One Great Scorer" (God) comes to "write against your name,"

He marks—not that you won or lost—

But how you played the game.[10]

Ultimate Purpose in Other Purposes

Once we grasp that our ultimate purpose in life is to glorify God, and that we do so by bearing fruit in accomplishing the work He gave us to do, our every calling has a fixed point of direction on the compass. All our choices and actions—in our family lives, our work, our churches, our communities, our friendships and associations, our appointments, our conversations, our play and recreation, our every chance encounter— point toward a single objective and are judged by a single standard: Do they produce fruit that glorifies God?

Jesus, looking back on His life shortly before His crucifixion, said to the Father, "I glorified you on earth, having accomplished the work that you gave me to do" (John 17:4). His work was to serve as the Savior of the world. That was His calling, or purpose, and by fulfilling it, He brought glory to His Father.

The rest of us do not have such lofty callings. But we do have callings, and they are important in their own way.

I am currently a husband, father, grandfather, judge, and court administrator. I am satisfied that these roles are callings, divine appointments for my life. Therefore, in each of them I am to glorify God—not that I always do, but that is the end to which each of these callings point. It is not too much to say that if in any of these roles I do not glorify God, then whatever else I may accomplish really doesn't matter.

To glorify God in these roles, two things are requisite: the grace of God administered to me through His Holy Spirit and godly virtues engraved in my character through practice and habit. Both are foundational; they are merged one to the other, and God is the source of both.

I do not know what tomorrow will bring. Maybe all will go well. Maybe my plans will work smoothly. But if I am challenged, if some person gets in my way or insults me or strikes me on the right cheek, if a traffic jam makes me late to an important meeting, if plans fail or I receive bad news—in such circumstances all kinds of vices will be aroused, such as pride, greed, fear, and anger. The question is whether in God's grace there will be virtues—humility, faith, wisdom, love—in my character, worked in over the years with such depth and strength that in the power of the Holy Spirit I will react in a way that is to God's honor.

Even when there is no special test or challenge, in each of our roles there is still before us the purpose of glorifying God in all we do, and this requires all the virtues we will discuss in part two. Of course, we fall short. The point here is that once we have determined our ultimate purpose, then all of life must be directed toward it, and so directing life requires character. *Purpose demands character. Without character, there is no purpose in purpose. And, we might add, without purpose there is no need for character.*

Julia, my friend, the great pray-er, brings glory to God even though she is crippled by arthritis. Her primary calling is that of an intercessor. We, likewise, can glorify God whatever our limitations or particular situations. As glorifying God is the "end" of our life here on earth, the purpose for which Christ has called us, then our focus must be on developing a strong character in God's grace—having virtues engraved in us—so that we can become trees that bear sweet fruit for God's glory.

Critical to this process are the biblical principles God gives us to live by and the source of power He provides: His Holy Spirit. These are the subjects of chapter three.

A Postscript

We have seen that our ultimate purpose is in two parts: "to glorify God <u>and</u> enjoy Him forever." Fortunately, the two parts are tightly joined. As we live a life to God's glory, we will enjoy Him deeply here on earth and forever in eternity. Development of the second part of our ultimate purpose is not within the scope of the discussion in this book. For two books which concentrate on the second part I would suggest John Piper's *Desiring God*[11] and Randy Alcorn's *Heaven*.[12]

Character Questions

1. Do you agree with the Westminster Catechism that our ultimate purpose is to glorify God and enjoy Him forever? Why or why not?

2. What are our "good works" and how do they bring glory to God?

3. What is your calling in life, and what would it mean for you to fulfill your ultimate purpose within the context of this calling?

4. Do you agree that purpose demands character and if so are you satisfied with your character as it relates to your ultimate purpose?

3

Principles and Power for Character

Listen to the sounds of a godly man in anguish.

Even at his mature age, and with his lengthy experience as a believer, he can still be amazed at himself for what he will do when his sinful nature gets the upper hand. Bemused, he begins by admitting, "I do not understand my own actions."

Deep down, he really wants to obey God's flawless directives in Scripture, but does he do that? No. Rather, he does the opposite. "I do not do what I want, but I do the very thing I hate." Instead of righteousness, sin. Instead of light, darkness.

Trying to analyze his situation, he decides this must be true: "I have the desire to do what is right, but not the ability to carry it out. For I do not do the good I want, but the evil I do not want is what I keep on doing. Now if I do what I do not want, it is no longer I who do it, but sin that dwells within me."

He has concluded, in short, that sin is an ever-living force inside him, always combating his attempts to do right, never entirely susceptible to his own attempts to put it down. A hopeless situation, it would seem. "Wretched man that I am!" he wails.

I'm sure by now you've recognized the apostle Paul in this anguished man. He described his battle with sin in Romans 7:15-25. But his struggle could be that of any one of Christ's followers who has attempted to live right and failed.

Fortunately, Paul did not just anguish over his problem but also shared the solution to his dilemma with us. "Who will deliver me from this body of death?" he asks. And the answer came in the next breath. "Thanks be to God through Jesus Christ our Lord!" In other words, not in his own resources but in the power of Christ was there hope for defeat of the force that was keeping him from being the man he ought to have been.

Herein lie some lessons for our own pursuit of character.

We have seen that the first part of the context of our character is purpose. The second is principle. After we ascertain the purpose of our lives, we ask, what are the moral rules we are to follow as we live into our ultimate purpose? We know these two considerations—purpose and principle—are vital for all people. (They apply to organizations as well, as we will discuss in chapter twelve.) The two must be aligned. But that is not all.

We need help beyond ourselves to adhere to God's principles, because our sinful natures are strong and the temptations of the world are great. Our own strength is inadequate, so we must look to the strength of God. In the character context, we have not only an ultimate *purpose* and biblical *principles* but also Holy Spirit *power*. Together, these three form the essential groundwork for building a godly character.

Every championship team has rules and expectations relating to conditioning, behavior, practice schedules, team meetings, and the like. No team wins championships without strong discipline. The same is true for every successful business. And it is true for all of us who seek to pursue the central purpose of our lives.

It is to the role of principles in character development that we now turn.

A Most Precious Possession

One of the ancient Hebrews' greatest contributions to the world was to receive and transmit our Creator's principles for the moral order. The law of God given to the Jews through Moses is the moral foundation for all biblical people. The Jews recognized this law, which is anchored in the Ten Commandments, as a soul-nourishing gift of inestimable beauty and value that they were to meditate on day and night.

As Dallas Willard says, "The law that God had truly given to Israel was, until the coming of the Messiah, the most precious possession of human beings on earth." And it continues to be a most precious possession.

Jesus was devoted to the law, though He clearly taught that all law was to serve the ethic of love. When asked separately by a young man and a lawyer what they should do to inherit eternal life, Jesus tells both of them, in effect, "Keep the law" (see Matthew 19:16-19; Luke 10:25-26). Jesus says that "until heaven and earth pass away, not an iota, not a dot, will pass from the Law until all is accomplished" and that whoever follows the commandments and teaches others to do so will be called "great in the kingdom of heaven" (Matthew 5:18-19). He, too, issued commandments, culminating in the commandment to love one another.

Hebrew Scripture teaches that God has written within the order of creation a moral code that reflects His infinite wisdom and goodness. By developing character so that our lives can be conformed to this code, we not only please God and glorify Him but also align ourselves with the moral precepts of the universe and with God's blessing for peace and happiness during our time on earth. Conversely, if we reject God's law and live in disobedience to Him, thus setting our lives against the moral ordering of creation, we subject ourselves to heartbreak and disappointment.

Nevertheless, American believers have trouble with the notion of biblical commandments, or law, and we resist the notion of being "discipled." Two powerful lines of thought have converged to support this view. First, liberal philosophers for more than two centuries have taught that we need to be free of tradition and authority. Second, within the church, there has been an emphasis (a sound one, theologically) on salvation by grace apart from anything we do in obedience to the law.

However, in the last generation, the bankruptcy of any notion that there are no absolute moral principles to guide our lives has been made all too clear. We believers have come to understand that, although salvation is by grace apart from works, the law is still the command of a wise and moral God. Following salvation, the role of grace is to cause our souls to delight in the moral law and to develop virtues within us that empower us to obey the law. Law and grace do not oppose each other; they work together for our happiness.

When we turn to the teachings of Jesus on how to live in accordance with the Bible's moral principles, we see that His emphasis was on the development of habits in doing the things He taught. In His teachings, grace and law are most perfectly fused.

Jesus' Apprentices

In concluding His Sermon on the Mount, Jesus taught, "Everyone who hears these words of mine and *puts them into practice* is like a wise man who built his house on the rock" (Matthew 7:24 NIV, emphasis added). By telling us to put His teachings into practice—or "work them into our lives" (see MSG)—Jesus was using character precepts. He was telling us not to just go home and think or talk about His teachings but to get off the couch (metaphorically speaking) and begin to practice them, repeatedly, as a golfer practices his swing or a musician practices a scale. Then, and only then, will the virtues of Jesus' character become so engraved in our own that we become trees that produce good fruit for the Lord.

Oswald Chambers, whose *My Utmost for His Highest* has been the most popular devotional book for the last century, states that while God saves us and sanctifies us, He "will not give us good habits, He will not give us character, He will not make us walk aright. We have to do all that ourselves. We have to work out the salvation God has worked in."[1]

The biblical word "disciple" means essentially what our word *apprentice* means today, referring to one who learns by practical experience under an expert. So when Jesus commissioned the Church to make disciples, He was talking about more than teaching or Bible study; He was talking about learning an obedient way of life through daily living (Matthew 28:19-20). For Jesus, discipling was character development, not lip service.

Going back to our reference to the rules that guide a championship team, we might say that morally we are no complicated sports program. But there are a multitude of facets that are involved in a disciple's life.

Jonathan Edwards adopted seventy resolutions for his life. Here are a few of them, just to give us an example of principles we might put into practice:

7. Resolved, Never to do anything, which I should be afraid to do if it were the last hour of my life ...

14. Resolved, Never to do anything out of revenge ...

41. Resolved, To ask myself, at the end of every day, week, month, and year, wherein I could possibly, in any respect, have done better ...

56. Resolved, Never to give over, nor in the least to slacken, my fight with my corruptions, however unsuccessful I may be ...

67. Resolved, After afflictions, to inquire, what I am the better for them; what good I have got by them, and what I might have got by them ...

70. Let there be something of benevolence in all that I speak.[2]

Dallas Willard tells the story of a woman coming to a pastor who had been emphasizing discipleship and saying to him, "I just want to be a Christian. I don't want to be a disciple. I like my life the way it is. I believe Jesus died for my sins and I will be with Him when I die. Why do I have to be a disciple?" Dr. Willard asks how we would answer that question.[3]

The answer is that discipleship is the path to an abundant life, and our Lord Jesus requires it. He calls us to deny ourselves, to take up our crosses, to learn from Him, to put His teachings into practice, to live a life as disciples who obey *"all that* [he] commanded" (Matthew 28:20 emphasis added).

For this, we must put on the character of Christ. That's the ultimate reason why character counts.

A Commitment to Revealed Truth

I received Christ at the age of thirty-seven (a story I tell in a later chapter). But at the same time when I accepted Christ as my Savior, I made a second, critical commitment: I decided (as a matter of faith) to believe the Bible as it is written. I concluded that God was good, and therefore was not a con man, and that the Scriptures He had given to His Church could not lie.

Of course, I now realize that this process of commitment was not really mine; it is the ministry of the Holy Spirit to teach us all things and to lead us into all truth by turning our hearts to the Bible, and that was what He did for me.

Until my conversion, though I considered Jesus Christ to be a wise teacher, I did not consider His teachings (or anything else in the Bible) to be sacred or authoritative. To the extent I paid any attention to the Bible, I considered it an exalted but fallible piece of literature—fallible because human authors wrote it and human councils put it together. So I accepted only the parts of the Bible I agreed with. In essence, I made my own mind the highest court of appeal for all things religious.

When converted, I realized that I could no longer reject those parts of Holy Scripture that I happened not to like. From that point forward, I have considered the Bible—all of it—to be trustworthy and authoritative. It, and not my all too fallible mind, has become the court of last resort on truth.

What became clear to me was that if a human being is ever to know who God is, what His character is like, and how we are to relate to Him, God would have to reveal it to us. We have not the slightest hope of knowing on the basis of our own minds.

It finally dawned on me that it was both prideful and silly to think that I was in charge of figuring out who God is. He will tell me, or else I will never know. By faith, I accepted the Bible as God's true way of revealing to us who He really is and what are His character and ways.

The change in my attitude toward the Bible does not mean that I take every word of it literally. When Jesus says that He is the "gate," for example, we all know He is speaking figuratively. But it does mean that I take every sentence of the Bible seriously and seek to understand its plain meaning.

Because God is both the source of the truth of the Christian faith and the source of all truth, there can be no truth, scientific or otherwise, which is not thoroughly consistent with His revelation.[4] Faith is not gullibility. Instead, it's a new lens through which we can see the truth of all reality, scientific and otherwise, as a harmonious whole.

This is an essential step in pursuit of biblical character. Since the moral order for the universe is found in the Scriptures, both Old and New Testaments, we need to have a commitment to the Bible—studying it, believing it, putting it into practice so as to develop the virtues that empower us to live in accordance with its principles.

We now may turn to the third part of character's context—power. We have seen that character must be "formed" or "engraved" in relation to our purpose and so as to enable us to live in accordance with biblical principles. But where do we get the strength to do this?

Grace: The Source of Supernatural Strength

Every successful organization, be it a business, a sports team, a church, or whatever, is comprised of people highly motivated to achieve the organization's mission. No matter how lofty the purpose and principles, if there is not exceptional motivation and energy to accomplish the mission, according to the rules that support it, the organization will fail in its purpose.

When Lombardi arrived at Green Bay, twenty minutes into his first meeting with Bart Starr (who was to become his Hall of Fame quarterback), Starr saw "a new world" and "felt an insatiable hunger for more."[5]

We all need such an "insatiable hunger" as we commit ourselves to live into our purpose in accordance with God's principles.

Central to the gospel is the truth that we have, not just the law of Moses and the words of Christ and His apostles, but also the power of Christ working within us to develop the virtues that lead away from sin and toward a life that will glorify God. The word used for this power is *grace*, referring to the unmerited gift of God. It is manifested in us through the Holy Spirit. The old rhyme teaches us well:

Run, John, run; the law commands
But gives neither the feet nor hands.
Better news the gospel brings;
It bids us fly and gives us wings.[6]

The "wings" of the gospel is grace.

Grace has a dual meaning in scripture. First and fundamentally, grace is God's unmerited favor to us through Jesus Christ. Secondarily, in many places grace means God's divine power for us through the Holy Spirit. Christ speaks of this dimension of grace when he counsels Paul, "My grace is sufficient for you" (2 Corinthians 12:9). Paul has this aspect of grace in mind when he writes to the Corinthians, "And God is able to make all grace abound to you, so ... you may abound in every good work." (2 Corinthians 9:8).

This second dimension, God's divine assistance, is included in the first, God's unmerited favor. It is the second face of grace that provides the power which is represented by the third point of our character framework triangle.

But how do we receive this grace? The answer is found (among other places) in the same passage of Scripture where we learn that we are to bear much fruit: John 15:1-11. The pivotal teaching on our ultimate purpose is also a key to understanding the source of strength for accomplishing our purpose.

In John 15 Jesus provides a metaphor describing a vital, personal union when He says, "I am the true vine, and my Father is the vinedresser. Every branch of mine that does not bear fruit he takes away, and every branch that does bear fruit he prunes, that it may bear more fruit" (John 15:1-2). Both the Father and the Son are working to make us fruitful. That's a pretty good coaching staff!

The Father, as vinedresser, carefully forms our characters into Christ's image and tends each branch of the vine, preparing us to live fruitful lives of Christian virtue. He cuts off those branches of our lives that bear no fruit and throws them into the fire. But He trims our fruit-bearing branches so that they will bear even more fruit. "This is to my Father's glory, that you bear *much* fruit" (John 15:8 NIV, emphasis added).

Then Jesus empowers us to bear much fruit. In His teaching that He is the true vine, He issues an invitation: "Abide in me, and I in you. As the branch cannot bear fruit by itself, unless it abides in the vine, neither can you, unless you abide in me. I am the vine; you are the branches. Whoever abides in me and I in him, he it is that bears much fruit, for apart from me you can do nothing" (John 15:4-5).

The Father has prepared us to produce fruit. Now Jesus empowers us to do so. His life flows through us, nourishing us. We are the branches, the living conduits, essential links in the process. Because we are to be vigorous and active participants, we need to be fit for our roles. Through putting Jesus' words into practice, and through abiding in Him, we become fit. We develop the virtues. They become habits. In grace, we grow into robust branches that bear much fruit for the glory of God. That is what we were created to do.

Having seen that God's grace is an essential part of Christian character formation, we need to consider our own roles in character formation in relation to grace.

Becoming "Little Christs"

In biblical terms, character formation is putting on the character of Christ. In the words of C. S. Lewis, it is becoming "little Christs."[7] The task of discipleship is character formation.

The Bible uses various derivations of the word "form"—a character word—in talking about our development in Christlikeness. To the Galatians, Paul wrote, "I am ... in the anguish of childbirth until Christ is *formed* in you!" (Galatians 4:19, emphasis added). We are "predestined to be *conformed* to the likeness of his Son" and we are to be "*transformed* into his likeness" (Romans 8:29 NIV; 2 Corinthians 3:18 NIV, emphasis added). But who does the forming?

There is today, and has been for centuries, a tendency to see our role in the formation of Christlike character – what theologians call "sanctification" — as essentially passive. Our role, it is said, is to surrender and empty ourselves. We abide in the vine, and the rest is up to Christ working through us by His Spirit. Such an approach misapprehends the role we are to play in growth in Christian character formation.

Sanctification is a joint work between the Holy Spirit working inwardly and us (through our minds and wills) working outwardly. The touchstone passage for this truth is Philippians 2:12-13, where Paul says, "My beloved, as you have always obeyed...work out your own salvation with fear and trembling, for it is God who works in you, both to will and to work for his good pleasure." We often forget that the word "work" appears twice in this sentence. Paul says we are to "work out" as God is "working in," just as Oswald Chambers described it in the quote cited previously.

J. I. Packer, one of the great evangelical thinkers of the twentieth century, wrote that "'yielding' and 'abiding' are matters not of passivity, but of *resolute habitual obedience*, in which you pray as hard as you work and you work as hard as you pray because you know God works in you to make you will and do." These words come from a preface Packer wrote to Bishop J. C. Ryle's collected sermons on holiness. After recounting how he had been converted to a saving faith while a student at Oxford, Packer tells how, following his conversion, he "was getting nowhere fast in his quest for greater godliness." The teachings he received told him "to yield, surrender and consecrate oneself to God," but his experience as he tried "was like that of the poor drug addict whom he found trying with desperate concentration to walk through a brick wall."[8] It was Ryle's assertion that holiness is a matter of putting the teachings of Christ into practice that set Packer on the right track.

Sanctification is indeed the work of the Holy Spirit, but His work is joined with our work in putting biblical law and Jesus' teachings into practice. Only then will our characters begin to be transformed into the likeness of Jesus. C. S. Lewis put the effect of our role into perspective this way (again emphasizing the tight relationship of being and doing):

> Every time you make a choice you are turning the central part of you, the part of you that chooses, into something a little different from what it was before. And taking your life as a whole, with all your innumerable choices, all your life long you are slowly turning this central thing either into a heavenly creature or into a hellish creature: either into a creature that is in harmony with God, and with other creatures, and with itself, or else into one that is in a state of war and hatred with God, and with its fellow-creatures, and with itself.[9]

One choice we can make, as we cooperate with the Holy Spirit in moving toward greater Christlikeness, is to take advantage of the means God has provided to bring grace into our lives. We can actually increase the flow of His grace to the places where we need it for character formation.

The Means of Grace

God does not inject His grace into our lives in some random or unordered way; rather, grace flows into our lives through established channels. These are usually called the "spiritual disciplines." I like to call them the means of grace. They include such practices as worshiping, partaking of the Lord's Supper, reading Scripture, participating in Bible study, praying, fasting, and confessing sin. They all presuppose a life surrendered to God and committed to His will.

A prominent writer on this subject, Richard Foster, states that "the Disciplines allow us to place ourselves before God so that He can transform us." Foster explains that the means of grace are a way of sowing to the Spirit, putting us where God's Spirit can "work within us and transform us."[10] Using the metaphor of becoming a tree that produces good fruit, we see that the means of grace are a way of assuring that the tree's roots extend to the living water.

The means of grace allow God to work from the inside out on what Foster calls the "ingrained habits of sin," replacing these habits with the virtues and character of Christ. The disciplines are what release the *power* part of the character triangle to engender and strengthen the virtues. Since we cannot eliminate any sin habit by willpower, relying upon God's appointed means of grace is the only way our character can be transformed. Foster says this truth has been experienced "by all of the great writers of the devotional life."[11] When I read their writings, I am assured of this truth, and I am sure this is true for all of us who give it thought.

Take any ingrained habit of sin. It may be greed or lust or pride. It may be the gluttonous pursuit of diversions in shopping or golf or more addictive habits like gambling. It may be a bad temper or envy and an unwillingness to forgive someone who has wronged or beaten or humiliated us. A resolution to discard such habits never works. If anything, as we concentrate on "beating them," we energize them. The only way to "beat them" is to let God's grace transform our characters from the inside out as the old habits are weakened and dissolved and the new virtues are put on. The means of grace are the channels that allow this grace to go to work.

In my life, it is a process that is measured in years and decades more often than days or weeks. The means of grace take time and repetition if they are to do us any good.

Repetition of Grace

Foster begins his book with a bold claim: "Superficiality is the curse of our age."[12] He is right. (Remember what we said about the personality ethic.) We simply do not understand that the matters of forging godly virtues through faith in grace require much time, thought, and practice for them to sink in deeply, permanently engraved in our souls. The means of grace are an essential part of the process.

Most of the means of grace require repetition. Bible reading and study, for example, should be daily exercises. So should prayer. We ought to worship with others at least once a week. Confession must be ongoing, since sin that is not exposed to light develops deep roots.

Furthermore, within each of these practices, we will have repetition. In liturgical churches, for instance, the same liturgy is used over and over in worship services.

What is at work here is the same principle behind the concept that virtues are habits. Our souls do not accept the workings of God in thought or deed easily.

I recently heard a presentation by a pediatric surgeon on how clubfeet are treated nowadays. With this condition, at birth the foot is twisted around so it points backward. For a long time, medicine had no treatment for this condition, and those born with the deformity were crippled for life. Then physicians sought to correct the defect with surgery. Now, though, they slowly twist the foot around, using a series of casts to preserve the progress, until the foot is essentially normal.

This process is similar to the process of character formation. We are all born with deformed souls, twisted and dysfunctional. The process of getting our souls right so that our thoughts, desires, and needs align with God's plan takes a lifetime of repetition and practice in what we think and do, and in the means of grace, because the forces that resist never go away.

We might like to think that an hour or two a week at church and a short session of prayer each day will be enough for us. But if we think this way, I doubt we will find a mature Christian in the world to agree with us. If that is our thinking, the truths of Scripture and the ways of God in all probability escape us.

Take a simple teaching from Scripture: "Are not two sparrows sold for a penny? And not one of them will fall to the ground apart from your Father. But even the hairs of your head are all numbered. Fear not, therefore; you are of more value than many sparrows" (Matthew 10:29-31). Here are three verses. They teach God's providence and care for each of His children. Do we really, deep inside, believe this? Do we really "fear not"?

These words need to be worked into our souls. We need to meditate on them, listen to sermons on them, discuss them with others, pray them, and most of all, experience them in what we do. They are true, but it takes time for their truth to sink in. And the same is true for every message God gives us in His Word.

The means of grace take time and repetition.

Consumed with Longing

Foster calls his book *The Celebration of Discipline*, and in this celebratory book he seeks to combat the tendency to think that the means of grace, such as prayer and Bible reading, are drudgery. Instead, he goes to great length to show that "joy is the keynote of all the Disciplines." All that is needed is a "longing after God."[13]

How do we get to the place where practicing the means of grace can be joy and can be the product of a longing after God? I can't tell you how it will work for you, but I can tell you how it has worked in my own life.

After my conversion to Christ at the age of thirty-seven, I joined the work of Prison Fellowship, Chuck Colson's prison ministry. As I attended Prison Fellowship meetings in Birmingham, I found in others an ardor for the things of God—a hunger and thirst for righteousness—that I did not have. Their prayer was deep and personal and flowed smoothly and naturally. Though I was studying the Bible and praying the best I could, I knew it was more from the head and less from the heart than it should have been. Friends joked with me that I was a "hair shirt Christian." My wife told me that I was the only person she knew who seemed to enjoy life by giving up all its pleasures. The fruit of the Holy Spirit was too little evident in my life.

In these circumstances I sat down with a veteran prison minister, Jim Merritt, and discussed my concerns with him. We entered into a prayer covenant that lasted many years. We would each pray that the fruit of the Spirit would be evident in the life of the other. This was a favorable bargain for me, as Jim's life abounded in the fruit of the Spirit. On the other hand, he had quite a challenge in praying for me.

Another member of the Prison Fellowship team kept trying to get me to go to a Pentecostal church in Birmingham. After some resistance, I relented and attended several services. Thereafter, late one Friday afternoon, I ended up in the sanctuary of the church in prayer with a man named Brother Ellis. It was this afternoon that—as much as my will and mind were capable—I surrendered my life in every respect to Jesus Christ. There followed, after prayer and confession throughout the weekend, what can only be described as a filling of my heart with the Holy Spirit.

Jesus teaches, "If anyone thirsts, let him come to me and drink. Whoever believes in me, as the Scripture has said, 'Out of his heart will flow rivers of living water'" (John 7:37-38). John explained that "rivers of living water" describe the Holy Spirit (v. 39). The thought that lived in my heart that weekend was that a deep spring of living water was flowing through me.

I recount this part of my life because thereafter, wholly apart from my own will, my prayer life and hunger for the things of God were dramatically transformed. I began to read the Bible because I loved it. The teachings of Scripture became ever more vivid. Delving more deeply into biblical truth, far from being drudgery, became lively and exciting. My prayer life became deeper, flowing from the heart and becoming sweet (no better word to describe it). My prayer times lengthened and kept on lengthening. I felt that I could identify with the composer of the 119th Psalm, who wrote, "My soul is consumed with longing" (v. 20).

An outgrowth of this experience was that I began to keep a journal that is little more than a written prayer diary. As I prayed on one thing or another of crucial significance in my life, I found it warming to the heart to write the prayer down. I kept the journal for no reason other than that I was fed spiritually by doing it. It took my prayer life to a deeper level, full of rich blessings.

All this in no respect was of my own doing. If I did anything, it was only to surrender, and that all too awkwardly. The rest was the work of the Holy Spirit, but as I write this twenty-one years later, I can say that the ardor for the things of God then engendered has not diminished.[14]

We all need to commit to regular practice of the means of grace—the spiritual disciplines. If the longing is not there, as for a season it was not in my life, then pray, beg, entreat Christ that He will give such a longing through His Holy Spirit. We need to pray earnestly to be saturated with the Holy Spirit. The words of an old hymn give us the words:

I surrender all,
I surrender all,
All to Thee, my blessed Savior,
I surrender all.[15]

As the Holy Spirit flows into us in an ever-increasing stream, and as we put the teachings of Christ into practice, we will be empowered to live by the principles God has given in His moral teaching and live into the ultimate purpose of our lives. Whether we live into this purpose in accordance with biblical teachings and whether the power of God can be released in us through lives that count depend on the content of our character – our virtue. It is to a discussion of key virtues and how they relate to purpose, principles, and power that we now turn.

Character Questions

1. What are some of the fundamental principles from Scripture that you believe you should be using to guide your behavior?

2. What exactly is the relationship between God's grace and our own self-effort when it comes to our morality? Or is their combination a mystery we can never hope to resolve in this life?

3. What has been your experience with the spiritual disciplines up to this point in your life? How could you better utilize these means of grace to help you in developing a more Christlike character?

Part 2

The Content of Character

The only thing that counts is faith expressing itself through love.

—Galatians 5:6 NIV

Introduction to Part 2

Despite what some relativists might believe, good character is not whatever we choose to make it. Good character, in fact, is made up of specific virtues that are commended in the Bible and that wise men and women throughout human history have recognized as essential. To grow in these virtues is to have a godly character.

In this book we will look at eight key virtues as essential character qualities. They include the four cardinal virtues recognized since classical times: wisdom, courage, self-control, and justice.[1] They also include the three theological virtues of faith, hope, and love, all of them elevated to high status by the apostle Paul (1 Corinthians 13:13). This book adds one more theological virtue to the list—humility—since this quality is fundamental to strong, godly character.

The four cardinal virtues have been called "pagan" virtues by some because they were promoted by such pre-Christian thinkers as Plato. But there is nothing pagan about these virtues. Along with the theological virtues, the cardinal virtues are all extolled in Scripture. All eight are biblical qualities and are crucial for a Christian to pursue.

Granting this, some still might take a look at the list of eight virtues and wonder about what is missing. Why *these* eight virtues? Are there not other biblical virtues that should be considered? What about patience, for example? Or mercy? Or any of a dozen other virtues, each arguably indispensable to a godly character?

Everyone needs a core set of virtues. We might focus on six, eight, ten, or some other number of virtues. But personally, I find that if I get much beyond eight, it is more than I can keep in mind with study and regular prayer. And the fact that the cardinal and theological virtues have been the focus of study by great saints down through the Christian centuries assures us that we cannot go far wrong with these. There is no reason to downplay other virtues, but the eight chosen here are worthy of any believer's attention.[2]

It has been said that the theological virtues produce saints, whereas the cardinal virtues mold heroes. One thesis of this book is the two categories of virtues combine in Christianity to produce a complete character that honors God. Both sets of virtues are qualities that God wants to form in every one of us, though we do not think of ourselves as either saints or heroes.

Furthermore, these eight virtues do not comprise a random collection, as if one could focus on any one of them apart from the others with equal results. They actually are interrelated in a particular and sequential way; they embody a natural progression. Essentially, the cardinal virtues connect the first three theological virtues with the supreme virtue of love. To picture this, we can think of the virtues as a tree—a tree of character that produces good fruit.

The Tree of Character

The tree imagery is not new; Scripture uses it more than once. In Jeremiah, for instance, we read the following:

Blessed is the man who trusts in the LORD,
    whose confidence is in him.
He will be like a tree planted by the water
    that sends out its roots by the stream.
It does not fear when heat comes;
    its leaves are always green.
It has no worries in a year of drought
    and never fails to bear fruit (Jeremiah 17:7-8 NIV).

This word picture gives us an excellent framework for thinking about the virtues that make up Christian character.

The stream can be likened to "living water," which John tells us is the Holy Spirit (John 4:10). To bear fruit for God's glory, we must be filled with the Holy Spirit.[3] And throughout the Bible, this river of life is associated with good fruit. The tree portrayed in Jeremiah "never fails to bear fruit" (Jeremiah 17:8

The Tree that Produces Good Fruit

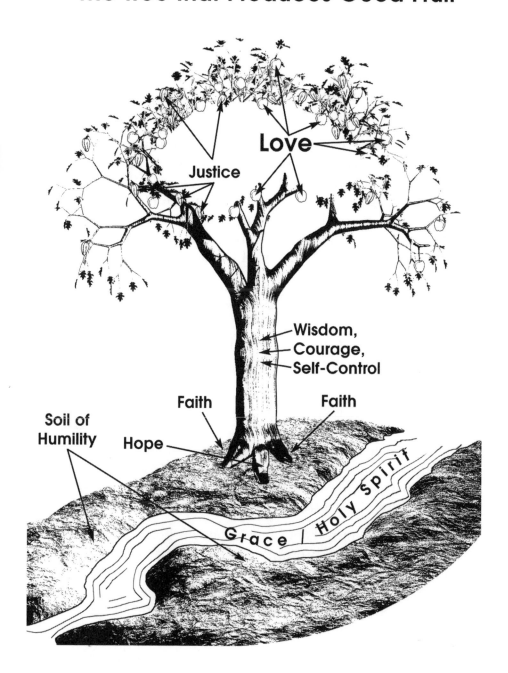

NIV). Our ultimate destination is the celestial city, where on either side of "the river of the water of life" is a tree bearing "twelve kinds of fruit, yielding its fruit each month" (Revelation 22:1-2).

The tree must also be planted in good soil, which we can think of as humility. No other Christian virtue can become strong without being joined with humility. Only through the soil of humility can the living water nourish the tree.

Faith and hope can be seen as the tree's roots. It is the man who "trusts in the LORD, whose confidence is in him" who is likened to a fruitful tree (Jeremiah 17:7 NIV). Through faith, our heart and soul are opened to the nourishment of the living water. Furthermore, hope acts as a taproot to strengthen the tree to weather life's storms or, to use a biblical metaphor, as the "sure and steadfast anchor of the soul" (Hebrews 6:19).

While humility, faith, and hope are the foundation of Christian character, love—the fourth theological virtue—is the fruit of the tree. It is that which the rest of the tree exists for; it is the purpose of the tree. (We will also call justice a fruit, for as we will see, it is an elementary expression of love.)

The cardinal virtues of wisdom, justice, courage, and self-control are there to transfer the power of the living water, humility, faith, and hope to love. We can understand the cardinal virtues of wisdom, courage, and self-control as the tree's trunk and branches. The apostle Paul says, "The only thing that counts is faith expressing itself through love" (Galatians 5:6 NIV), and it is the cardinal virtues that make such expression possible.

Like the heavenly hosts bowing down before the throne of God, the virtues of humility, faith, hope, wisdom, justice, courage, and self-control all exist for love—we can even say they exist *only* for love. So, too, do we. Without love, we cannot glorify God, and we enjoy God forever only in His love for us and through our love for Him.

The more we study the virtues, the more we recognize, not only a certain sequence in their operation, but just as much a natural and tight interdependence. As the roots, trunk, limbs, leaves, and fruit of a tree are all essential to each other, so the virtues are naturally united with one another. Without wisdom, for example, love is easily misplaced, as we see when we spoil our children. Without courage, we cannot love effectively. Without self-control, we cannot be wise. Without hope, our faith will likely wither in the face of trials.

Just as each part of the tree is indispensable to its life, so each of the virtues is indispensable to a character that will allow us to move into our ultimate purpose.

Keys to Virtue

There are two keys to all virtue: self-denial and perseverance. And so these keys represent themes we will see threading their way through the chapters to come.

If we are to live into our ultimate purpose, we must accept with the utmost seriousness the condition of the Master who invites us to follow Him: "If anyone would come after me, let him deny himself" (Luke 9:23). If we are to "find" or "save" our lives, we must first lose them for Christ's sake (v. 24).

Spiritual agriculture, we might say, begins with self-denial. Jesus taught, "Unless a grain of wheat falls into the earth and dies, it remains alone; but if it dies, it bears much fruit" (John 12:24). It's true in farming, and it's true in character growth as well.

Seen in this way, Christ's call to self-denial is not a way of taking enjoyment out of our lives. It is, in fact, precisely the opposite: an invitation that provides the foundation for Christlike character that will give us abundant life and great joy. Indeed, joy will come only to the person who possesses the virtues discussed in this book, all of which grow out of the humility that empowers us to deny ourselves.

We cannot love others or have faith or hope in God if we put ourselves first. Nor can we be humble, wise, just, courageous, or self-controlled while we are at the same time selfish. As

William Ellery Channing says, "All great virtues bear the imprint of self-denial."

Though Channing didn't say it, the virtues also bear the imprint of perseverance—the second key.

Because all virtues need to be engraved into our soul, they are not acquired overnight. There are natural processes to producing a crop, and these require time and cannot be cut short. Likewise, the engraving that transforms our character into Christlikeness takes much time and, absent a miracle, cannot be abbreviated.

To use another biblical image, God is the potter and we are the clay, and His work in shaping us is ever ongoing. If we want to jump off the potter's wheel, we can, but God's work must cease for as long as we are off it. If we want to take on the shape He has for us, we must endure the process of molding.

Humility, faith, hope, wisdom, justice, courage, self-control, and love are formed in us over time, especially through trials and difficulties. Any offer of a process that is quick and easy misses the mark. Denying ourselves, taking up our crosses and following Jesus, is a lifetime journey.

These pictures help us understand that the first part of our ultimate purpose—bearing the fruit of love for the glory of God—is not something we can seek directly. We do not express love except in conjunction with a host of virtues that precede it.

The following chapters contain a brief sketch of the primary virtues of the Christian life. Each of the virtues deserves a full book, if not a full library. The purpose of part two of the book is merely to provide a biblical frame of reference for beginning prayer, meditation, and discussion about these great virtues and, most of all, for putting them into practice.

We need to remember that we should practice the virtues continuously. When we are in deep trouble or in a fiery trial and we need courage or wisdom, faith or love, in a special way, we cannot turn these virtues on like a light bulb. Just as a seed does not produce a tree bearing good fruit overnight, neither can we produce fruit quickly in our characters.

As an athlete goes to a practice field to hone his skills, so we must go to the "practice field" again and again to cultivate our virtues. Over the days and years, the virtues need to be engraved in our characters as we practice them daily so they become second nature to us. Then, when one of life's crises comes our way, our souls will be prepared to work through it in a way that honors God. We will be, in God's grace, a tree that bears godly fruit.

4

Humility: Understanding Reality

Bill Wilson—known as "Bill W." to the more than two million men and women who have joined Alcoholics Anonymous (AA) since he founded the organization in 1935—established anonymity as a central component of AA's program. "We believe that the principle of anonymity has immense spiritual significance," Wilson wrote. "It reminds us that we are to place principles before personalities; that we are actually to practice a genuine humility."[1] Yet Wilson did not easily die to his own desire for personal distinction.

In *My Name Is Bill*, biographer Susan Cheever tells what happened when Yale University sought to give Wilson an honorary degree. "He saw how much the publicity might help A. A.," Cheever writes. "He also wanted the degree and the recognition for himself." Yet by that point in his life Wilson "was sufficiently sophisticated in his own principles to know that accepting it was somehow a bad idea." And so Wilson decided to leave the decision to his organization's board of trustees.

"His spirits were buoyed to find that all but one of the trustees thought he should accept the degree," Cheever reports. The lone dissenter was Archibald Roosevelt, who explained to Wilson that his father, Theodore Roosevelt, had worried about his own attraction to power and had vowed never to accept a personal honor, making an exception only for the Nobel Prize.

"Bill knew that he was hearing the right message [from Roosevelt]," writes Cheever. "He was human, though." Wilson refused the degree for himself but asked that it be given to Alcoholics Anonymous as an organization. Yale rejected the suggestion.

Cheever's book goes on to describe Wilson's eventual victory over pride. "Later he declined to be on the cover of *Time* magazine, even, as the editors suggested, with his back to the camera. He also turned down at least six other honorary degrees and a number of overtures from the Nobel Prize Committee."[2]

Like Wilson, we all must grow into humility. That is, we must seek it if we want to have a character like Christ's. This virtue is primary in biblical character, for the virtues that glorify God are all the offspring of humility. Or to put it another way, humility is the soil in which other virtues flourish.

Our word *humility* comes from the Latin term *humus*, meaning "earth." In today's terminology, *humus* is the result of decomposing vegetable matter and is a common garden fertilizer. And just as *humus* helps our gardens flourish, so the soil of humility provides a fertile source for the tree of character to grow in our lives and to bear fruit for God.

The study of Christian virtue always begins with humility. It is a precondition of all other virtues.

What Is Humility?

Josef Pieper, an astute Roman Catholic student of virtue, writes that "the ground of humility is man's estimation of himself according to the truth. And that is almost all there is to it."[3] This leads us to a sound definition of humility: *understanding through grace the truth of who God is and who we are.*

Someone once asked St. Augustine what he considered to be the most important precept of Christianity. He began his response by telling of a great speaker who was asked to state the chief rules for eloquence. The speaker replied that the first rule was "delivery," the second rule was "delivery," and the third rule was "delivery." In the same way, St. Augustine says, "If you ask me concerning the precepts of the Christian religion, first, second, third, and always I would answer 'humility.' "[4]

Echoing Augustine, Jonathan Edwards called humility "the most essential thing in true religion." The American theologian went on to state, "All, everything in grace is calculated to bring humility into the hearts of man."[5] All, everything—remember that. As much as we may struggle with humility, we can take courage because God is always at work in our lives, helping us to become more humble. For then, and only then, can He produce great things in us and through us.

And where does it all begin? With repentance.

Shift of Mind

"Repent" was the first word of Jesus' ministry, as He told people, "Repent, for the kingdom of heaven is at hand" (Matthew 4:17). It was also the last. In His parting words in Luke's Gospel, Jesus says, "It is written, that the Christ should suffer and on the third day rise from the dead, and that *repentance and forgiveness of sins should be proclaimed in his name to all nations*" (Luke 24:46-47, emphasis added).

Repentance is our translation of a Greek word that means "shift of mind."[6] In its most fundamental sense, repentance is nothing more than a change toward clear thinking—understanding the truth about who we are and who God is. As Oswald Chambers advises, "It is astounding how ignorant we are about ourselves! ... We have to get rid of the idea that we understand ourselves, it is the last conceit to go."[7] The truth is, we are all sinners—foolish rebels against an all-powerful God.

The Bible is filled with stories of repentance. In each of them, our spiritual forebears were struck with horror when they realized their sinfulness. Reading Isaiah 6, for example, we can almost sense the pain that the future prophet Isaiah felt when he had an unexpected encounter not only with God but also with himself—with his own failings as a sinner.

It all began with a vision Isaiah had of the holiness and glory of the Lord. The cherubim in the vision were present before God, worshiping Him and saying,

Holy, holy, holy is the LORD of hosts;
the whole earth is full of His glory! (Isaiah 6:3).

Immediately Isaiah cried out: "Woe is me! For I am lost; for I am a man of unclean lips, and I dwell in the midst of a people of unclean lips" (v. 5). Isaiah's words show his shift of mind to a state of understanding the truth about himself and his sinfulness before the holy God.

For Isaiah, humility began with an understanding that his sin had created a chasm between God and himself. This problem—understanding our sinfulness in light of the majesty of a holy God—recurs virtually every time in Scripture when a person encounters the divine: consider Job (Job 42:5-6), David (Psalm 51:1-12), and Peter (Luke 5:8). The same process of humility applies to us.

When the Lord expelled Adam and Eve from paradise, He placed an angel with a flaming sword at the gate east of Eden to prevent the couple from coming back into the garden, where the tree of life grew. That describes our condition. We are banished from paradise and there is nothing we can do on our own to reenter it. As we seek to understand Christian character, we first of all must allow this truth to enter our heads.

We are often led to believe that if we are sincere, if we give it our all, the doors of heaven will be flung open for us and we can pass by the flaming sword and go back into paradise. But this is not true. We enter the gates of paradise through the sacrificial death of Jesus Christ and the spiritual cleanness that comes from faith that He alone can render us righteous before God. He is the one mediator between God and man.

This key to repentance and humility is beautifully expressed in the words of a couple of old hymns. One attests, "Nothing in my hands I bring, simply to the cross I cling." Another states, "Just as I am without one plea, but that thy blood was shed for me...."[8]

And for those of us in liturgical churches who may not have these hymns in our hymnals, we need only take note of the

Kyrie, in which three times each Sunday we cry out for God's mercy. The cry for mercy is the plea of one who has no case and no rights and who begs the forbearance of the judge. That is the truth that repentance leads us to understand.

"What Is Man?"

In addition to its message of spiritual repentance, the Bible points us to humility by reminding us of our insignificance in the face of God's grandeur and majesty. Scripture compares us to mist and grass and reminds us how brief our time is on earth (Psalm 90). Nature broadcasts the same message.

Just look at the sky. Astronomers now believe that our sun is one of seventy sextillion (that means seventy thousand million million million) observable stars in the universe. That's about ten times the number of grains of sand on all the beaches and deserts on the earth![9] Considering these facts, we must wonder prayerfully with David,

> When I look at your heavens, the work of your fingers,
> the moon and the stars, which you have set in place,
> what is man that you are mindful of him? (Psalm 8:3-4).

The deeper we go into our exploration of microbiology and quantum theory, the more the most brilliant of our scientists are coming to understand how little we know. Blaise Pascal was right when he said that our knowledge, when compared to all the wisdom in the universe, is as minuscule as a single human body compared to all the matter of the universe.[10] God was making no idle boast, but rather was stating the plain facts when He declared,

> My thoughts are not your thoughts,
> neither are your ways my ways ...
> For as the heavens are higher than the earth,
> so are my ways higher than your ways
> and my thoughts than your thoughts (Isaiah 55:8-9).

In all this, perhaps the most amazing thing is that we continue to think of ourselves as highly as we do. A joke makes the point well.

It seems a number of the world's most gifted scientists scheduled a meeting with God. In their pride, they were confident they could get along without Him. They thanked God for starting with the human race, but now, they said, they "know everything." They can even clone humans and understand the mystery of the atom. So they told God to leave them alone, because the human race can get along just fine without Him.

God replied, "It's up to you. But are you sure you know it all? What if I asked you to create a human?"

The scientists replied, "We can do that; we cloned one last year."

God said, "No, I mean like we did in Genesis."

The scientists, now a little daunted, looked at the ground and replied, "You mean make a human out of dirt?"

God said, "No, you first need to make the dirt."

A true sense of our insignificance as well as our sinfulness leads us to bow before God. After repentance, we are called to continue on in humility throughout our life's sojourn.

Submitted Before God

In the ordinary affairs of life—what we do most of the time—submission is a chief mark of the Christian. Following Jesus, we deny ourselves and take up our crosses daily (Matthew 16:24). We submit ourselves first to God, our highest authority, and second to one another for the sake of Christ.

The apostle Paul, as pastor to many of the early churches, wrote often about how submission is to extend to every facet of Christians' lives—church, family, work, citizenship, and more. He expressed this theme perhaps most succinctly in Romans 12:1.

Paul had spent the first eleven chapters of Romans talking about the mercies of God. He had explained how the sacrificial death of Jesus has purchased for us eternal life, access to God's grace, and an inheritance with Christ. He had also explained that in Christ we are more than conquerors. Then he began chapter 12 by saying, "I appeal to you therefore, brothers, by the mercies of God, to present your bodies as a living sacrifice, holy and acceptable to God, which is your spiritual worship" (v. 1)

By using the word "bodies," Paul was saying that the response we make to God's mercies needs to appear in what we do just as much as in what we think and in what we believe. Our response is not to be spiritual only but also to affect our daily activities.[11]

Paul's more detailed instructions regarding submission are contained in both Ephesians and Colossians. In these letters he laid out what submission should look like in our closest relationships (see Ephesians 5:22-6:9; Colossians 3:18-4:1). For the Christian, this kind of submission among human beings is actually an expression of submission to God.

In Ephesians, Paul began his counsel of submission by stating that we are to "submit to one another out of reverence for Christ" (Ephesians 5:21 NIV). In other words, the principle of submission is rooted in a devotion to Jesus Christ and His sacrificial death for us. That is where the focus should remain.

Similarly, in Colossians, Paul defined the life of submission within the framework of devotion to Jesus Christ. He introduced his instructions on submission by first writing that the "peace of Christ" should rule in our hearts, that His Word should "dwell in [us] richly," and that, whatever we do, we should do it "in the name of the Lord Jesus" (Colossians 3:15-17).

Only after providing this context did Paul, in both Ephesians and Colossians, instruct us to be submissive in our family life and in our work.

For husbands the injunction is to "love your wives, as Christ loved the church and gave himself up for her" (Ephesians 5:25).

Paul was telling husbands that authority is to be exercised within the home through love with a sacrificial spirit. It is the person who through love is willing to lay it on the line, to sacrifice all on another's behalf, who has authority in the Christian sense.

The same dynamic is at work in the relationship between children and parents. The command for children to honor their father and mother is one of the most basic in all of Scripture (Exodus 20:12; Ephesians 6:2). And we all know the consequences of failure to obey this command. Whatever benefits of comfort and convenience we Americans enjoy in today's affluent society, certainly the biggest negative we face is the breakdown of the family—the failure of children to honor their father and their mother and the failure of fathers and mothers to live sacrificial lives on behalf of their children, showing God's love to them.

Relations within the family—those between husbands and wives and between parents and children—are fields of practice for us to develop humility through submitting to one another and, ultimately, to God. But our lives are made up of more than family relationships. One other important part of our daily activities is our work, and there, too, we are to practice humility. In this case humility is, more specifically, a matter of practicing servanthood.

Masters Who Serve

Servanthood is a subset of submission, as Paul made clear in both Ephesians and Colossians. After discussing submission within the family, he went on to discuss the relationship between master and servant. Here he gave a simple rule for all work: "Whatever you do, work at it with all your heart, as working for the Lord, not for men, since you know that you will receive an inheritance from the Lord as a reward. It is the Lord Christ you are serving" (Colossians 3:23-24 NIV). Again, we need to note the focus on Jesus Christ in all we do. In this simple instruction on work, Paul refers to Christ three times, twice showing that service to our earthly masters is really service to Jesus Christ.

Jesus made it clear that the usual relationship between master and servant is not to exist within Christian circles. To His disciples, He was the Master, yet He took up a towel and washed the disciples' feet after His triumphal entry into Jerusalem. This is what He told His disciples about His actions: "Do you understand what I have done to you? You call me Teacher and Lord, and you are right, for so I am. If I then, your Lord and Teacher, have washed your feet, you also ought to wash one another's feet. For I have given you an example that you also should do just as I have done to you" (John 13:12-15).

Again, the message here is that the one in authority is the one to make the sacrifice. Truly enough, the servant obeys the master, as serving the Lord. Yet the master also serves the servant, following the example of the King of kings and Lord of lords.

Just as with family relationships, work relationships are a field where we can practice submission and servanthood and thereby render ourselves as living sacrifices for the grace of humility to be formed in us. Indeed, we can be certain that if we do not desire an attitude like that of Jesus Christ, we will not have a heart and soul through which the Holy Spirit can work to develop humility within us. The Holy Spirit will do His work, but only as we put into practice the teachings of Scripture on relationships.

Servant Lord

What does a human life look like when it is rooted in profound humility? To find out the answer to that question, we need only look to Jesus, the humblest man who ever walked the earth.

Scripture paints a detailed picture of Christ's humility. In the second chapter of Philippians, for example, Paul taught that our attitude "should be the same as that of Christ Jesus":

Who, being in very nature God,
> did not consider equality with God something to
> be grasped,
but made himself nothing,
> taking the very nature of a servant,
> being made in human likeness.
And being found in appearance as a man,
> he humbled himself
> and became obedient to death—even death on a
> cross! (Philippians 2:5-8 NIV).

Paul was telling us that our status and titles don't matter. Jesus was God—surely there can be no greater status or title than that. Yet He "made himself nothing" when He came to be with us. So although we may be head coaches, senators, or CEOs, Paul's message is clear: our position doesn't count. Humility is for everyone.

All authority in heaven and on earth had been given to Jesus. Through Him all things were made and in Him all things hold together (Colossians 1:16-17). Yet when He came among us, He was the lowliest of servants. "The Son of Man came not to be served but to serve, and to give his life as a ransom for many" (Matthew 20:28). His authority was based solely upon the authority of His word, character, and example.

So, what can we conclude from looking at this most perfect image of humility? For one thing, as Rick Warren says in *The Purpose Driven Life*, "It's not about you." (Or her, or him, or me.) It's about God. We are here to serve Him, obey His law, and carry out His purposes for our lives. We also are here to serve each other for Him. Whatever our status or title, we are servants of everyone in our communities.

Ascending to Heaven

Novelist Saul Bellow tells a tale of the rabbi in a small Russian town. This rabbi would disappear each Friday morning for several hours. The rabbi's disciples boasted that during those hours the rabbi would ascend to heaven and talk to God.

A stranger moved into town and was skeptical of the reports about the rabbi. He decided to hide and watch what the rabbi did one Friday morning.

That morning, the rabbi said his prayers, dressed in peasant clothing, and then, grabbing an axe, headed off into the woods. There he cut some firewood, which he afterward hauled to a shack on the outskirts of the town—the home of a widow and her sick son. The rabbi left the pair enough fuel for a week and then snuck back home.

Having observed the rabbi's actions, the stranger stayed on in the village and became the rabbi's disciple. And whenever he would hear one of the villagers say, "On Friday morning our rabbi ascends all the way to heaven," the newcomer would quietly add, "If not higher."[12]

The rabbi was humble enough to serve others in a way calculated to go unseen. In the same way, we are to serve others—whatever their station in life and whatever ours.

If by this time you are thinking that a future full of servanthood, submission, and humility looks grim, fear not. Being humble does not mean that we won't accomplish much in life. In fact, consider this possibility: Humility will *increase* our effectiveness at whatever we do.

Humble Excellence

Jesus taught, "Unless a grain of wheat falls into the earth and dies, it remains alone; but if it dies, it bears much fruit" (John 12:24). Jesus was talking here about His own death, but His words apply to us as well. For it is only through humility—dying to self, to our own purposes, and to our conceits—that we are free to bring forth much fruit.

This brings us to a couple of misconceptions that hover around a biblical understanding of humility. First, there is nothing about humility that keeps a Christian from aspiring to excellence or success, from going after lofty goals, or from being as tough as nails when justice or love calls for it. A humble person can have a winning attitude and exude great confidence.

Second, nothing about humility prevents us from being as highly competent as our God-given gifts allow us to be. In fact, Scripture tells us to "aim for perfection" (2 Corinthians 13:11 NIV). We all know that nothing short of excellence will glorify God, so we should be satisfied with nothing less.

Thus, it is entirely consistent with biblical humility for an artist to strive to produce the finest works of which he is capable and to discipline his life to achieve this goal. Being fully humble in the biblical sense of the word, a high school student can seek grades to qualify for the best colleges and can study diligently to achieve that privilege. The offensive tackle on a professional football team, altogether consistent with humility, can lay a pancake block on the opposing lineman time and again. (It might help every so often to extend a hand to help the lineman up.)

How is it that we can attain such accomplishments and still remain humble? Because the primary objective of the humble person is not to win but to glorify God by doing his best and then to leave in God's hands whether he will *be* the best. The humble person understands how little if any of our success we can attribute to ourselves. In that sense, humility is a form of wisdom. It is thinking clearly. It is simply being realistic. It is knowing who really deserves the credit and the glory for what we do.

Let's take the example of a tailback who wins the Heisman Trophy. This Heisman winner gets his name in the paper and his face on ESPN. But where did he get the DNA that created the strong body? And where did he get the great coordination that helped him win the prize? How many of the 100 trillion cells in his body did he create?

We are told that for each of these cells there is a bank of instructions more detailed than the thirty-two volumes of the *Encyclopedia Britannica* put together. Does this tailback understand even one of these instructions? (For that matter, does even the smartest doctor or biologist in the world fully understand the marvel of a single human cell?)

"But I worked so hard," the tailback might say. "I went to the weight room. I practiced harder than anyone else on the team."

To him we could reply: "But who taught you to work that hard? Who built the weight room? Who bought the equipment? Who built the university, including the stadium you played in? Who cut the grass there and laid out the lines and boundaries? Did you hire or pay your coaches? Did you recruit your team-mates? Did you open up those holes in the line that you ran through?"

If this tailback has humility, he will express nothing but overflowing gratitude when he wins the Heisman—to his parents, to his teachers, to his coaches, to all the players on his team, to everyone who helped him along the way. Most of all, time and time again, he will express gratitude to God. And because of that gratitude, he will be motivated to work all the harder, so as not to let down those who have invested in him and who depend on him.

This ageless thought says it all: *We drink from wells we did not dig and we are warmed by fires we did not build* (see Deuteronomy 6:11). In this light, humility is only logical. It ought to become our daily habit.

The Humility Habit

Humility begins with the grace of repentance. But after that shift of mind occurs, we can and must engrave humility into our characters by practice, so that it becomes second nature to us.

But what, exactly, should we practice? There's a catch-22 here: To the extent we try to *look* humble, we quickly fall victim to pride. In truth, we can only *be* humble. We will be humble if we continually focus on the profound wisdom of who we really are, and who God really is. We will be humble if we abandon pretenses based upon ego—that is, believing we deserve credit for our intelligence, looks, abilities, accomplishments, or wealth. We will be humble if we gratefully give credit to God for all we are and have.

A number of specific practices help to make humility a habit.

First, we should make it a point to avoid using "I," "me," and "my" when referring to accomplishments. Mindful of the truth about who is really responsible, we will come to see how words such as "we," "us," and "ours" are always more accurate.

Second, we can keep in our minds (and thus reflect in our attitudes) the Latin phrase *Soli Deo gloria*—"to God alone be the glory." And we can practice the disciplines of simplicity, submission, and servanthood.

Finally, throughout our days—and, really, all the time, every day—we can offer up prayers of gratitude to God for His many gifts to us. This discipline will honor God and remind us of who is responsible for all good things.

God-confidence

When Douglas Freeman completed his magisterial four-volume biography of Robert E. Lee, he searched for a way to summarize the character of this great man, for an incident that would epitomize the heart of the general. These words referring to Lee's funeral, conclude the biography:

Had his life been epitomized in one sentence of the Book he read so often, it would have been in the words, "If any man will come after me, let him deny himself, and take up his cross daily, and follow me." And if one, only one, of all the myriad incidents of his stirring life had to be selected to typify his message, as a man, to the young American who stood in hushed awe that rainy October morning as their parents wept at the passing of the Southern Arthur, who would hesitate in selecting that incident? It occurred in Northern Virginia, probably on his last visit there. A young mother brought her baby to him to be blessed. He took the infant in his arms and looked at it and then at her and slowly said, "Teach him he must deny himself."[13]

The ultimate outgrowth of humility is self-denial. Indeed, as we have elsewhere noted, self-denial is critical to the development of every godly virtue. Faith, hope, wisdom, courage, self-control, justice, love—none of these virtues can be engraved in our characters if we put ourselves first.

Repeatedly, Jesus tells us to deny ourselves, take up our cross, and follow Him (Matthew 10:38-39; 16:24-25; Luke 17:33; and John 12:24-25). The plain language of *The Message* makes vividly clear what His words mean for our everyday lives. In Matthew 10:38-39, for example, Jesus says, "If your first concern is to look after yourself, you'll never find yourself. But if you forget about yourself and look to me, you'll find both yourself and me." And in Luke 17:32-33 Jesus tells His disciples, "If you grasp and cling to life on your terms, you'll lose it, but if you let that life go, you'll get life on God's terms."

Living on those terms, we will no longer strive for the values that our modern culture esteems: self-assertiveness, self-assuredness, self-confidence. But that doesn't mean believers can't feel good about themselves or be assertive, assured, or confident.

Let's go back to our tailback. If he is six feet tall, weighs 220 muscular pounds, has good hands and great moves, and runs the forty-yard dash in 4.4 seconds, he can certainly be confident that he can get the job done. He can fulfill his role as a servant of his team with assurance and poise. But if he views his skill with humility, his assurance will be based, not on faith in himself, but in systems others have developed that bring out the best in him and his teammates. Beyond that, his confidence will be in the Lord. He is God-confident, not self-confident.

This level of self-denial does not grow in us overnight. In God's grace, it is worked into us as we practice submission and servanthood in thought and deed, giving all the credit and thanksgiving to God and to others. This is living as we ought, planting the tree of our character in the rich soil of humility.

As we will see in the next chapters, humility allows us to put down strong roots of faith and hope.

Character Questions

1. Most people struggle with pride in certain areas more than in others. For example, someone may not be vain about his appearance but might be proud of his intellect. In what area(s) do you have the most trouble being humble, and why?

2. Jonathan Edwards stated, "All, everything in grace is calculated to bring humility into the hearts of man." What has brought humility into your heart?

3. What will be your next step in making humility a habit?

5

Faith: Trusting God, No Matter What

Faith is basic to the Christian life and a foundational virtue. In terms of the tree of character, faith is one of the root virtues. And we know that without strong roots, we won't be able to produce good works for God's glory.

Along with faith, the other root virtue is hope. Both of these biblical virtues anchor and empower us. And both can become so engraved in our characters that faithfulness and hopefulness become second nature to us. We will look at the virtue of hope in the next chapter, but first we must explore the character quality that starts us off in the Christian life and enables us to persevere until the end.

The Nature of Faith

Faith connects the humble heart with the grace of God. The apostle Paul says that "the only thing that counts is faith expressing itself through love" (Galatians 5:6 NIV) and that "whatever does not proceed from faith is sin" (Romans 14:23). And from Hebrews we know that "without faith it is impossible to please God" (Hebrews 11:6 NIV). Clearly, faith must fill every nook and cranny of our lives, from our thoughts and emotions to our decisions and deeds.

Faith is a gift we receive from God. Paul states it this way in Ephesians: "By grace you have been saved through faith. And this is not your own doing; it is the gift of God, not a result of works, so that no one may boast" (Ephesians 2:8-9). We don't deserve faith. We can't buy it or earn it. But we *can* desire it and pray for it. We can also prepare to receive it, by humbly surrendering to God's will and turning to God as our hope.

The Bible tells us that a tree planted next to a stream is always green and always bears fruit (Psalm 1:3; Jeremiah 17:7-8). The roots that draw from the living water in the stream are the roots of faith. As the Bible tells us, through our faith we have access to God's grace (Romans 5:1-2). Faith, therefore, connects us to God. We ought to devote the whole of our lives to keeping this connection strong and free-flowing.

Faith has three faces, showing itself in three different ways in our lives. *First, faith is belief in Christ for salvation. Second, faith is trust in the God whom the Bible reveals, regardless of the problems we face. Third, faith is action committed to the glory of God.*

Faith as Belief

What defines the Christian life? Is it doing the things that Christians do—going to church, being baptized, and so on? Or is it, perhaps, mentally assenting to a body of doctrines? It is nothing like this, though people make the mistake of thinking so all the time. The true Christian life begins with, and can never exist without, belief in Christ as God's Son and our Savior. This kind of belief is saving faith, a commitment of all we have and all we are to Jesus, initiating an eternal relationship with Him.

Through God's grace, I was given faith at age thirty-seven. I did not go looking for it. In fact, at that point in my life, I had rejected the concept of saving faith. I was satisfied that, if indeed there was such a thing as salvation, sincerity of heart and an above average amount of good works would be enough to qualify me for it. Though I had been raised in a Christian family, the only attention I paid to the new birth was to try to avoid conversation with any believer who wanted to lead me to it! My heart was changed, and with it my head, when I read Chuck Colson's book, *Born Again.*

Colson was one of President Nixon's top advisers, and when the Watergate crisis hit the Nixon administration, Colson was implicated in its cover-up and ultimately pled guilty to a criminal indictment charging him in the efforts to conceal the crimes of the administration. On his way to prison Colson met with one of his trusted friends and former law clients, who led him to receive Christ and be born again. Thereafter, Colson, the ex-Marine enforcer of the Nixon administration, committed his life to Christ and upon release from prison formed and began leading a worldwide prison ministry called Prison Fellowship.

Ironically, I had picked up the book to learn more about Watergate, not religion. There was no crisis in my life. Indeed, by any worldly measure, all was well with me and mine. My life was on cruise control. But as I read Colson's words, everything changed for me. Awkwardly and in tears, I began to pray, "Dear God, whatever happened to Chuck Colson, let it happen to me."

A few weeks later, our youngest child, Sissy, was baptized in the Episcopal church. The service for infant baptism calls on the parents and godparents to answer several questions on behalf of the infant. "Do you turn to Jesus Christ and accept Him as your Savior?" "Do you promise to obey Him as Lord?" "Will you put your whole trust in His grace and love?"

As I answered "I do" to these foundational questions of the Christian faith for my daughter, I was vividly aware that I was answering them for myself as well. It had taken me thirty-seven years to understand that receiving Jesus Christ, obeying Him as Lord, and trusting Him is what the Christian faith is all about.

The single most important question in all of life is the first one I answered that day: "Do you turn to Jesus Christ and accept Him as your Savior?" My yes to that question had nothing to do with my brain. It was not that I had thought through this fundamental idea and found it convincing. Quite the opposite, in fact. To the natural mind, it is impossible to fathom that God, who is sovereign, would allow mankind's situation to get to a point where it required the crucifixion of His Son to repair it. It is precisely because this essential salvation truth makes no sense intellectually that we must receive it in our hearts by faith.

This sort of belief in Christ as Savior is not all there is to the virtue of faith. A second dimension of faith is trusting God to take care of us as He has promised.

Faith as Trust

Almost always in the New Testament, when we read the word "faith" or "believe," it is translated from a Greek word that means "to trust or have confidence in." This is the most fundamental meaning of Christian faith.

In John's writings, the word "believe" could just as well be translated "trust." In my case, this use of the word "believe" was unfortunate, because it caused me to concentrate too much on what was in my head when my concerns should have centered on my heart, deepening my trust in God. To be sure, we must have intellectual knowledge of, and belief in, the object of our faith. The stronger this knowledge, the more powerful and effective our faith. But faith is far more than mere belief. As James makes clear, even the devil believes the Christian creed (James 2:19). He just rebels from the truth.

The call to have faith in God—that is, not just to believe in Him but also to trust Him—is the basic theme of the Bible. From Genesis to Revelation, Scripture's essential truth is that God is sovereign and all-powerful, that He created the world and that everything at all times is under His control, and that He is holy, good, and steadfastly loving. It is this God in whom we are to put our trust.

The issue of trust boils down to who or what will control our lives. The secular world offers an array of choices in which we are tempted to place our trust—money, a company, a nation, another person, and ourselves, to name a few. But biblical faith puts God in control. Proverbs says:

Trust in the Lord with all your heart,
     and do not lean on your own understanding.
In all your ways acknowledge him,
     and he will make straight your paths (3:5-6).

Note here that trust is to be wholehearted. Any secondary trust in our lives must be both under and aligned with our trust in God.

The New Testament makes clear that Jesus Christ is the Lord of our lives. Having faith in Him means making Him sovereign over our lives all the time and in every way. It means we invite Him to reign on the throne of our lives.

Viewed in this way, faith is co-existent with humility. When what we trust is our own strength—in other words, when we try to play god in our lives—there can be no faith in the biblical sense. We are on our own. But when, in humility, we understand God's sovereignty and our total dependence on His mercy and grace, we have faith. It has been said correctly that faith is "utter humility."[2]

The School of Adversity

The virtue of trusting God is like a muscle which must be exercised and strengthened or it will wilt and become useless. The exercise that develops the faith "muscle" comes only in circumstances where we have lost or relinquished control of a situation and have been forced to turn to God. If we want to find people whose faith is great, we need to look to those who have been tested by adversity—illness, heartbreak, poverty—and who have persevered in faith.

Though not written from an explicitly biblical perspective, psychiatrist Scott Peck's best-selling book *The Road Less Traveled* offers insight about the role of trials in our lives. The book begins with three stark words: "Life is difficult."[3] Peck's theme is that we grow in character only to the extent that we face our difficulties head-on and work through them.

Similarly, Rick Warren, in the book that Ashley Smith read to Brian Nichols, has stated: "Life is a series of problems. Every time you solve one, another is waiting to take its place. Not all of them are big, but all are significant in God's growth process for you."[4]

As we work through trials, God's grace is with us. God uses our difficulties to perfect us so that we may bear more fruit for His glory.

Paul's letter to the Romans clearly shows the relationships among grace, faith, adversity, and character. The first four chapters of Romans tell us that salvation is by faith alone, without any works that we might add. Chapter 5 tells us that by this saving faith we have become reconciled to God. We have peace with Him and access to His grace, which equips us to serve Him in all He calls us to do. Then Paul writes, "We rejoice in our sufferings, knowing that suffering produces endurance, and endurance produces character, and character produces hope" (Romans 5:3-4).

In a sense, then, suffering is something we can welcome, since we know that Jesus is using our tough times to teach us to persevere, thereby strengthening our character. James has a similar message, saying that "trials of many kinds" will test our faith, that they will teach us to persevere, and that through this perseverance our characters may become "mature and complete," lacking nothing (James 1:2,4 NIV).

George Müller, a German minister who lived in England in the mid nineteenth century, offers a powerful example both of trust in God and the sort of fruit that trust can yield.

A Life of Trust

God called George Müller to minister to orphans, and Müller answered the call. But that was not all. In faith, he resolved not to ask anyone for a single pound or pence for the orphanage he established in Bristol, England. He would pray and trust that God would provide whatever the ministry needed.

Money was incredibly tight. Many days, when one meal for the children ended, there weren't yet sufficient funds to serve the next. Müller's problems were not month to month; they were meal to meal. Yet Müller trusted God and spent his time praying. And time and again, without fail, funds sufficient for at least the next meal were provided. Over the course of twenty-five years, Müller's orphanage grew from a few children to seven hundred and from a few small rooms to three large buildings owned by the ministry—all without anyone asking someone else for a donation.

Few of us have the sort of trust in God that Müller demonstrated. But it is easy to see how experiences such as his would serve to strengthen faith in the Lord. In his autobiography Müller writes of the benefits of adversity to the growth of trust in God. His logic was simple. "The more I am in a position to be tried in faith ... the more shall I have the opportunity of seeing God's help and deliverance ... Every fresh instance in which He helps me and delivers me will lead toward an increase in my faith."[5]

As a result of his own experience, Müller had some advice for others, including us. "On this account, therefore, the believer should not shrink from situations ... in which his faith may be tried but should cheerfully embrace these opportunities where he may see the hand of God stretched out on his behalf to help and deliver him."[6] The result, of course, is that the believer's faith is strengthened.

Here we can see how faith is a virtue in the sense we have defined it. It is strengthened by being put into practice. Faith is not given to us by Christ fully formed. He perfects it over time as we train in discipline under Him. Twenty-six years into his orphan ministry, Müller says, "The selfsame faith which is found in every believer" had for him been increasing "little by little for the last six and twenty years."[7]

It is easy to presume on the truth of how faith develops and to put God to the test. I was once advising a ministry that wanted to launch an expansion program so bold that, if it were to be successful, "only by God's power" could it have been accomplished—to use the words of the ministry leaders. I advised against the program because a foundation for it had not been laid over the previous life of the ministry.

By contrast, Müller started with a handful of orphans. His ministry grew "little by little," as did his faith. His vision was bold, but so was it wise. He moved in God's time.

Müller's example makes us all ponder how we can build our trust in God over the course of a lifetime. For all of us, no doubt, the greatest difficulty comes when we are facing hardship and trials, which, of course, also provides the greatest opportunity.

The Will to Trust

When times are tough, I have often turned to Jerry Bridges' *Trusting God*, a great book on this subject. Bridges makes a critical point: Trusting God is a matter of the will. We can choose to honor God by trusting Him even when we don't want to, even when we wonder why God would allow us to get into such a fix. Bridges advises that, just as we learn to obey God "one choice at a time," so we must learn to trust God "one circumstance at a time." Speaking for himself (but it is true for me and probably for you too), Bridges says, "I never feel like trusting God when adversity strikes, but I can choose to do so even when I don't feel like it. The act of will, though, must be based on belief and belief must be based on truth."[8]

Bridges goes on to tie trusting in God to our ultimate purpose, telling us that "our first priority in times of adversity is to ... glorify God by trusting Him.... God's honor is to take precedence over our feelings.... As we seek God's glory, we may be sure that he has purposed our good and that He will not be frustrated in fulfilling that purpose."[9]

Of the three faces of faith—belief, trust, and action—trust is by far the most difficult for me. Reading, studying, and memorizing the Bible are food for my soul. I revel in work and challenges, and as best I can, I commit all my actions to God's honor. But trusting Him is no easy thing.

God has been ever so merciful to me. He has given me good health, a wonderful family life, successful employment, and a lifetime in the greatest, most prosperous, most just nation on the planet. My life can't compare to the experience of those who suffer illness, injustice, or deprivation, nor with that of the millions of believers throughout the world who even today are persecuted for their faith. Yet, although the Bible counsels that I

99

should have peace in the midst of trouble, I continue to wrestle with anxiety and distraction when I have made bad decisions or let others down.

I make this confession simply to let you know that if you have a problem with trust, I am in your company. Neither of us may ever become a George Müller, but God will honor our attempts to trust Him and by His Spirit will grow in us the ability to trust.

Faith as Action

If belief and trust were all there were to faith, you could rightly ask, "So what? How do believing and trusting fulfill my ultimate purpose? How do they make the tree of character grow within me? Where is the fruit?"

This is where the third aspect of faith comes into play. Remember what was said at the beginning of this chapter: Faith is like a root of the tree that brings God glory. When we trust and believe, we are connected to the grace of God. And just as water and nutrients flow into plants through their roots, so through our faith grace flows into us, equipping us to accomplish the good works that God has prepared beforehand for us to do.

The Bible is clear on this point: All the belief and trust in the world are worthless if we don't put the teachings of Jesus into practice through faith. As James tells us, faith without works is dead (James 2:26).

Once the commitment to act is made, the person of faith can declare with Paul, "I can do everything through him who gives me strength" (Philippians 4:13 NIV). Just as Paul counsels Timothy as he was planting a church, so we can "be strong in the grace that is in Christ Jesus" (2 Timothy 2:1 NIV). When Paul prayed for relief from a thorn in his side, Christ told him, "My power is made perfect in weakness" (2 Corinthians 12:9 NIV). We can know such power.

In his *Commentary on Romans*, Martin Luther writes that "faith is a living, daring confidence in God's grace, so sure and certain that the believer would stake his life on it a thousand times." We should note the object of faith: God's grace. Luther went on to say that because of this faith a person "is ready and glad to do good to everyone" and to "suffer everything out of love and praise to God ... It is impossible to separate works from faith, just as impossible to separate heat from light and fire."[10]

When Luther spoke of that "living, daring confidence in God's grace," he was talking about belief and trust. Look at the amazing *work* that George Müller's *belief* and *trust* enabled him to do. Certainly Müller's works were as impossible to separate from his faith as heat and light are from fire.

Luther and the Catholic church had a long-running dispute over the role of faith in the life of the believer. The dispute continues in some measure today. But on the fruit of faith being action, Protestantism and Catholicism are in complete agreement.

In a letter titled *The Splendor of Truth*, written in 1993, Pope John Paul II tells us, "Faith is a lived knowledge of Christ, a living remembrance of His commandments, and a *truth to be lived out*. A word ... is not truly received until it passes into action, until it is put into practice. Faith is a decision involving one's whole existence ... It entails an act of trusting abandonment to Christ, which enables us to live as He lived (cf. *Gal* 2:20), in profound love of God and of our brothers and sisters."[11]

Note the words Luther and John Paul II used to describe faith. They talked of "living" faith, of "staking our lives" on it. They used verbs like "do." The Pope instructed that believers are to put their faith "into practice." This is the language of virtue and character. Faith results in living and serving and working and practicing and doing good works.

It's important to note that when the Pope spoke of a "trusting abandonment," he was describing the depth of our humble trust and confidence in God, not instructing us to abandon our own efforts to do the work God has assigned us. We are not to "let go and let God" but rather, as Colossians tells us, to work at whatever we are called to do with all our heart, trusting that the results are in the hands of God (Colossians 3:23). When Proverbs says that "the horse is made ready for the day of battle," that's talking about our part. But having given it our all, "victory rests with the Lord" (Proverbs 21:31 NIV).

Faith has been compared to putting a car into gear. It attaches the machine to the power source. It allows us to let Jesus do His work in and through our lives. Believing that Christ is who Scripture proclaims Him to be, we can trust that He "is able to do immeasurably more than all we ask or imagine, according to his power that is at work within us" (Ephesians 3:20 NIV).

One occasion when God did immeasurably more than anyone could have expected was when He used a tiny old woman to quell a prison riot.

Mother Antonia

On Halloween night, 1994, a prisoner inside the La Mesa state penitentiary in Tijuana, Mexico, called a guard over to him. According to plan, arms passed through the bars and grabbed the guard, stealing his gun and keys. The prisoners quickly released themselves, set mattresses on fire in the cell block, and started shooting into the air.

Fearing what might happen, the remaining guards abandoned their posts and shut off electricity to the prison. The prisoners were now in charge of most of the facility, which was dark except for the flames rising from top-floor windows. Meanwhile, SWAT teams assembled on the streets for the expected takeover.

Then there appeared a small woman in a white habit. She was Mother Antonia, an elderly American sister who voluntarily lived in a cell and served the prisoners in any way she could.

She wanted to go in to talk to them now. After some debate, the warden agreed.

Mother Antonia entered the darkened prison, hearing the shots and smelling the smoke. Some of the prisoners came out of hiding, surprised to see Mother Antonia instead of riot police. "Mother Antonia!" shouted one inmate. "Get out of here. You'll be shot!"

But Mother Antonia continued advancing toward the main body of rioting prisoners. "What's going on here?" she said. "The whole city is terrified." She told them that an army was outside getting ready to come in and that if they didn't put down their guns, their children would be orphaned.

"Mother," said one inmate named Blackie, "we've been up here so long they've forgotten us. That water's gone, and we're desperate."

"We can take care of those things, but this isn't the way to do it. First, you have to give me the guns."

"Mother," Blackie said softly, "as soon as we heard your voice, we dropped the guns out the window."

Because one woman put her faith into action, Mexico's Night of the Dead did not become a night of killing in 1994. Mother Antonia's faith made a difference far beyond what anyone could have expected.

Likewise, as we believe in the truth of Scripture by following Christ, trust in God whether times are good or bad, and live out our faith through working and serving for Christ's sake, faith will grow in us and nourish a magnificent tree of character. Fruit bearing begins with strong roots.

Character Questions

1. Based on what you have read in this chapter, how would you define faith?

2. The author said he finds that faith as trust is the hardest kind of faith for him. What is the hardest kind for you, and why?

3. This chapter tells the stories of several people of faith. The author surrendered his life to Christ in faith, as Charles Colson had done. George Müller believed that God would provide for his ministry's needs. Mother Antonia walked into a prison riot because she believed God wanted her to bring peace to the situation. Which of these people would you like to be more like, and why? What can you do about it?

6

Hope: Waiting on the Lord

Psychologist Viktor Frankl spent two-and-a-half years in Nazi concentration camps near the end of World War II. Afterward, in his book *Man's Search for Meaning*, Frankl tells the story of a fellow prisoner who in February 1945 dreamed their camp would be liberated on March 30 of that year. The prisoner was filled with hope, for he was convinced the dream was prophetic. "But as the promised day drew nearer," Frankl wrote, "the war news which reached our camp made it appear very unlikely that we would be free on the promised date." On March 29 Frankl's fellow prisoner became ill with typhoid fever. On March 30, instead of being rescued, the man became delirious and lost consciousness. The next day he died. Frankl concluded that the man died because his hope had collapsed.[1]

Hope is basic. We can't live without it, at least not for long. Hope is also an essential part of the Christian character, a virtue God grows within us by His grace. We might define the virtue of hope as *the expectation of those who commit their lives to God that He will do good things for them in this life and in the life to come.*

As this definition implies, our hope comes in two dimensions. One is hope for a life in the heavenly realm after our life here below is over. This is termed in Scripture "our blessed hope" (Titus 2:13) and "a living hope" (1 Peter 1:3), and indeed, where would we be without this hope for eternal life with God? But with that one comes the other kind of hope, or hope for God's blessing in our earthly life. For example, if we are ill, we hope for healing; if we feel bound, we hope for release; if we have been put upon, we hope for justice.

Along with faith, hope (whether of the earthly or the heavenly variety) is one of the roots of the tree of character. Just as the roots of a physical tree are intertwined and reach deep into the earth in search of life-giving nutrients, so faith and hope are intertwined in our spirits and give life and support to our character as a whole. With strong faith and hope, our lives may be swayed but not buckled by the winds of adversity or temptation.

So important is the intertwining of hope with faith that, if we want to understand hope better, we must begin by exploring how hope is birthed by and nourishes its partner virtue: faith.

Hope: The Logical Extension of Faith

If faith gives us a "living, daring confidence" in God's grace, according to the description of Martin Luther,[2] then hope is the stabilizing, long-term dimension of faith. Luther's fellow Reformer John Calvin wrote much the same in his *Institutes*:

If faith ... is a sure persuasion of the truth of God—that it can neither lie to us, nor deceive us, nor become void—then those who have grasped this certainty assuredly expect the time to come when God will fulfill His promises, which they are persuaded cannot but be true. Accordingly, in brief, hope is nothing else than the expectation of those things which faith has believed to have been truly promised by God. Thus, faith believes God to be true, hope awaits the time when His truth shall be manifested; faith believes that He is our Father, hope anticipates that He will ever show Himself to be a Father toward us; faith believes that eternal life has been given to us, hope anticipates that it will some time be revealed; faith is the foundation upon which hope rests, hope nourishes and sustains faith.[3]

Turning to Scripture, we learn that hope is tightly joined with both faith and love, the other eternally abiding virtues (1 Corinthians 12:31; 13:13). The Bible tells us that "love hopes all things" (1 Corinthians 13:7) and that "hope does not put us to shame, because God's love has been poured into our hearts through the Holy Spirit" (Romans 5:5). Likewise, hope is joined with faith. In his letter to the Romans, Paul writes that we should trust in God so that we "may overflow with hope by the power of the Holy Spirit" (Romans 15:13 NIV). And Hebrews tells us, "Faith is the assurance of things hoped for" (11:1).

Faith believes in the promises of God, yet we often feel disappointed when that which we had been trusting God for fails to come to pass. How can such a thing be? The fact is, God's plan is not our plan and His time is not our time. The Bible teaches that God's thoughts and ways are far above our own (Isaiah 55:8-9), and as a result, His choices are often far different from what we had wanted.

In my life as a Christian, I have lifted up heartfelt prayers daily, sometimes for decades, requesting what I have believed to be acceptable blessings from God, either for myself or for others. "Two or three" other believers have often joined with me in these prayers (Matthew 18:20). I have prayed "believing" (Matthew 21:22 KJV). Nevertheless, there have been times when God has not answered my prayers with a yes. I'm sure you can say the same has been true in your experience of prayer. In this way our faith is tested. But hope sustains faith.

Paul tells us that "in our sufferings ... hope does not disappoint us, because God's love has been poured into our hearts by the Holy Spirit, whom he has given us" (Romans 5:3-5 NIV). In a sense, the rest of Romans 5 and all of Romans 8 are an elaboration of this profound truth, as Paul continues to explain that, because of God's unfailing love, hope will not disappoint. That's what he is saying in Romans 8:28 when he tells us that "in all things God works for the good of those who love him, who have been called according to his purpose" (NIV).

He finishes this theme in 8:35-39, where he declares that nothing will separate us from the love of Christ—neither tribulation nor disasters nor persecution nor famine nor nakedness nor danger nor the sword. "In all these things," through God's love, "we are more than conquerors" (v. 37). And here is the finale: "I am sure that neither death nor life, nor angels nor rulers, nor things present nor things to come, nor powers, nor height nor depth, nor anything else in all creation, will be able to separate us from the love of God in Christ Jesus our Lord" (vv. 38-39). This is the substance of our hope, a taproot of the tree that bears good fruit.

The Hope That Sustains

Along with Alabama's future senator Admiral Jeremiah Denton, Admiral Jim Stockdale spent a part of the Vietnam War in the "Hanoi Hilton" POW camp. Stockdale had an experience startlingly similar to that of Viktor Frankl, cited at the beginning of the chapter. Stockdale credits his own survival during eight years of imprisonment to the fact that he "never lost faith in the end of the story." But not all were so fortunate. Asked by a writer which prisoners didn't survive, Stockdale replied that it was the optimists, the ones who had their own timetable for freedom, who generally failed to make it. Some would confidently proclaim that they would be out by Christmas or Easter, and Christmas and Easter would come and go. Stockdale says they "died of a broken heart."

In reflecting on his ordeal, Stockdale gives us some critical advice about trusting God through adversity. He tells us, "You must never confuse faith that you will prevail in the end—which you can never afford to lose—with the discipline to confront the most brutal facts of your current reality, whatever they might be."[4]

When Stockdale talks about the "faith that you will prevail in the end," he's talking about biblical hope. A man of great faith, he never stopped believing the day would come when he would be released. But both he and Frankl avoided the presumption that such a day would come quickly or at a specific time. Both remained hopeful until God did His work.

There is hardly any better advice for working through our daily challenges. We must face the facts of our situation, but no matter how discouraging they may be, we can know that in Christ we will prevail in the end.

If we hope humbly and patiently, then when all else has failed and fallen apart, hope will still be standing. Love and faith abide with hope, but in the dark night of the soul, hope is the final refuge. Of Abraham's hope for a male heir through Sarah, Paul writes, "In hope he believed against hope" (Romans 4:18). Job, bereft of any reason to hope, cried out defiantly, "Though he slay me, yet will I hope in him" (Job 13:15 NIV). C. S. Lewis, in *The Screwtape Letters*, made the point that hope can endure, pointing out that Satan's cause is lost when the believer, "no longer desiring, but still intending, to do [God's] will, looks round upon the universe from which every trace of Him seems to have vanished, and asks why he has been forsaken, and still obeys."[5] *And still obeys.* That is what hope will do.

Hope Amid Suffering

Perhaps you, as I, have struggled with the biblical injunction that we should rejoice in our suffering (Romans 5:3; James 1:2). What is there about suffering to give joy? But of course it is not our suffering itself that gives us joy. Rather, we can have joy *amid* suffering and *despite* suffering because we know that God still loves us, still cares for us, and in His inscrutable way is working out what is best for us. We have every reason for hope, even though we are hurting.

Perhaps the most beautiful expression of hope in the Hebrew Scriptures is found in the third chapter of Lamentations. Judah had been conquered by the Babylonians; the temple had been desecrated; the Hebrew people had been uprooted and cast into slavery. A once proud and prosperous nation lay in ruins. And so the first twenty verses of chapter 3 are as bleak and pessimistic as any in the Bible. Yet at that point Jeremiah says,

> But this I call to mind,
> and therefore I have hope (Lamentations 3:21).

Then Jeremiah adds the sublime words on which the hymn "Great Is Thy Faithfulness" is based:

The steadfast love of the LORD never ceases;
>   his mercies never come to an end;
> they are new every morning;
>   great is your faithfulness (Lamentations 3:22-23).

We've heard it said that "the arc of history is long, but it tends toward justice." These words get at an important truth about hope: God's steadfast love works according to His own timetable—often over a long period, even centuries, and never at the snap of our fingers.

God's chosen people were enslaved in Egypt for hundreds of years before He appointed Moses to deliver them. Six hundred years passed between the great messianic prophecies and the coming of Jesus Christ. The early Church expected Jesus' immediate return, and yet two thousand years have passed and still we wait. In such circumstances the human heart cries out,

> How long, O LORD? Will you forget me forever?
>   How long will you hide your face from me?
>   (Psalm 13:1 NIV)

Such has been the cry of the persecuted, the enslaved, the oppressed, and the heartbroken from the time our ancestors were expelled from the garden. And such is our cry today. And thus we need hope.

The Long-term Perspective

Paul, the great apostle of hope, spells out the mind-set and habits of our earthly hope: "Rejoice in hope, be patient in tribulation, be constant in prayer" (Romans 12:12). This is the best counsel for any of us whose faith is tested by a trial that appears unendurable. We are to rejoice in hope; God's steadfast love and mercy cover us. We should be patient and steady in hope; there will be a resolution to our troubles. We should pray constantly in hope; we will have peace through fellowship with God, knowing that He is working all things for our good.

Later in Romans, Paul advises that our hope is in Christ. Then he pronounces a blessing and prayer: "May the God of hope fill you with all joy and peace as you trust in him, so that you may overflow with hope by the power of the Holy Spirit" (Romans 15:13 NIV). It is as if Paul is saying that peace is an outflow of hope, and as we keep on trusting, we overflow with a confident hope by the power of the Holy Spirit.

In America, far too often we think only of the short term. We want events to unfold according to our own personal schedules. We expect instant relief from trouble. Yet while God's mercies may sometimes result in a quick fix, far more often, in His wisdom, He defers His answers to our hearts' cries, sometimes for years. Hope, therefore, is a long-term virtue, and we do well to remember the words to the hymn "In His Time":

> In His time, in His time
> He makes all things beautiful in His time.
> Lord, please show me every day
> As You're teaching me Your way
> That You do just what You say
> in Your time.[6]

While it is true that in hope we persevere, Paul tells us twice in Romans that biblical hope comes *after* perseverance (Romans 5:3-5, 15:4). His point is that Christian hope is a virtue for the mature, for those who have learned to endure hardship. A child expects an instant solution and loses his temper when relief does not come immediately. The mature parent has learned to wait upon the Lord. In the terminology of character, the virtue of hope is engraved slowly and deeply— and only on those who have learned that God sets the timetable. In its confidence in God's promises, hope nurtures a godly patience. More than any other virtue, hope waits upon the Lord.

Hope Revived

In *Shawshank Redemption*, Andy Dufresne is imprisoned for a crime he did not commit. He endures the abusive, unjust environment for nearly twenty years before breaking free.

Andy's ability to endure and his determination to escape come from one source: hope.

His friend and fellow prisoner, Red, questions Andy's faith that good might ever be a part of their lives again. Red is imprisoned for a murder he committed decades ago; he sees no hope of parole, no hope of redemption, no hope of freedom. Yet Andy tells him, "There's something inside that they can't get to, that they can't touch, that's yours ... hope."

"Hope?" Red asks. "Hope is a dangerous thing. Hope can drive a man insane. It's got no use on the inside [of a prison]. You'd better get used to that idea."

Red doesn't know it, but Andy's hope is active and growing—he is slowly chipping away at his prison wall. Eventually Andy escapes and finds a safe haven in Mexico, where he lives his dream of owning a boat and chartering rides on the Pacific Ocean.

When Red is approved for parole after forty years in prison, Andy tells him in a letter, "Remember, Red, hope is a good thing, maybe the best of things, and no good thing ever dies."

Red comes to life again when he gives himself permission to hope—hope to find Andy, hope to begin a new life. The final words of the movie come from Red as he goes to join Andy in Mexico: "I hope I can make it across the border. I hope to see my friend and shake his hand. I hope the Pacific is as blue as it has been in my dreams. I hope."[7]

For believers, hope has a solid object: God. And as it is revived within us, likewise it revives us.

Those who hope in the LORD
> will renew their strength.
They will soar on wings like eagles;
>> they will run and not grow weary,
>> they will walk and not be faint (Isaiah 40:31 NIV).

The Sin of Despair

John Claypool, a well-known Episcopal priest and writer who led my church, St. Luke's Episcopal Church in Birmingham, Alabama, for many years, has written extensively on hope. In his book, *The Hopeful Heart*, Claypool says that Paul's words in 1 Corinthians 13 — "We know in part and we prophesy in part" and "Now we see in a mirror dimly" (vv. 9, 12)—provide two different "avenues to hopefulness" even when situations are dire. "Humility before what we do not know and acceptance of what we do know from Scripture can lead us into 'the promised' land of hope," Claypool writes.[8]

To show how humility supports hope, Claypool tells the story of his own experience of hopelessness. In 1960 he and an elderly Jewish rabbi were working together in the civil rights movement in Louisville, Kentucky. After a group of African-American ministers got up and left a particularly contentious meeting, Claypool told the rabbi that he thought the racial problem was so old and deep that there was no hope of its resolution. The rabbi, whose family had been through the Holocaust, took Claypool aside and told him, "To the Jew, there is only one unforgivable sin, and that is the sin of despair."

Viktor Frankl would agree. So would the great Jewish prophets. The point Claypool's friend was realizing was that despair—the absence of hope—is presumptuous, in that by it we declare that we know more about God's provision for us and our loved ones than does God Himself. In fact, such despair is, at bottom, rebellion against God's goodness and love. God can make the dead come back to life, and the resurrection of His Son promises that, for those who belong to Him, death is the gateway to eternal blessedness. What room is there, then, for despair?

Though we don't know the future, Claypool writes, we do know some things. Specifically, we know what the Scriptures assure us to be true, and that provides more than enough cause for hope.

The sign over the gate of Dante's hell may read, "Abandon hope all ye who enter here," but none of us who follows Christ need ever abandon our hope.

Our Blessed Hope

Scripture promises, and faith believes, that Jesus will come again to put an end to the present fallen creation and will establish His reign over all. He will judge, condemn, and extinguish all evil. Paul therefore declares in his celebrated taunt-song to the final enemy,

> O death, where is your victory?
>> O death, where is your sting? (1 Corinthians 15:55).

Surely, Horatio Spafford knew the full and profound meaning of these words.

In 1873, Spafford was a successful Illinois attorney, happily married, with four daughters. He was a devout Presbyterian and follower of evangelist D. L. Moody. Spafford decided to go to England with his family to assist with a Moody crusade. Detained by a business crisis, Spafford sent his wife and daughters ahead without him. The Spafford women's ship was struck by another ship as they crossed the Atlantic, and within minutes it had sunk. All four of Spafford's daughters died, though his wife survived.

Grief-stricken, Spafford set sail to meet his wife. When his ship passed the spot where his daughters had drowned, Spafford, with a comfort that could only come from blessed hope, wrote this great hymn:

> When peace, like a river, attendeth my way,
> When sorrows like sea billows roll—
> Whatever my lot, Thou hast taught me to say,
> It is well, it is well with my soul.[9]

Though we may not know what tomorrow will bring, nor what awaits us in any of our remaining days, we do know the end of the story of redemption. For those who belong to Jesus

Christ, it is glorious. In His kingdom, to be established when He comes again, there will be everlasting joy and peace. Peter states it this way: "According to his great mercy, [God] has caused us to be born again to a living hope through the resurrection of Jesus Christ" (1 Peter 1:3). Peter tells us this hope is to "an inheritance that is imperishable, undefiled, and unfading," to be "revealed in the last time" (1 Peter 1:4-5). And Paul tells us that "our blessed hope" is "the appearing of the glory of our great God and Savior Jesus Christ" (Titus 2:13).

This aspect of hope should have life-shaping power over how we live today. God's plan and purpose for our lives is not limited to the few years we have on earth but extends throughout eternity. We will indeed enjoy hope forever. His plan for all creation is one that will conclude in perfect justice and—for those whose names are written in "the Lamb's book of life" (Revelation 21:27 NIV)—in everlasting joy, peace, and delight in God.

It was this second form of hope that motivated the great heroes whose courage is described in Hebrews 11. The writer of Hebrews says of these men and women, "They desire a better country, that is a heavenly one. Therefore God is not ashamed to be called their God, for he has prepared for them a city" (Hebrews 11:16). And He has prepared for *us* a city. It is this hope, confirmed by the "great cloud of witnesses," that is before us as we "run with endurance the race that is set before us" (12:1).

An old quip describes a person as "so heavenly minded that he is no earthly good." We forget that Jesus encourages us to be heavenly minded, especially with our earthly possessions. "Lay up for yourselves treasures in heaven" (Matthew 6:20). Being heavenly minded in hope should make us more earthly good. Because, if we think clearly, our future eternity in heaven overwhelms any concern we need have about earthly life.

Heavenly minded Christians should be ready to make great and even ultimate sacrifices in love for others here on earth. Life here in light of the blessed hope is only a temporary way station as we pass through our earthly home headed to our heavenly one forever. Clearly one of the greatest challenges for the American church, and for me as well, is to become more heavenly minded and therefore more earthly good for God's glory. The blessed hope by God's grace needs to be deeply engraved in all of us. Even for Jesus it was the "joy that was set before him" that empowered him to "endure the cross, despising the shame" (Hebrews 12:2).

The blessed hope is the foundation of the book of Revelation—in many ways the most mystifying, but also the most glorious and inspiring, of the books of the Bible. Written by John on the basis of a revelation from Jesus Christ, Revelation offered encouragement and comfort to the early, emerging churches that experienced great distress as the threat of Roman persecution spread. Its themes of justice and the victory of Jesus Christ remain a profound comfort today, reminding us of the everlasting blessedness of all who belong to Him.

> Never again will they hunger;
>> never again will they thirst.
> The sun will not beat upon them,
>> nor any scorching heat.
> For the Lamb at the center of the throne will be their
>> shepherd;
>> he will lead them to springs of living water.
> And God will wipe away every tear from their eyes
>> (Revelation 7:16-17 NIV).

Cultivation of Hope

Hope—whether it is hope for an eternity with God or merely hope that tomorrow might be easier than today—is in one sense a gift from God. He implants hope in our hearts by the Holy Spirit.

Yet, in another way, hope is a virtue we are capable of cultivating within ourselves. Hope is susceptible to strengthening through habitual practices, just as are all the other virtues. We can seek to become more hopeful and thereby nourish the Christian character in our lives.

Hope is most exercised—and most needed—when we find ourselves in difficult spots. It is when we are sick or suffering the pangs of betrayal or out of a job that we develop more strongly our ability to hope. Of course, nobody would ask to be put in that kind of situation. But while we do not enter the field of the testing of our hope voluntarily, when God puts us there, He grows hope in us as we exercise whatever measure of faith we have.

Here again, we see the interrelationship of faith and hope. Times of trial strengthen our faith and hope together, just as aerobic exercise strengthens an athlete's heart and lungs together. And just as we exercise faith by an act of the will, *choosing* to believe and to trust, so we exercise hope by *choosing* to hope in the promises of God. And then as we do act on our hope, we become more prepared to rely on hope the next time we need it.

Gratefully, I acknowledge that my life has been easier than what many others have experienced, and that's been because of the mysterious grace of God. Yet, because I have entered onto the field of adversity less often than have others, I have had fewer opportunities to cultivate the virtue of hope. But I can assure you that whenever I have hoped in God, He has never let me down. He may not always do what I would like, nor do it as soon as I would like, but He is always right and He *always* fulfills His promises—for this life and the next.

Meanwhile, the Lord loves it when we attempt to faithfully hope in Him. "The LORD takes pleasure ... in those who hope in his steadfast love" (Psalm 147:11). And as we cooperate, He helps us to hope in Him even more, year after year, decade after decade, as we grow to resemble more nearly His Son.

The greatest witness to hope of the last century was Pope John Paul II.[10] The Pope lived through the tyranny and dreariness of Communism and the horrors of World War II, but speaking to the United Nations in 1994, he left us with this uplifting prophecy for the twenty-first century and beyond:

117

We must not be afraid of the future. We must not be afraid of man. It is no accident that we are here. Each and every human person has been created in the "image and likeness" of the One who is the origin of all that is. We have within us the capacities for wisdom and virtue. With these gifts, and with the help of God's grace, we can build in the next century and the next millennium a civilization worthy of the human person, a true culture of freedom. We can and must do so! And in doing so, we shall see that the tears of this century have prepared the ground for a new springtime of the human spirit.[11]

What is hope? It is the vision implanted by God that sees in "tears" the preparation for a "new springtime."

Hope, along with faith, provides the firm grounding that the tree of character requires. And because of the strength and nourishment these provide, the additional virtues that comprise the trunk and branches can grow. The first of these other great virtues is the ability to discern what is right to believe or to do in a given situation. In a word, wisdom.

Frederick Douglass, a slave for much of his life, said he prayed and prayed for freedom, but the Lord didn't answer his prayer until he started to run. At some point we must move beyond hope to action. Wisdom enables us to make the right decisions about when and how to act.

Character Questions

1. Do you believe someone could die from a loss of hope, as Viktor Frankl has said? What makes you think that?

2. How hopeful are you? What is the basis of your hope?

3. What do you need to be hopeful about at this point in your life? How could you focus on cultivating this hope in your practice of the spiritual disciplines (prayer, Bible study, fasting, and so on)?

7

Wisdom: Making the Right Choices

It is customary at most public speaking events for the speakers to try to be inspirational without becoming controversial. Not all speakers, however, follow the rules.

While speaking before U.S. government officials at the National Prayer Breakfast in 1994, Mother Teresa of Calcutta declared the following:

> The greatest destroyer of peace today is abortion, because it is a war against the child, a direct killing of the innocent child, murder by the mother herself. And if we accept that a mother can kill her own child, how can we tell other people not to kill one another? ...
>
> If we remember that God loves us, and that we can love others as He loves us, then America can become a sign of peace for the world. From here, a sign of care for the weakest of the weak—the unborn child—must go out to the world. If you become a burning light of justice and peace in the world, then really you will be true to what the founders of this country stood for.[1]

Such wisdom rings with an unmistakable clarity, rising above the meaningless clamor of so much public speech-making.

Now let's ask ourselves this: Why was this wizened old woman, an Albanian Catholic missionary to India, able to put her finger on the truth when other intelligent, well-educated people could not? And why are many other men and women of God able to astound us with their profound insights? Because they are people in whom, over time, God has developed the virtue of wisdom, and therefore in the manner of Christ they speak with authority. They get to the heart of things.

That's wisdom. *Wisdom is a gift of grace that enables us to see reality clearly and thereby make decisions that are good for others and ourselves.* And as such, wisdom is a virtue of immeasurable importance. It is essential to any disciple who seeks to live a life that will glorify God. Wisdom makes us more Christlike.

Virtually all we know about Christ's early years is that He "increased in *wisdom* and in stature and in favor with God and man" (Luke 2:52, emphasis added). In Christ "are hidden all the treasures of *wisdom* and knowledge" (Colossians 2:3, emphasis added) and He has been "made our *wisdom*" (1 Corinthians 1:30, emphasis added). A core ministry of the Holy Spirit is wisdom (Isaiah 11:2). In short, God is wise, and so may we be by His grace.

The Carrier Virtues

So far, we have looked at the character strengths of humility, faith, and hope. Along with love, these make up the traditional "theological" virtues. But humility, faith, and hope do not lead immediately and automatically to love. They need the cardinal virtues of wisdom, courage, self-control, and justice to get us there.[2]

In terms of the tree of character, the river of living water, the soil of humility, and the roots of faith and hope are what give the tree its strong base and its vitality. But they are not its whole and they are not its crown. Just as a tree's trunk and branches transport nutrients to the leaves and fruit of a tree, so the virtues of wisdom, courage, and self-control transport the spiritual virtues into expressions of love.

As we saw in chapter one, being and doing are partners. The cardinal virtues connect being and doing, piety and deed. They allow the deep spiritual virtues to bear fruit. In this sense, we call them carrier virtues. The destiny of humility, faith, and hope is expressed in love, and the carrier virtues serve them in the same way as in the old days a horse and guide would carry a missionary from the port of a foreign land to a mission station far inland.

As we seek the fruits of justice and love in our lives, we should work in God's grace to mature in us the carrier virtues of wisdom, courage, and self-control. Some of us (most certainly I) may have been born with less of a natural capacity for one or more of these virtues than have others. And some of us may need these virtues more than do others—a soldier, for example, needs great courage and a business executive needs much wisdom. But all of these character qualities are valuable for all of us, and God, by His Spirit and through our faith, can grow these character strengths in any one of us.

Wisdom and Other Virtues

Wisdom is tightly intertwined, and mutually interdependent, with all the other virtues. All the virtues go awry without the guidance of wisdom. Without wisdom, humility can become weakness; faith can lead to naïveté; hope can become a pipe dream. Take away wisdom, and justice is impossible, courage becomes reckless bravado, self-control turns into stiff legalism. Without wisdom, love spoils children and enables dependency.

On the other side of the coin, one cannot be wise without humility. Without faith, wisdom does not understand supernatural reality. Faith gives shape to wisdom. Without hope, wisdom lacks optimism. Remove courage, and wisdom shrinks from the difficult decision. With self-control lacking, wisdom cannot even get started. If love is not at the core of wisdom, then—to quote the apostle Paul—wisdom amounts to "nothing" (1 Corinthians 13:2).

Wisdom is a virtue that we cannot have too much of. No one can be too wise, whereas without wisdom all the other virtues suffer from excess.

Thinking Clearly

Michael Novak, a Catholic writer and a scholar at the American Enterprise Institute in Washington, D.C., tells us that the first moral obligation is to think clearly. At first blush no one agrees with such a statement. Morality begins with love or justice, we are all taught. But Novak's intention is not to denigrate love and justice; rather, his point is that if we are to love others or to practice justice effectively, we must first be able to think clearly, to understand reality.

Clear thought is as critical to loving as it is to practicing medicine or building a bridge. If love (as we will discuss in a later chapter) is longing and acting for the good of another, how can we love if we are not wise enough to know what is really good for the other? To take one example, how much misery have we created for our children, and even for the poor, with the well-meaning but misplaced compassion of some welfare programs? Without wisdom, love is a noble sentiment but not a nutritious fruit.

Paul writes that "the only thing that counts is faith expressing itself through love" (Galatians 5:6 NIV). Here he ties the roots to the fruit and asserts that this is the "only thing that counts." Stated otherwise, without faith joined to love, everything else is worthless. Wisdom, together with the other carrier virtues, is the key to this connection. Without it, faith does not express itself in love.

Jack Welch, the long-time CEO of General Electric, had as one of his primary tenets of management, "Face reality as it is, not as you wish it were." He and Novak are on the same page. Before we love or seek to do justice—or make a business decision—we must think clearly so as to understand the real situation. That is what wisdom is all about.

The Wisdom of the Humble

At this point, we might be worried that we don't have the capacity for wisdom. We can, nevertheless, be assured that wisdom is not about education or even intelligence. Some who pretend to be wise are in fact foolish, while others who are simple in their lifestyle are truly wise. Indeed, as Paul tells us, the gospel itself is foolishness, if viewed from a worldly perspective (1 Corinthians 1:18-2:16).

People with exceptionally high aptitude often lack wisdom. Philosophers Jean-Jacques Rousseau and Friedrich Nietzsche made wrecks of their private lives, and their writings led to disasters for the societies that subscribed to their views. Oliver Wendell Holmes, purportedly the smartest person ever to graduate from Harvard Law School, held that mankind amounts to no more than an anthill. All that mattered, according to his philosophy, was power.

On the other hand, there have been extremely wise people with no formal education—David, a shepherd boy, being a notable example, and the carpenter Jesus being another. But we don't have to go to the Bible for examples; we have them before us in our own day.

The tsunami that struck the shores of Southeast Asia in December 2004 killed hundreds of thousands. But it did not take the life of even one of the Moken, or "sea gypsies" of the Andaman Sea, even though they were camping on the beaches of Thailand at the time. This fishing tribe preserved legends about the sea receding and then rushing back to swallow whatever life it can reach. When spear fisherman Saleh Kalathalay saw the signs of the impending tsunami, he ran about warning others of his tribe. The Moken consequently fled to higher ground, where they were safe when the water came pouring back. These simple people were wise in the ways of the sea.

One of the wisest people I know is a woman who never received any formal education. She was ironing and babysitting for ten cents a day when she was nine years old. Now ninety-three, Catherine White began her connection with our family many years ago when she took a position as housekeeper in my grandparents' home. All of us have been drawn in love to Catherine ever since. When our daughters went off to college, it was Catherine's counsel to them, not mine, that resonated most deeply in their hearts. In essence, she told them, "Whatever happens, know that you have a friend in Jesus. You can always turn to Him for guidance and strength."

Ph.D.'s or high school dropouts, we can become wise by seeking wisdom as a gift from God and putting the foundations of wisdom into practice. James tells us, "If any of you lacks wisdom, let him ask God, who gives generously to all without reproach, and it will be given him" (James 1:5).

Because the decisions humans have to make are infinitely varied, there is no book or course on the content of wisdom. As with every virtue, the study of wisdom is one of learning how to become the sort of person who thinks and acts wisely. Here the Bible has much to teach us.

The Beginning of Wisdom

In the Old Testament, Proverbs is our foundational source for understanding wisdom. Here wisdom is more highly extolled than any other virtue. We are told to "seek it like silver and search for it as for hidden treasures" (2:4). "Wisdom is better than jewels," we are assured, "and all that you may desire cannot compare with her" (8:11). Wisdom tells us, "Prefer my life-disciplines over chasing after money, and God-knowledge over a lucrative career" (8:10 MSG).

In Proverbs, the reason given for seeking wisdom is to produce a peaceful and prosperous life. Speaking of wisdom, Proverbs says, "Long life is in her right hand; in her left hand are riches and honor" (3:16; see also 8:18). Though here "riches" applies to spiritual riches, it does not exclude financial wealth as a by-product of a wise life. Furthermore, all the paths of wisdom are "peace" (3:17). With wisdom, "if you lie down, you will not be afraid; when you lie down, your sleep will be sweet" (3:24).

Proverbs is filled with instruction on wisdom as well as wise teachings on a wide range of topics. But this couplet must rank as the book's motto:

The fear of the LORD is the beginning of wisdom,
> and the knowledge of the Holy One is insight
> (9:10).[3]

In other words, we can't have wisdom and insight without both fear and knowledge of the Lord. But in this context, what exactly is meant by "fear" and "knowledge"?

At its simplest level, "fear of the LORD" is awe and reverence for God. Beyond that, the Bible teaches that to fear God is to keep His commandments (Deuteronomy 5:29; 6:2,24) and obey His voice (Haggai 1:12). It is to walk after Him (Deuteronomy 10:12) and to serve Him (6:13; 10:20). To begin to grow in wisdom, therefore, we must first obey God. Rebels from God's Word cannot be wise.

Fear of God includes "knowledge of the Holy One"—that is, understanding of His greatness, His power, His holiness. After all, this is what generates awe and reverence. As a corollary, it implies understanding who we are in relation to God and our accountability to Him. The foundation of wisdom, therefore, is virtually identical to the shift of mind we discussed in the chapter on humility. Wisdom begins with knowledge of God's holiness and sovereignty and our sinfulness and dependence.

One way to summarize the meaning of the Proverbs "motto" is to say that wisdom begins with a biblical worldview and, even more basically, with faith.

The Way We See

A worldview is the lens by which we see life. All our day-to-day decisions relate back to this view, just as our visual view of the physical world relates back to the lens of our eyes. Everyone has a worldview; the question is, what is the content of our worldview?

Secularists believe we are a collection of particles without purpose or inherent dignity. Some are existentialists—life is no more than what we make of it. Some are pragmatists—what matters is what works. Some are sensualists—eat, drink, and be merry, for tomorrow we die!

Christians, on the other hand, fear God and see all of reality through a faith lens that believes God to be uncreated, all-powerful, and holy. God is love, and we understand that He has made us for fellowship with Him. The world is distorted by sin, but God has a plan to redeem believers and to bring great glory to Himself.

So confident of our minds, it is easy for us to say that we have mastered this part—what's next? But probably we haven't mastered it. Pollster George Barna says that only 9 percent of born-again believers and 4 percent of all adult Americans possess what he defines as a biblical worldview. Of Protestant pastors, about half hold such an outlook on life.

Barna makes clear that a worldview is not simply a matter of intellectual assent. It must be both "taught and caught—that is, it has to be explained and modeled." Nor is there any crash course that works. "It is a long-term process that requires a lot of purposeful activity: teaching, prayer, conversation, accountability, and so forth."[4] This is character talk.

We Americans, so insistent on instant solutions, do not like such advice, but upon reflection, we know it is true. We come to understand who God is and who we are through experience, not study. We can be told that God loves us and that He is sovereign over all the details of life, but we come to know these truths when we experience them in the dark valleys of life. We can be told and even affirm that we are sinful and that there is no righteousness in us, but most of the time it takes a painful experience for us to finally see it.

Indeed, as we go through troubles, we can all declare to God along with Job, "I had heard of you by the hearing of the ear, but now my eye sees you" (Job 42:5). We need to remember that Job was no prodigal son; he was spiritually mature before his troubles began. The Bible records that he was "a blameless and upright man, who fear[ed] God and turn[ed] away from evil" (Job 1:8).

The Holy Spirit, together with humility (repentance), faith (trust in God), and experience, are the sources of the biblical worldview and therefore are the fountainhead of wisdom.

Character That Engenders Wisdom

If Proverbs is the key book on wisdom in the Old Testament, then the book of James plays a similar role in the New Testament. This practical book gives us sound advice about true and false wisdom.

Who is wise and understanding among you? By his good conduct let him show his works in the meekness of wisdom. But if you have bitter jealousy and selfish ambition in your hearts, do not boast and be false to the truth. This is not the wisdom that comes down from above, but is earthly, unspiritual, demonic. For where jealousy and selfish ambition exist, there will be disorder and every vile practice. But the wisdom from above is first pure, then peaceable, gentle, open to reason, full of mercy and good fruits, impartial and sincere. And a harvest of righteousness is sown in peace by those who make peace (James 3:13-18).

Here, James teaches us about the agriculture that produces wisdom.

The apostle begins by telling us that wisdom is known by its "good conduct" and "works" (v. 13). Forrest Gump was taught by his mother, "Stupid is as stupid does"; we might say the opposite—"Wisdom is as wisdom does." If a man's life is a wreck, he is likely not wise. Behavior, not big talk, proves wisdom.

James then moves on to the enemies of wisdom: the vices of jealousy and selfish ambition.

Examples abound of jealousy ("bitter envy" NIV) trumping wisdom and leading to disastrous decisions. Cain's jealousy of Abel blinded him to the reality that he was his brother's keeper with the result that Cain murdered his brother and thereby ruined his own life. (Genesis 4:1-17) Saul's jealousy of David deceived him from grasping the truth that David was his most trusted and able general. As a result of his envy, Saul disowned Jonathan his valiant son, became a brutal murderer and was killed when his army was scattered by the Philistines (1 Samuel 18-31).

As for selfish ambition, Warren Buffett—probably the wisest businessperson of the current generation—was asked to speak to the University of Washington Business School on what it takes to succeed in business. He told the class that some of them would be very successful and some would not. For those who would not prosper, he said, "It will be because you get in your own way, not because the world does not allow you." It is primarily through our selfish ambitions that we get in our own way.

A leading account of the Enron debacle is a book entitled, *The Smartest Guys in the Room.* Smart indeed, but not wise, was the Enron executive gang who had enormous potential to build a great company providing innovative services to the energy market. Why did Enron fail? Selfish ambition blinded CEO Ken Lay and his cohorts, making them fools. Likewise the brilliant group at the hedge fund, Long Term Capital Management. Roger Lowenstein's account of their disaster which came close to sinking many of the mightiest Wall Street investment houses is entitled *When Genius Failed*. Why did genius fail? Selfish ambition.

Selfishness, whether it manifests itself as envy, pride, greed, or lust, is the archenemy of clear thinking. It is a tool of Satan to make us fools and, through the ensuing stupidity, to subvert marriages, careers, and lives and to destroy the honor due to Christ in our lives.

James next speaks of "wisdom from above" (James 3:17). This wisdom that "shows [its] works in ... meekness" is the wisdom that proceeds from a worldview that acknowledges the sovereignty of God and that knows God is working all things out in accordance with His providential will (v. 13). When our wisdom "gets to the heart of the issue" or "sees the truth of the matter," as we might say, then it is wisdom from above. That is, it is wisdom down here that connects our decisions with the sovereign will of God above. How do we do that?

James tells us we do it through a character that has a bundle of virtues: meekness, purity, peaceableness, gentleness, openness to advice, mercy, impartiality, and sincerity. These virtues assure us that self is out of the way and allow us both to seek and discern God's will and to think clearly.

We should note that wisdom does not fall on us, dropped out of the sky. It is the product of a number of habits developed over the course of our life. When a crisis comes in our life and we cry out for wisdom, without these companion virtues, it is not likely we will find it (barring God's intervention with a miracle).

To see how companion virtues support wisdom, let us look at peaceableness and gentleness. These are two interconnected qualities.

When we, through vices (bad habits) of anger or envy, want to fight back and get even, we cannot make wise decisions nor discern the will of God. When we cannot put an affront or insult behind us, then focusing on the hurt and its perpetrator, and not on the real situation, deafens us to wise advice and blinds us to reality. A lack of peaceableness has made us foolish.

When Paul counsels about how to deal with anxiety, he first advises us to let our "gentleness" be known, for then through prayer and petition the Lord will give us "peace" (Philippians 4:5-7 NIV). Anxiety or fear, along with selfish ambition or greed, prevents clear thinking. All of us some of the time, and most of us all of the time, see reality through a lens that includes our fear of the unknown or failure. We need God's peace, and this is part of the wisdom from above.

Strong emotion is a barrier to wisdom. Not only anger and fear, but other strong emotions as well, cloud our ability to think well. (Just think for a moment how many millions of bad decisions will be made just today because sexual desire has interfered with people's thought processes.) We must keep our passions and emotions in check (which is the role of self-control), and then we will be able to exhibit peaceableness, gentleness, and all the other fine character qualities—wisdom above all.

Wisdom from Action

We all know to be true what I have already said: that wisdom derives from experience, not from a classroom or a sermon. And the experience that counts most for character development is that which comes from facing obstacles and enduring through trials. James writes that we are to "count it all joy" when we face "trials of various kinds," because through steadfastness in the face of tests we become "perfect and complete, lacking in nothing" (James 1:2-4).

God's way of giving us wisdom is to leave us free to make our own decisions in a world full of trials and troubles, and as we do, He disciplines us so that our characters are fashioned to make decisions that honor Him. Proverbs teaches that God "will make straight [our] paths" when we "in all [our] ways acknowledge him" (Proverbs 3:6). We should note that it is while we are on our "paths" that we look to God for His guidance. He guides as we move out and do things, and that inevitably entails hardships of many kinds.

Malcolm Muggeridge, a devout believer and one of England's foremost journalists in the last century, wrote, "Everything I have learnt, whatever it might be ... has been learnt through suffering ... It is a mystery that the only way in which God can help us grow is through suffering."[5] This brings us back to the point that we must have a worldview that trusts in both God's steadfast love and His sovereignty.

When we pray for wisdom, we are clearly praying "according to his will" (1 John 5:14), and James assures us that God will give us such wisdom "generously" (James 1:5). But all may go awry before He does. The specific decision over which we have prayed may explode in our face—such has happened to me more than once. But God's sovereign will is still at work, and the wisdom we seek will yet be given to us, though perhaps only through our suffering for a season.

Of course, if we stay off the path and do nothing, or fail to persevere and quit we may avoid risks and steer clear of heartbreak. But then wisdom will not be ours. And if wisdom is not ours, it is impossible for our lives to count for their ultimate purpose, which is to live for God's glory, bearing fruit as we can do only through wisdom.

I am sure we all pray for wisdom as James invites us to. I certainly do. But as an old expression has it, "Be careful what you pray for."

When we delve into a biblical understanding of wisdom, we learn that God may not give it to us directly. He may first decide that our greed and selfish ambition, or our lust or bitter jealousy or sloth, needs to be worked on so that we will be in a position to see reality clearly. And therefore what we are really praying for (as God sees it) when we pray for wisdom is for light to shine on our sin so we can confess it and deal with it. We are praying for a few tests to be put in front of us so that our learning will sink in and become meaningful. We may need these tests for humility to grow into the faith and hope on which wisdom may rest.

Wisdom from Others

We have seen that the character that makes wise decisions first holds to a biblical worldview, second depends on those virtues that get self out of the picture before a decision is made, and third moves out in action so God can work in us and direct us. There is one additional quality that is essential to making wise decisions—what James calls being "open to reason" (James 3:17).

Wise people listen to others because they know that their objective is to think clearly and that other viewpoints and perspectives are essential to thinking clearly. Proverbs says it this way: "Without counsel plans fail, but with many advisers they succeed" (Proverbs 15:22). Elsewhere we are counseled, "Oil and perfume make the heart glad, and the sweetness of a friend comes from his earnest counsel" (27:9). We need to surround ourselves with friends who will give us earnest counsel.

None of us has a wise perspective on all of life's challenges and problems; each of us has a lens shaped by our own individuality that is necessarily limiting. Thus we have the adage, "Somebody who knows more than anybody is everybody." To raise children wisely, husbands and wives need each other. To lead a football team, a head coach needs other coaches and trainers so that he can understand everything that is going on with the team. We have all found it incredible when we see people, especially youngsters, mess up their own and others' lives because they will not listen. Truly, pride goes before a fall.

Walter Wangerin comments, "At the beginning of his reign, King Solomon prayed one superior gift from God. Not wealth, not long life, but something far more valuable—he asked for 'an understanding heart,' which may be translated, *a hearing heart*. He asked, we say, for wisdom. But the genius of wisdom ... is the ability to open a room in one's heart for the talk—and so for the presence—of another. Wisdom is none other than the ability to listen."[6]

Is there room in our hearts for the talk of another? Do we welcome advice and criticism? I try to live like this, but if you were to ask my wife or my children and those who work with me, you would find that I often do not. We all, and most of all I, need humility and openness to others if we are to be wise.

Wisdom does not come easily. That is the reason the Bible compares it to precious metals and jewels—it is an all-too-rare commodity. "All that you may desire cannot compare with her" (Proverbs 8:11). Love may be a "more excellent" virtue (1 Corinthians 12:31), but surely the riches of wisdom are incomparable, and without wisdom the more excellent virtue will count for little.

Wisdom is an essential carrier virtue—crucial to helping faith express itself in love. Another, and equally crucial, carrier virtue is that which sends us out to the battlefield when we would much prefer to drop our weapons and run: courage.

Character Questions

1. Do you agree with Michael Novak's statement that the first moral obligation is to think clearly? Why or why not?

2. Have you ever considered that you have a worldview? What ways of thinking do you believe make up your worldview?

3. If you were to *really* view wisdom as more precious than gold and jewels, as Proverbs describes it, how would that change your life?

8

Courage: Engaging in the Struggle

We usually think of Martin Luther King Jr. as intrepid in his leadership of the civil rights movement. And we are right in doing so. But we have this impression of his fearlessness only because King successfully passed through a crisis of courage early on.

When he was twenty-seven years old, shortly after moving to Montgomery to become pastor of Dexter Avenue Baptist Church, King was given leadership of the Montgomery bus boycott. He was soon thereafter arrested briefly and also began receiving a series of threatening phone calls. On January 27, 1956, he returned home late one night after a meeting and was about to retire when the phone rang. The caller said, "N——, we are tired of you and your mess now. And if you aren't out of this town in three days, we're going to blow your brains out, and blow up your house."

King was unable to sleep after this call. He knew the threat put his wife, Coretta, and their five-month-old daughter in mortal danger, so he made a cup of coffee and sat down at the kitchen table to think. In his mind, he went over the problems his movement was facing and the grave risks to which he was subjecting his wife and baby. It seemed to him that he couldn't take it any longer. He was forced to reconsider the faith that until then had been little more than a family inheritance to him.

Commenting later on what he would consider the most important night of his life, King stated:

> I bowed down over that cup of coffee ... I said, "Lord, I'm down here trying to do what's right. I think I'm right. I think the cause that we represent is right. But Lord, I

must confess that I'm weak now. I'm faltering. I'm losing my courage. And I can't let the people see me like this because if they see me weak and losing my courage, they will begin to get weak."

And it seemed at that moment that I could hear an inner voice saying to me, "Martin Luther, stand up for righteousness. Stand up for justice. Stand up for truth. And lo, I will be with you, even until the end of the world." ... I heard the voice of Jesus saying still to fight on. He promised never to leave me, never to leave me alone. No, never alone.[1]

King went back to bed that night with a sense of peace.

And his newfound courage stuck with him. Some days afterward, when he learned that his house had been bombed as threatened by the nighttime caller (King's family had been present but were unhurt), others were surprised by how calmly he took the news. King later commented about his reaction, "My religious experience a few nights before had given me the strength to face it."[2]

King loved his fellow African-Americans and wanted to see their lot improved. But he needed courage to enable him to express that love in action. For each of us as well, we need courage if we are to bear fruit and live out our ultimate purpose of bringing glory to God in whatever calling He has for us.[3]

Kinds of Courage

Courage is another of the cardinal virtues, traditionally labeled *fortitude* and placed after prudence (wisdom) and justice in the usual listing. In this book we treat justice later on since, in the context of the tree of character, justice is a fruit. Yet certainly, in one sense, it is appropriate that courage should follow both wisdom and justice, for if an action is not wise and undertaken for a just cause, then we should not call it courageous.

For this reason, courage is not simply a daredevil spirit. Motorcycle stunt performer Evel Knievel was daring, but his showman acts scarcely merit the label of courage. Similarly, although brave men and women climb to the top of Mount Everest and we celebrate their "courage," perhaps *boldness*, *determination*, and *daring* are better words to describe their achievement. Speaking of those who sacrificed themselves for Christ in the early Church period, Augustine says, "Not the injury, but the cause makes the martyrs."

In our frame of reference, courage is a carrier virtue, every bit as indispensable as wisdom in transmitting the strengths of humility, faith, and hope to expression in love. It is a great and noble Christian virtue.

If wisdom is the brains, courage is the brawn; wisdom the head, courage the muscle. Nothing worthwhile succeeds in this world without courage—from raising a child in the knowledge and love of God, to sustaining a marriage, to building a bridge or a company, to establishing and sustaining a democratic republic.

If we resist these bold assertions, it is probably because we tend to restrict courage to the category of valor (courage in the form of putting our lives or bodies in danger), when it is much more. *Courage includes not only valor but also perseverance in the face of difficulty and moral courage—doing the right thing even when it is costly.*

When the virtue of courage is seen in its fullness, we can agree with C. S. Lewis that "courage is not simply *one* of the virtues, but the form of every virtue at the testing point, which means, at the point of highest reality. A chastity or honesty or mercy which yields to danger will be chaste or honest or merciful only on conditions. Pilate was merciful till it became risky."[4]

Winston Churchill, certainly one of the most courageous men of the twentieth century, puts it this way: "Courage is rightly esteemed the first of human qualities, because it is the quality which guarantees all others."

The reason courage is so essential is that life in all its dimensions is a constant struggle. Paul teaches us that the desires of the flesh are in conflict with the desires of the Spirit, that we wrestle the forces of evil (Ephesians 6:10-18). Maintaining our health is a struggle, one we are destined to lose in this world (absent Jesus' return). Competition is built into the roots of the world, appearing in economics, politics, romance, education, athletics, the courts, and so on. Oswald Chambers summarizes our situation: "Life without war is impossible either in nature or in grace. The basis of physical, mental, moral, and spiritual life is antagonism. This is the open fact of life."[5]

Later on, in the introduction to part three, we will discuss the relation of virtue and freedom. The most critical virtue in creating and defending our personal (and national) freedom is courage. Without courage, the forces of the world and the devil will enslave us. Drug and alcohol abuse, promiscuous sex, elevated school dropout rates, and other such human pathologies all derive essentially from the failure of persevering and moral courage, resulting in one kind of bondage or another.

If we as a society could only understand the importance of courage to a worthwhile life, how differently we would raise our children. Too often our instincts are to protect them from competition. We see this attitude in grade inflation, social promotions, and laws and court rulings that tie the hands of administrators and teachers to discipline. We see this in our homes when we as parents indulge the instincts all children have to quit or give in when the going gets tough.

Courage is learned primarily in the school of adversity and conflict. This is true for each type of courage, starting with heroism.

Courage as Valor

In the Hebrew Scriptures, perhaps the greatest story of God's providing courage to a faithful leader is that of Joshua leading the children of Israel into the Promised Land.

Moses, God's anointed leader, had died and the mantle of leadership had fallen on Joshua to take the Israelites into Canaan, where they were to meet fierce resistance from trained armies. The Israelites were wholly inexperienced in warfare. So before Joshua's victories in Canaan, including the famous battle of Jericho, the Lord spoke these words to Joshua:

> Just as I was with Moses, so I will be with you. I will not leave you or forsake you. Be strong and courageous, for you shall cause this people to inherit the land that I swore to their fathers to give them. Only be strong and very courageous, being careful to do according to all the law that Moses my servant commanded you. Do not turn from it to the right hand or to the left, that you may have good success wherever you go. This Book of the Law shall not depart from your mouth, but you shall meditate on it day and night, so that you may be careful to do according to all that is written in it. For then you will make your way prosperous and then you will have good success. Have I not commanded you? Be strong and courageous. Do not be frightened, and do not be dismayed, for the LORD your God is with you wherever you go (Joshua 1:5-9).

It was the key words from this passage, well known to Dr. King (the son and grandson of preachers), that our Lord repeated to the civil rights leader in imbuing him with the same courage given Joshua.

The Lord's message to Joshua also states the virtuous cycle included in God's relationship with all His people. Walk by the law God has given us; be careful to do everything in accordance with it; then have no fear or discouragement, for God will never leave us nor forsake us and "good success" awaits us.

Besides Joshua, many other biblical figures behaved heroically, and the renown for their achievements stands as a lasting testimony to their courage. Among the numerous biblical pictures of courage, those that come immediately to my mind include the following: A teenaged David striding up to the giant Goliath with nothing but creekside gravel for ammunition. Daniel willing to share a pit with lions rather than disobey God. Esther interceding for her people with her capricious and autocratic husband.

Moving to the present, our troops in Iraq—all of them volunteers, many of whom have sought to serve in Iraq as a fulfillment of patriotic duty—have enormous valor, just as have all the brave Americans who over the years have given their lives or exposed themselves to mortal danger to defend our freedoms. So, too, in the wake of September 11, have we been reawakened to the valor of our law enforcement officers and firefighters all over the country.

Because of God's common grace, courage, like all the other cardinal virtues, may be present in anyone, regardless of his or her faith commitment. But as we have said before, the virtues are uniquely activated in those who possess the Holy Spirit as a result of their faith in Christ. The Christian tradition, consequently, is rich in examples of heroic courage.

The Courage of Christ and His Followers

Courage requires vulnerability. One cannot be courageous if there is no threat of pain, and only the Christian God was vulnerable by becoming a man and suffering scorn, torture, and death for our sake. The vulnerability of Christ in His passion is properly recognized by Christians as the highest expression of courage, though it is of an altogether different order from anything that ordinary people experience. Not only did Jesus on the cross have to brave something no one else has ever experienced (having the sins of the whole world heaped upon Him), but also the purpose of His courage was more sublime than any other could be (the salvation of all who are His own).

Following the example of Christ, many believers down through the ages have exhibited extraordinary courage of the valorous type—some to the point of death.

One of the most renowned of the early martyrs was Polycarp, elderly bishop of Smyrna, who was burned at the stake about A.D. 155 for refusing to take an oath to Caesar. Repeatedly, his executioner beseeched him to avoid death by taking the oath. But when on the day of his execution he was pressed by the Roman proconsul to renounce Christ and swear by Caesar, Polycarp replied, "Eighty and six years I have served Him, and He did me no wrong. How can I blaspheme my King who saved me?"

As the bishop entered the stadium for his execution, it is reported that a voice from heaven came to him, saying, "Be strong, Polycarp, and play the man." This encouragement echoes the words of David's General Joab, who before a battle with a superior force tells his men, "Be of good courage, and let us play the men for our people, and for the cities of our God: and the LORD do that which seemeth him good" (2 Samuel 10:12 KJV).[6]

These same words of Polycarp's were picked up fifteen hundred years later in England when Bishop Latimer refused to forsake his faith to obey the king and was burned at the stake along with his devoted friend, Thomas Ridley. As the fire was kindled, Latimer spoke his last to Ridley: "Be of good comfort, Master Ridley, and play the man. We shall this day light such a candle by God's grace in England as I trust shall never be put out."

The accounts of the heroic courage of Christians, whether they be martyrs or missionaries or sacrificial servants such as Mother Teresa, are endless. Millions of such examples are with us worldwide. Yet, while these stories inspire and encourage us, it is likely that most who read this book will not be called to serve the Lord so boldly. Ours are likely to be more modest callings. The courage we most need to understand is of a more everyday sort, though it is still essential for achieving our ultimate purpose. This is the courage to face, and persist in overcoming, the challenges we have in daily life—spiritual, relational, vocational, and moral. It is primarily in this type of courage that character is developed.

Courage as Perseverance

The critical importance of persistence—persisting through trials and difficulties to finish a task—is a pervasive theme in the Bible. We have seen, in discussing faith, that Paul extols perseverance as the foundation of character (Romans 5:3-4) and James teaches that perseverance is the result of the testing of our faith and thereby becomes a bridge to our being "perfect and complete, lacking in nothing" (James 1:4). In Hebrews we are exhorted to run with "perseverance" the race set before us (Hebrews 12:1 NIV). In exhorting and commending the deeds of the early churches in Revelation, perseverance is at the center of Jesus' attention (Revelation 2:3,10,19; 3:10).

The significance of perseverance is twofold. First, as we noted in the introduction to part two, perseverance is a key to the development of all virtue. We grow in character and each of its virtues by sticking with our tasks, including their difficulties and discouragements, until we finish.

The inclination to quit, to give up before we finish, is generally of the devil—and it is all too prevalent today. We are too prone to having a consumer mentality toward everything, so that when the short-term pain outweighs the short-term gain, we give up or switch to something else that appears more pleasurable. We forget the wisdom of psychiatrist Scott Peck that "the tendency to avoid problems and the emotional suffering in them is the primary basis of all human mental illness."[7] The high school dropout is handicapped first of all because he quit; the failure to complete an education is serious, but the failure in the character realm is more dire.

Second, perseverance is critical if our life is to glorify God. We glorify Him not when we quit but when we finish. Jesus prayed to His Father, "I have brought you glory on earth by completing the work you gave me to do" (John 17:4 NIV). Jesus' "food" was to "finish" His Father's work (4:34 NIV).

The whole world admires perseverance. Sticking with God's calling on our life through difficulty and heartbreak brings great glory to Him. In fact, those who do so are every bit as much heroes as is a military conqueror.

Sports movies generally do not have an explicitly Christian theme, yet we are deeply moved by them. Cinderella Man overcomes unbelievable obstacles to win the heavyweight championship. When in *Hoosiers* the small-town basketball team overcomes great odds to win the state championship, we all cheer. In fact, it is such performances in the faith realm that are cheered by the heavenly "great cloud of witnesses" (Hebrews 12:1 NIV).

The leaders we revere persevered through great difficulty and strain to finish their work—Washington in the Revolutionary War; Lincoln who prevailed, and Lee who did not, in the Civil War; Winston Churchill in the Second World War. Churchill's most famous words are, "Never give in. Never give in. Never, never, never, never—in nothing, great or small, large or petty—never give in, except to convictions of honour and good sense. Never yield to force. Never yield to the apparently overwhelming might of the enemy."[8]

Sticking with It

Ray Kroc, the founder of McDonald's, posted on his wall his favorite inspirational message: "Nothing in the world can take the place of persistence. Talent will not; nothing is more common than unsuccessful men with great talent. Genius will not; unrewarded genius is almost a proverb. Education will not; the world is full of educated derelicts. Persistence, determination alone are omnipotent."[9]

The final line is not good theology. God alone is omnipotent. But the gist of the message is certainly correct. We succeed in all our purposes, most importantly our ultimate purpose, only to the extent that we persist and finish the work.

William Wilberforce, as a young man, stated his life's mission in a diary entry on October 28, 1787: "God Almighty has set before me two great objects, the suppression of the

Slave Trade and the reformation of manners." In regard to the former goal, this Parliamentarian not only used every weapon in his considerable political arsenal, but also he used every means in his power to turn public opinion in Britain against slavery. It was forty-six years after writing the crucial diary entry—and just three days before his death—when the bill for the abolition of slavery throughout the British Empire passed its second reading in the House of Commons. That's perseverance on an amazing level.

Moving from the sublime to the everyday world, we are all foot soldiers. Ours is to do God's bidding day by day. It is often monotonous. Sticking with it without complaint requires persevering courage.

Oswald Chambers reminds us that "drudgery is the touchstone of character." In combating the notion that we should do "exceptional things for God," Chambers reminds us that sinful pride can motivate us to do the great things and even to make it through the crisis. But he says "it ... require[s] the supernatural grace of God to live twenty-four hours in every day as a saint, to go through drudgery as a disciple, to live an ordinary, unobserved, ignored existence as a disciple of Jesus ... We have to be exceptional in the ordinary things, to be holy ... among [average] people, and this is not learned in five minutes."[10]

But in grace such drudgery becomes divine. As the poet George Herbert puts it:

Teach me my God and King
    In all things Thee to see.
And what I do in anything
    To do it as for Thee! ...

All may of Thee partake;
    Nothing can be so mean,
Which, with this tincture "for Thy sake"
    Will not grow bright and clean.

A servant with this clause
　　Makes drudgery divine:
Who sweeps a room, as for Thy laws
　　Makes that and th' action fine.

This is the famous stone
　　That turneth all to gold;
For that which God doth touch and own
　　Cannot for less be told.[11]

Herbert well expresses the real work of Jesus Christ in the world. It is seen in us ordinary people following Him faithfully in giving extraordinary care and devotion to ordinary tasks. Ordinary people thereby, unseen to most, transform the mundane into the divine for His glory.

Whereas the opposite of valor is cowardice, the opposite of perseverance is laziness. The old-timers called this sin *sloth*. Though theologians rank pride as the primal sin, sloth deserves second place. Next to pride, it creates the greatest barrier to the development of Christlike character. We will never make much progress in our pursuit of character without perseverance.

Moral Courage

Moral courage is the virtue the average person thinks of most in our general conversation about character. It is this courage to which Lewis refers when he says that courage is the "form of every virtue at the testing point." Moral courage determines the choices we make when the going gets tough.

Though moral courage often includes valor, it need not. Nor is it necessarily attached to perseverance. Yet it is essential to any life that will glorify God.

The practice of moral courage ought to be a daily exercise. As we saw in President Reagan's words quoted in an earlier chapter, in God's grace we build such courage "piece by piece, bit by bit" into "habits of duty and honor and integrity." And as

Reagan reminds us, its default are habits of "dishonor and shame."

It takes moral courage for teenagers to refuse to go along with the crowd, to stay away from drugs, alcohol, and sexual irresponsibility, and this courage is tested daily and therefore must be practiced daily. It takes courage to stick with a friend or relative who has failed or embarrassed himself to the point where all others have turned against him. It takes courage for a boss to criticize a loyal subordinate when he is not getting the job done or for a coach to suspend a star player before the championship game for breaking team rules. It took courage for Joseph to say no to Potiphar's wife and for Daniel to refuse Nebuchadnezzar's food and wine.

It takes moral courage to tell the truth. Much if not most lying is meant to avoid facing the consequences of mistakes we have made or problems we have created. As a child, I broke a water pipe at our house but lied about it to avoid my father's anger. There were many similar lies in my childhood. We might chalk such lies up to immaturity, but we see presidents (Nixon and Clinton come to mind) lie to cover up their misdeeds. They were men of no small courage, yet they did not have the moral courage to tell the truth.

It also takes moral courage to receive the truth about ourselves when it is not good. Proverbs tells us repeatedly that it is a blessing when others criticize and correct us. For example, it says, "Reprove a man of understanding, and he will gain knowledge" (Proverbs 19:25). But how many of us welcome criticism and thank the critic? It takes courage (and humility) to do so.

My boss once told me that I was the most difficult person to criticize he had ever met. My wife would agree. I thank God they both had the guts to tell me the truth.

It takes moral courage, also, to stand for justice when the cause is unpopular among our peers.

One day, not long after the end of the Civil War, services were being held at St. Paul's Church in Richmond, Virginia. When it came time for Communion, a black man—a former slave—knelt at the Communion rail and held out his hands to receive the bread and the wine from the common cup. Up to this point, at St. Paul's, slaves had not been served Communion at the railing alongside whites. The black man was making a point about the change that had taken place with emancipation.

The priest stood in his place, not knowing what to do. The congregation was hushed, with members looking around at each other uncomfortably. What would happen next? Just then a figure got up from a pew, walked to the front of the church, and knelt beside the black man. It was General Robert E. Lee. By his actions alone, Lee had made a statement about equality before the Lord, despite ingrained habits of discrimination in the church. That took moral courage.

It takes courage as well to bear the consequences of the problems our bad decisions or poor leadership may cause. When General Eisenhower released the Allied troops for the invasion of Normandy, he wrote a letter of resignation the day *before* the invasion so there would be no problem in removing him if the invasion failed. When Warren Buffett took over the reins of the investment firm Salomon Brothers, which faced the likelihood of being barred from the government bond market (equivalent to its death sentence), he opened his press conference by saying, "I will talk to you in the manner of a man who has never met a lawyer." Such approaches are a far cry from that of so may CEOs today who, when accused of wrongdoing, blame it on subordinates. Leaders who have moral courage bear pain; they do not transfer it.

Courage and Fear

Courage is not the absence of fear. In fact, it presupposes fear. Courage is moving out and continuing on in the face of fear. Courage always involves risk, as does love. It is infrequent that we face significant risk of bodily harm (except that we all will face death—and it will take courage to do so with honor). The fears that most confront us are the fear of failure and the fear of disapproval or rejection. In my life, both fears are well nigh constant, and thankfully my faith helps me cope with them. I do know that in the natural sphere the greatest risk of failure and rejection lies in taking no risk. The old saying "Better to have tried and failed than not to have tried at all" is certainly true.

And we all fail from time to time. Before he became president, Abraham Lincoln lost in six elections and failed in two businesses. Thomas Edison tried more than six thousand alloys and substances before he hit on a carbonized cotton thread for the filament of the first light bulb. This caused him to coin his phrase that genius is "99 percent perspiration and 1 percent inspiration." John D. Rockefeller was turned down dozens of times as he searched for his first job as a bookkeeper.

It is with respect to fear that courage and faith are most tightly joined. We have the courage to move out in the face of fear because of our faith. Joshua's and Dr. King's experiences teach us this. And our faith is given expression in a life that honors God because courage strengthens us to move through fear.

And what strengthens our courage? God Himself takes on that role.

The Spirit of Power

The Scriptures teach that the Holy Spirit is the third member of the Godhead and that He is mighty. In Isaiah 11 the Holy Spirit is identified as "the Spirit of ... power" (v. 2 NIV). In John's Gospel the Holy Spirit is described with a Greek word that means "one who walks beside us" (John 14:16,26; 15:26; 16:7). This word has been translated in some Bible versions as "Comforter," an English word that literally means "with power."

With this background in mind, it is less surprising to read that Jesus, before leaving His disciples, tells them to wait in Jerusalem until they would be "clothed with power from on high" (Luke 24:49). In Acts we learn that this power came through the Holy Spirit, given to the believers at Pentecost (Acts 1:4-5; 2).

No more radical change in character is noted in all of Scripture than that of Peter after the Holy Spirit was given to him at Pentecost. Just weeks earlier, the disciple had in craven fear denied Jesus three times (Luke 22:54-62). But from the day of Pentecost, he preached the gospel with boldness and stood up to the dire threats of the religious leaders (Acts 2; 4).

In this same vein, the New Testament is filled with assurances that Christ, through His Spirit, provides believers with the power to accomplish all He has called us to do.

- "The kingdom of God does not consist in talk but in power" (1 Corinthians 4:20).
- "He is not weak in dealing with you, but is powerful among you" (2 Corinthians 13:3).
- "Now to him who is able to do far more abundantly than all that we ask or think, according to the power at work within us ..." (Ephesians 3:20).
- "Be strong in the Lord and in the strength of his might" (Ephesians 6:10).
- "I can do all things through him who strengthens me" (Philippians 4:13).
- "God gave us a spirit not of fear but of power and love and self-control" (2 Timothy 1:7).

The power that was given to the great leaders of the early Church for bold preaching and for signs and wonders is available to all who have the Holy Spirit today as we serve with the strength God provides.

149

The Practice of Courage

How do we put courage into practice? As with all other virtues, courage can become a habit, ingrained in us as our character is transformed.

Heroic courage requires facing fears and not *overcoming* them but *going through* them. We do what our duty to valor calls for even though we don't want to. We exercise our will to act in faith that God will take care of us no matter what and will honor our attempts to do the right.

As we face our lesser fears, we will be prepared to face greater ones. We might think that if we are not firefighters, police officers, or soldiers, we won't need great valor. And that may be true. But then again, there may come a time when we'll have to say, "Let's roll," as did Todd Beamer and the other brave passengers on United flight 93 on September 11, 2001.

Persevering courage is the easiest to practice. As a matter of will, we simply finish what we start.

As Jesus taught us, before we start, we ought to "count the cost." If we do not, we may not be able to finish, and all who see us will mock us (Luke 14:28-30). Stated differently, we should seek God's guidance, and that of others, before we start anything of consequence. If in faith we resolve to go forward, we should be determined to complete what we have begun.

As we pursue any course of action for God, we should look upon obstacles as God's ways of developing our character, not as reasons to quit. This is not to say that we should never give up; it is to say that we should be very reluctant to do so and that it should be the rare exception.

Procrastination is a form of temporary quitting, and it is likely to turn into a permanent form. There is no better rule for character development than to delay gratification and each day take the most difficult and disagreeable assignments first.

As for moral courage, we need to begin with the small stuff. Telling the truth, even if it hurts, all the time. Taking the road less traveled when relatively little is at stake. Over time, the virtue of moral courage will in God's grace become ever stronger, so that when the point of highest reality comes upon us we can stand up.

Maybe someday God will use us to effect great change in this world, as He used Wilberforce and King. But it won't happen if we don't first develop our moral courage by practicing it over time.

Without courage (of whatever type), we can never advance beyond the elementary stages of character development. Without courage, as well as the other carrier virtues of wisdom and self-control, we can never bear the fruit of good works and glorify our God in heaven.

Character Questions

1. For you, which of the following is hardest, and why?

    • Facing physical danger in the course of doing what you are supposed to do;

    • Sticking with some kind of labor even though it is hard and the payoff is uncertain;

    • Doing what is morally right despite being strongly opposed by others.

2. How could being more courageous enable you to bring greater glory to God through your life?

3. Write a brief prayer for courage. Memorize it and use it in your devotional time for the next few days.

9

Self-control: Denying Self for Christ's Sake

Popular author and pastor Max Lucado comes from a family with alcoholism in its history, and so he knew he had to be extra careful about drinking. "If there's anything about this DNA stuff," he commented, "I've got it." For a long time, he didn't drink at all. But a few years ago, he started drinking in what he considered to be safe quantities.

It didn't stay safe for long.

Lucado recalled, "I lowered my guard a bit. One beer with a barbecue won't hurt. Then another time with Mexican food. Then a time or two with no food at all."

Then one warm Friday afternoon, on the way to speak at a men's retreat, Lucado got thirsty and began to think about where he could buy a beer without being seen by anyone who knew him. He drove to a convenience store, waited for all the other customers to leave, and then went in to buy his beer. Afterward, he hurried to the car, holding the beer close by his side so no one would notice it.

Suddenly Lucado took stock of what he was doing. "I really felt a sense of conviction," Lucado remembered, "because the night before I'd had a long talk with my oldest daughter about not covering things up."

Lucado chose not to drink the beer. Instead, he threw it in a Dumpster and asked God's forgiveness for exposing himself to danger and acting hypocritically. Since then, his rule has been: no alcohol.

He commented later, "I think I could have been getting close to a cliff and not known it."[1]

Lucado exercised one of the cardinal virtues: self-control. This virtue was called *temperance* by the ancients. Today, however, the term *temperance* is usually applied in a more limited way to refer to abstinence from alcohol. That is still an important kind of self-control for many, as it is for Lucado, but self-control applies to every facet of our lives. It is a critical virtue.

Self-control, along with fellow cardinal virtues wisdom and courage, is a part of the trunk and branches in the tree of character. If courage provides power and muscle, self-control must be there for structured strength. It, too, is essential if faith, hope, and humility are to be expressed in the fruit of love. And thus self-control is fundamental to achieving the ultimate purpose of the Christian life. Without it, not only will we not produce fruit that will glorify God, but we will instead produce a bitter fruit that brings dishonor to His name and misery to ourselves and those we would love.

Soul Peace

Temperance originally meant "order," and it is still helpful to see self-control as the virtue that provides order, or peace, for the soul.

The perennial problem with the soul is that the passions overrule the choices of mind and will and so all kind of problems arise in a person's life. It's like the country song that describes a boy in a peck of trouble with the father of the girl he sneaked out of the house late at night. The refrain is "I know what I was feelin', but what was I thinkin'?"

Self-control is the virtue that creates order by subduing or aligning the passions with the mind and will to provide peace to the soul and happiness in life. It is an essential virtue for the Christian life—really, for any successful life. Yet of all the virtues, it is the one we most resist. We do not want controls on our passions. We want to be free, even of our conscience.

We resist self-control because we do not think clearly. (Or to put it more accurately, we resist it because the seductions of the world *keep us* from thinking clearly.) So, to think more clearly, let us go back to the mind game (first introduced in chapter two) of going to our own funeral. We have seen that it is not the best way to determine our purpose in life, but it is not a bad way to measure foolishness.

Who among us would want others to attest at our funeral that we were sexually immoral or stingy or full of anger? And who would want the speakers to say that, as a result of these vices, we were severely limited in our freedom to love our spouse and children, to serve our employer, and to glorify God? None of us wants such a scenario to come true, but until we have a life-threatening disease or our juices quit flowing with old age, for too many of us, our funeral seems distant. And so we do not control our passions as we ought.

And what about God? If there is one thing that is clear in the Bible, no matter how skillfully we seek to hide our sin from others, God knows all and He will hold all persons—believers and nonbelievers—accountable (Hebrews 4:13; 1 Corinthians 3:11-15).

The virtue of self-control is a profoundly spiritual matter. It must be understood in light of the battle that is going on for our souls.

Pride and Passion

We are made to glorify God by bearing the fruit of good works, and this is something we can accomplish only in freedom. But the forces of evil—referred to by Paul as "rulers," "authorities," "cosmic powers over this present darkness," and "the spiritual forces of evil in the heavenly places" (Ephesians 6:12)—are arrayed against our freedom and the good fruit that spring from it. Their goal is the bondage of our soul through

155

vices—bad habits that become internalized and that produce evil fruit.

The apostle Paul gives us a catalog of these vices: "sexual immorality, impurity, sensuality, idolatry, sorcery, enmity, strife, jealousy, fits of anger, rivalries, dissensions, divisions, envy, drunkenness, orgies, and things like these" (Galatians 5:19-21). They contravene the moral will of God, destroy our fellowship with Him, and lead to death. Paul warns, "Those who do such things will not inherit the kingdom of God."

Paul terms the vices "works of the flesh" (Galatians 5:19). He was not implying that the body was inherently sinful, but rather he was saying that our old sin nature can have an impact on us even after we become Christians. That's why the *New International Version* of the Bible terms these vices "acts of the sinful nature." The sinful nature is that part of our character that rebels against the sovereignty of God in our lives, and it has two components: pride and passion.

Pride spawns the cold-blooded sins, such as envy and greed. Pride is competitive and would eliminate all who stand in its way, including God. As has been said by others, all sins flee from God except for pride, which alone stands up to Him. There is no redeeming feature to the cold-blooded sins. They are diabolical, of the devil's own nature. They must be crucified, put to death (Romans 8:13).[2]

The passions, on the other hand, are warm-blooded. These are such things as desire and ambition. They need not be crucified but rather must be controlled and properly directed. Why is that? Because emotions can be good things.

Let's face it: Ambition, zeal, and desire drive the world. Without them, this place would be deadly dull. Desire is a good thing, and strong desire is a better thing, if through wisdom and self-control it is directed toward the right object. We are to love and serve God with all our heart (Matthew 22:37). Jesus gave His life to purify for Himself a people "zealous for good works" (Titus 2:14). We are to love our spouse and children deeply and serve our employer with all of our heart (see

Colossians 3:23 NIV). We should thank God for our desires, provided they are wisely directed.

Still, the passions can be destructive. Enjoyment of fine food is good, but gluttony is bad. Romantic love is good, but lustful desire for someone outside of marriage is bad. Ambition to do well at our job is good, but trampling over others to get ahead is bad.

Self-control can be compared to a wall of good habits around our life that keeps the lusts and seductions of the world from enslaving us.[3] More specifically, self-control is aided by two types of walls: internal and external. But before we get to our discussion of these walls, we need to clear up a couple of misconceptions about our ability to be self-controlled.

The Inadequacy of the Mind

The first misconception was apparently started by the ancient Greeks, who—lacking knowledge about the power of sin—believed that if they were wise enough, they would be moral people. We carry this error forward today with our confidence in education. We are too inclined to believe that a good education will solve all the problems of our youth. The truth is, while education is critical, education alone will produce neither good nor successful people.

The mind, in fact, is pitifully weak in controlling our passions. John Henry Newman, a nineteenth-century Roman Catholic cardinal, put it this way: "If you think you can tie a battleship to the dock with sewing thread, or quarry granite with a razor blade, you are more nearly right than if you think man can control his pride and passion with his mind."[4]

No one has understood this error more vividly than C. S. Lewis. In *The Abolition of Man* he rebukes the intellectual elites who thought they could eliminate objective, permanent moral norms and still successfully teach a form of virtue in the classroom that would maintain a vibrant society. He writes that "without the art of trained emotions the intellect is powerless against the animal organism."[5] By "animal organism," he means those lusts for pleasure that self-control must govern.

In a great phrase, Lewis writes that the "head rules the belly through the chest." The "chest," for Lewis, was "trained habit," or character. Virtue, he writes, was indispensable to "connect the head to the belly." And he gives a penetrating description of the folly of intellectuals who seek to raise students on a diet of relative moral values: "We make men without chests and expect of them virtue and enterprise. We laugh at honour and are shocked to find traitors in our midst. We castrate and bid the geldings be fruitful."[6]

I recently met with a dean of one of our national law schools who, following the scandals of Enron, WorldCom, Arthur Andersen, and others, explained that one of the major strategic initiatives for his school would be "professional responsibility." Many law schools are jumping on this bandwagon, and well they should. But they ought to begin by acknowledging their responsibility for the mess.

For the last two generations, the leading edge of legal scholarship has promoted a philosophy called "legal realism," which holds that there are no transcendent moral principles and that justice is what activist judges declare it to be. This philosophy asserts that there are no natural law principles providing a moral foundation for law, just man-made rules.

Indeed, we have castrated and bid the geldings be fruitful. We should not be surprised at the bitter fruit shown in the corporate and professional world or at belated calls for programs of "professional responsibility."

Don't get me wrong. I believe deeply in the importance of professional responsibility as well as study for it and training in it. We will get nowhere with it, however, if the underlying philosophy supports the idea that there are no objective moral norms.

An Ongoing Struggle

The second misconception is that, with prayer and sincerity on our part, the grace of God will swiftly and easily deliver us from the power of our sinful nature. This misconception misses how both God and sin work in our lives.

We have seen how the strategy of Satan and his forces is to take control of us and keep us in bondage and how bad habits destroy our ability to do what we want. This bondage created the dilemma of Paul's that we discussed in a previous chapter. He declares, "Wretched man that I am!" and asks, "Who will deliver me from this body of death?" because he failed to do what his better self wanted to do (Romans 7:24).

Paul announced in Romans 8 that the deliverance he sought is available through Jesus Christ and the ministry of Christ's Spirit within us, as we submit to His sovereignty, live according to His guidelines, and set our mind on Him. But there is nothing in chapter 8 that promises miraculous, immediate, or easy delivery. Chapter 8, in fact, depicts a life of struggle and of suffering as we await the future glory.

Paul gave no explanation of what specific problem created his own dilemma. But I know of many who have for some considerable time struggled with what in the past was called a "besetting sin." This is a sin that we hate, that we bring into the light, that we confess, that we plead with God to eliminate, and that we nevertheless continue to do (or at least to struggle against the temptation to do). I've been there. I expect you have too. We have company even with the great apostle, I suspect.

A vivid example of a besetting sin is one in the life of William Bennett, all the more extraordinary because Bennett, as much as any other person, has caused our nation to take the subject of character seriously. *The Book of Virtues*, his collection of stories and writings on virtue, has brought a deeper appreciation of this subject into hundreds of thousands of homes. *Our Sacred Honor*, another Bennett book, helped improve our understanding of how deeply our Founding

Founders revered the importance of character in the life of our democratic republic.

Yet although Bennett cares deeply about character, and although he is a devout Christian, he developed a habit to video poker. We can thank God that Bennett let his problems come to light and has overcome them, but it has not been without great pain. Most of all, we can thank God (I certainly do) that He raised Bennett up as a prophet in this country to call us to refocus on the critical importance of character.

Bennett's besetting sin was gambling. For us, a besetting sin might be something quite different and much less tangible. It might belong to the domain of pride—for example, we might try to change or control someone, and even though we know it is wrong and destructive, we persist in it. Or it might belong to the realm of desire—lust, workaholism, shopping, and so on. Whatever the case, we struggle with our sin repeatedly, despite God's grace and His Spirit in our lives.

Our situation is hard but not hopeless. If we keep our sin in the light, if we hate it and confess it, God will give us victory. As the Bible teaches us, "God is faithful, and he will not let you be tempted beyond your ability, but with the temptation he will also provide the way of escape, that you may be able to endure it" (1 Corinthians 10:13). Sometimes the victory comes only with the help of an external wall; always we need an internal wall.

The Wall Inside[7]

The virtue of self-control builds a wall around our soul that repels the power of deceptive seductions and frees our mind and will to be controlled by the Spirit rather than by the "sin that dwells within" us (see Romans 7:20). This is no easy wall to build. Satan and his powers in the world do not want it built, and the sinful habits of our old life are tough to break.

We need to keep in mind that sinful habits, just like good habits, must have an internal satisfaction if they are to be sustained. If someone has a sinful habit, such as playing video poker, he must take a perverse delight in it. The same is true for gluttony, greed, envy, and every other vice. This makes it hard for us to break our sinful habits.

Self-control cannot win this battle alone—that is what Romans 7 teaches us. It must be allied with other virtues. Wisdom must combat the deceptions and seductions of the world by helping us think clearly. Courage must buttress our decision to resist temptation or to repel a bad habit. Faith and hope show us that God is more powerful than any force arrayed against us and that victory can be ours. Living a fruitful life is never the challenge of one virtue alone.

And most of all, self-control must be buttressed by the Holy Spirit. Part of the fruit of the Holy Spirit is "self-control" (Galatians 5:23). The Holy Spirit is described as the Spirit of "power and love and self-control" (2 Timothy 1:7). But we must keep in mind that the Holy Spirit is never coercive. He will not contravene our decision to sin, and without "trained emotions" developed over time through practice, we are lost.

Self-control, therefore, deals with the internal virtuous wall, built in grace and love with the power of the Holy Spirit, placed around the soul to give it freedom to follow the promptings of the Spirit. For most of us, that wall is insufficient even when reinforced by other virtues. We all need external walls in addition to the internal one.

Walls Outside

External walls are human constructions that reinforce our internal wall and keep our sinful inclinations in check. Some of these walls are common to us all. Others are ones that, if we are wise, we build for ourselves.

One common external wall is governmental law. We might think that we would do the right thing without laws and regulations, but in all likelihood we would not. To take one example, suppose that the property tax were collected solely on the basis of an honor code—no one would ever audit a property owner or check to see if he had paid the tax. What would be the result, even among devout Christians? Clearly, laws play a crucial role in guiding us to do what is right.

Social disapproval is another external wall if there is sunlight to expose the evil deed. No one, for example, views pornography in the open. It is an activity that needs privacy—darkness, really. How much more sexual immorality among devout Christians would we have if there were plenty of time and darkness and we were sure that no other person would ever know what we did? We would succumb to the temptation to indulge in many more evil deeds if we knew that nobody would find out. And we *are* succumbing, as seen by the rapid rise of gambling and pornography on the Internet.

Authority is yet another external wall. An employee does not lose his temper in front of the CEO. A church member does not use profanity in front of a pastor or priest. A player does not cheat under the watchful eye of the referee. We respect authority and it helps to keep our behavior in line.

Now consider this irony. These examples of external walls prove that we *can* control ourselves. We control ourselves all the time when we must to avoid embarrassment or punishment. Truly, then, when we sin—and we all do—we are without excuse.

We are not done with the external walls aiding in self-control. To the walls that are common to most people, each of us needs to add custom-made ones for our own uses. These are walls we put up to help us deal with the weak areas in our lives. Someone who wants to stop his habit of viewing pornography, for instance, could put filtering software on his computer. A person who overspends could cut up his credit cards. An alcoholic could join Alcoholics Anonymous.

Such walls can be built and maintained through accountability partnerships, with a friend or church leader, in which we are free to confess our weaknesses. Evil loves darkness. If we confess our sinful deeds honestly, if we put them in the light and keep them there, almost surely we will free ourselves from them in God's grace.

We need to be honest about our weaknesses and find friends and teammates to help us. We might, for example, have a habit of making rash decisions—we need someone to slow us down. We might be wise but cowardly—we can team up with someone who is courageous but rash. As Alcoholics Anonymous has demonstrated, fellow sojourners who struggle with the same temptations can be an enormous help.

The point is that we all need help—both from God and each other. Others can help us to erect the external walls we need to strengthen our self-control. And we can use all the help we get.

There is one crucial way God helps our self-control that we have barely touched on so far. That is by giving us our conscience, which is a window to His Spirit's will.

The Window of Conscience[8]

The virtue of self-control works in concert with our conscience—an internal self-regulator that helps us know right from wrong in our thinking and in our behavior. If we are contemplating doing something that is not consistent with a Christlike character, then through communion with the Holy Spirit, our conscience is quickened to send a trouble signal to our mind.

The eyes of our conscience are illuminated through what can be understood as a windowpane. When it is clear, the light of God shines through and the conscience remains sensitive to the Holy Spirit. When we are off course, the conscience alerts the mind and will to make a change in course as the Spirit strengthens us to do so.

If we respond in repentance to an alert about our own error, then the window to our conscience remains clear. But if we ignore the promptings of the Spirit and avoid seeking forgiveness of our sins through Jesus Christ, the window becomes cloudy. In other words, in that case we begin to rationalize and excuse our misconduct, and there ensues a negative cycle that can result in the window becoming opaque—no light coming through at all. The Bible calls this condition a seared conscience (1 Timothy 4:2). We are sold out to sin, our freedom is lost, and the Holy Spirit has relented to our conscious disregard of His promptings.

For this reason, Jesus, who is the light of the world (John 8:12), is indispensable to self-control. Justice Brandeis, a Supreme Court justice, coined a phrase: "The streetlight is the best constable; sunlight is the best disinfectant." Whatever there is in our life that cannot bear sunshine must be stopped (or crucified, to use the biblical word) through grace operating with the virtue of self-control and be confessed for cleansing. We must keep the windows to our consciences clean. Self-control depends upon it.

How do we put self-control into practice? There are few questions more important in the ethical life, for if we fail in self-control—more than any other of the carrier virtues—we are most likely going to bring dishonor to the name of God and heartbreak, if not disaster, to our own lives.

If one were to offer a simple formula, it might best be sunlight and prayer. The forces of darkness are just that—they hate light. If we bring weaknesses and sin into the light, Satan's array of forces flee. And if the virtue of self-control is to grow in strength, our conscience must be kept clean. Certainly for us to bring our sins to light takes courage. As for prayer, it needs to include both confession and petition for power to overcome (see 1 John 1:6; 1 Corinthians 10:13).

Self-control in Scripture

Of all the cardinal virtues, self-control is the one most taught in New Testament Scripture. And it is there that we learn how to go about inculcating this virtue in our lives on the way to a more godly character.

An ideal starting place for a survey of the high points about self-control in the New Testament is a statement by the apostle Peter.

> [God's] divine power has granted to us all things that pertain to life and godliness, through the knowledge of him who called us to his own glory and excellence, by which he has granted to us his precious and very great promises, so that through them you may become partakers of the divine nature, having escaped from the corruption that is in the world because of sinful desire. For this very reason, *make every effort to supplement your faith with virtue, and virtue with knowledge, and knowledge with self-control*, and self-control with steadfastness, and steadfastness with godliness, and godliness with brotherly affection, and brotherly affection with love. For if these qualities are yours and are increasing, they keep you from being ineffective or unfruitful in the knowledge of our Lord Jesus Christ (2 Peter 1:3-8, emphasis added).

This teaching is a succinct statement of the major thesis of this book. Through divine power we are granted all things pertaining to life and godliness. But we are to "make every effort" to supplement this power with virtue leading to self-control and, through self-control, to love. Only then will we be kept from ineffectiveness and unfruitfulness in our relationship with Jesus Christ.

Chambers captures the rich depth of the apostle's wisdom when he says, "[Supplement] means all that character means. No man is born either naturally or supernaturally with character, he has to make character. Nor are we born with habits; we have to form habits on the basis of the new life God has put into us. We are not meant to be illuminated versions, but the common stuff of ordinary life exhibiting the marvel of the grace of God."[9] To that, I say "Amen."

Having listed a number of virtues, Peter goes on to implore us to "be all the more diligent" and "*practice* these qualities" so we will never fall (v. 10, emphasis added). Thus he reinforces the importance of our role in character formation. *Self-control—and indeed the whole of the biblical moral life—is a matter of adding to divine power our effort, our diligence, and our practice of virtue.*

As we go to the practice field, we find Paul. He teaches, "Every athlete exercises self-control in all things. They do it to receive a perishable wreath, but we an imperishable. So I do not run aimlessly; I do not box as one beating the air. But I discipline my body and keep it under control, lest after preaching to others I myself should be disqualified" (1 Corinthians 9:25-27). Our self-control is not for an athletic contest of consequence only for a moment; rather, we practice self-control with eyes on eternity, where we will receive an imperishable gift. For this we are to stay disciplined and under control.

In his letter to Titus, Paul amplifies our understanding of self-control:

"The grace of God has appeared, bringing salvation for all people, training us to renounce ungodliness and worldly passions, and to live self-controlled, upright, and godly lives in the present age, waiting for our blessed hope, the appearing of the glory of our great God and Savior Jesus Christ, who gave himself for us to redeem us from all lawlessness and to purify for himself a people for his own possession who are zealous for good works" (Titus 2:11-14).

Here Paul counsels that the grace of God "trains" us to live self-controlled lives. Grace does not just teach us by reaching our mind. Nor does it miraculously implant self-control in us. It takes us out to the practice field and trains us; it inducts us into boot camp; it works us out. The "well done" commendation of Christ (Matthew 25:21) will be ours after we have been trained, after we have in God's grace made "every effort" on the field of practice.

Sometimes we will fail. We will miss assignments. We will appear awkward. We will drop the ball (or knock it out of bounds). We will forget. But the perfect Trainer will always be with us, offering encouragement, exercises, and counsel until through grace operating in the power of the Holy Spirit we become what Christ gave Himself for us to be: "a people for his own possession who are zealous for good works" (Titus 2:14).

Character Questions

1. What is your temperature—are you cold-blooded or warm-blooded? In other words, when it comes to self-control, do you have a greater problem with your pride or your passions? What evidence do you have for that conclusion?

2. Do you agree or disagree with the idea that self-control is a part of spiritual warfare? Explain your reasoning.

3. Be your own coach. What is the workout plan for the practice field of self-control for you today?

10

Justice: Being Fair to All

In September 2003, Ben Rogozensky of Decatur, Georgia, having been arrested on charges of obstructing justice and giving false information to police officers, was scheduled to have a hearing before State Court Judge Antonio DelCampo. The thirty-one-year-old Rogozensky was meeting with his lawyer at the DeKalb County Courthouse when he asked sheriff's deputies if he could use the restroom. From there, Rogozensky maneuvered himself into a ceiling crawl space and headed for what he hoped was freedom. It all ended quickly when Rogozensky came crashing through the ceiling and landed ten feet below in Judge DelCampo's chambers. A technician working on the judge's computer nabbed the would-be escapee.

We do not always like the idea of justice. And it's not only when, somewhat like Rogozensky, we want to escape the consequences of justice for ourselves. Justice can seem negative and unmerciful, all about inflicting punishment—an eye for an eye.

Once I was asked to give two teachings at a large church in Alabama. I suggested to the pastor that I could give one speech on leadership and another on justice. He responded by asking me to skip justice and deliver two talks on leadership. I think the pastor's sentiment is no different from that of many Christians—we prefer more uplifting subjects than justice.

Justice is, however, a great and noble virtue. Somewhere deep inside, we all want to be just, and if we were, this world would be an immeasurably better place. Samuel Johnson had it right when he says, "Almost all the miseries of life, almost all the wickedness that infects society, and almost all the distresses that affect mankind, are the consequences of some defect in private duties."

In the secular world justice and not love is the "more excellent way" (compare 1 Corinthians 12:31 KJV). Aristotle said that neither "the evening star nor the morning star is as glorious as justice," which he called the "highest moral virtue." Cicero declared that "the luster of virtue appears in justice."[1] For Christians, of course, love is the most excellent way, and the luster of virtue appears in love.

Yet justice and love are not opposing virtues. In terms of personal behavior, together they are the fruit of character. We have already seen how humility provides the soil of character and how faith and hope reach into that soil as roots. Wisdom, courage, and self-control are the trunk and branches, enabling faith and hope to produce fruit. At last, then, we can begin considering the fruit that fulfills our ultimate purpose of bringing God glory. A part of the fruit in the tree of character is justice.

Giving What's Due

Justice is an enormous subject. Law libraries that cover tens of thousands of square feet are all about justice. In the Bible, the Law and the Prophets are largely about justice, and so is the book of Proverbs. Given all this information, can we say what justice really is?

One definition of justice has endured for thousands of years. It goes beyond complying with whatever laws of the land may be in effect in a given time and place. This definition is consistent with biblical teaching on justice and therefore represents the meaning that God Himself gives to justice. *Justice is rendering a person his due, constantly, without fear.*

The biblical understanding of what is due another is a lofty one—far above secular understanding—because in it every human being is seen in relation to God. We have been created in the image of God and thus have inherent dignity and value (Genesis 1:27). So all human beings, all the time, are to be treated with courtesy and respect, both to their face and behind their back.

The Christian standard for personal justice is seen in the Golden Rule. What is due another person? Under Christ, we are to do to another person as we would have done to us (Matthew 7:12). Fair treatment of others pleases our justice-loving God.

Scripture consistently records the Lord's concern for justice. It tells us that "righteousness and justice are the foundation" of God's throne (Psalm 97:2) and that the Messiah is about the business of establishing justice on the earth.

> He will not grow faint or be discouraged
>> till he has established justice in the earth;
>> and the coastlands wait for his law (Isaiah 42:4).

Through Amos, the Lord warned that He did not desire religious festivals or offerings. He would not receive songs and melodies from instruments until the people started acting justly.

> Let justice roll down like waters,
>> and righteousness like an ever-flowing stream
>> (Amos 5:24).

Yes, let it! Justice works all kinds of good in this world. And in our personal, everyday lives—which is what character is all about—justice, like love, brings honor to God.

Indeed, justice and love are inseparable partners. It can even be hard to determine where one begins and the other ends. Love is both the spring and the root of all justice as well as the finisher of all just action.

Justice: Elementary Love

Benjamin Rush, a devout Christian who signed both the Declaration of Independence and the Constitution, once said, "The world is more in need of justice than love. Indeed it is the want of justice that makes love everywhere so necessary."[2] This is a startling statement, but it is one that, upon reflection, we

171

recognize contains profound truth. To illustrate, let us look at marriage.

Most difficulties in marriage come from a lack of justice, not of love. I am no marriage counselor, but some who are have told me that the issues of bad marriages most often involve injustice. "He abuses me." "He's having an affair." "She lies to me."

What is fairly due to our spouses? First, we owe faithfulness to the marriage vows—to love and cherish and be faithful "till death do us part." These are our promises as married persons. And so an unfaithful marriage partner is, first of all, unjust.

Beyond the vows, what else is due one spouse from the other? If we look at the husband's responsibility, he at a minimum should always be courteous, considerate, gentle, well mannered, and honest. He should pay attention to his wife's conversation, be fair in financial arrangements and in duties relating to children, and put the needs of his wife and children ahead of fishing, playing golf, and watching football.

I know I am setting myself up for criticism here—my wife will tell you that I fall way short! Yet this is all simply justice, a matter of husbands giving wives their due. Husbands should do unto their wives what they, if they were in their wives' position, would wish to have done unto them.

Love, however, will do more. With love, husbands will delight in their wives and cherish them. In love, husbands will be sacrificially devoted to their wives, spontaneously giving more than is due. In this way, love completes justice and adds luster and enjoyment to the relationship. But let us never forget that justice provides the foundation without which love cannot operate.

Pastor and author John Piper sees the dimension of enjoyment that love adds to justice in marriage. In a love poem to his wife, Noel, he says:

I am a Christian hedonist
Because I know that if I kissed

My wife simply because it's right
And not because it's my delight
It would not honor her so well.
With pleasures I will praise Noel
And I will magnify my wife
By making her my joy in life.[3]

I have used marriage as a case study, but of course justice serves love in all kinds of relationships. Beyond marriage, we need to give what is due to our parents, our children, our boss, our fellow workers, our neighbors, our friends, and even our enemies. We owe, at a minimum, respect and courtesy to every person. Justice, in this way, is a sort of elementary, or beginning stage, love.

What, then, is the scope of Christian justice—giving the other what is due, or treating him or her as we would want to be treated. To justice, there belongs loyalty, faithfulness, fairness, honesty, integrity, promise keeping, unselfishness, courtesy, respect, attentiveness, quality, and excellence. So seen, most of life (say, 95 percent) is lived in the dimension of justice. The virtue of justice and the vice of injustice are constantly in practice.

What, then, is love? Love goes beyond justice in forgiveness, mercy, sacrifice, compassion (compassion means literally "suffer with"), not reciprocating (turning the other check), expecting nothing in return, overflowing (giving more than is expected), and being endless (long-suffering, persevering).

We will look at love in more detail in the next chapter. For now we merely need to note that love motivates and engenders justice, giving fullness and reality to it. Justice without love as its fountainhead is little more than a calculation, something a machine might do. The nobility of justice comes only as it is joined with love.

Considering how important justice is, especially as it is aligned with love, it is extraordinary that we are more dishonest about how just we are than about any other virtue.

Spinning Injustice

Few of us consider ourselves to be unjust. We might admit a lack of love or a failure in self-control. We might acknowledge cowardice, lust, or foolishness. But we all are skillful at ignoring or rationalizing injustice when it has a foothold in our lives.

At different times in history, large groups of devout Christians have rationalized economic systems that have consigned the poor to misery. In war, both sides claim justice. On every political issue, both parties assert the justice of their position—it's called "spin." I like the definition of politics in *The Devil's Dictionary*: "A strife of interests masquerading as a contest of principles. The conduct of public affairs for private advantage."[4] Some "principle" is almost always used to rationalize injustice, not just in politics, but in families, churches, and businesses as well. Of all the sins, injustice is the one to which our conscience most easily hardens.

I know this to be true from personal experience. After years of denial, I have recently been able to see the injustice (as well as the default of love) in my workaholism.

For my entire work life, my day has begun at 4:30 A.M. I kept up this pattern through my many years in a law firm and then through my tenure at Protective Life. Finally, I retired from Protective and thought my pace would slacken. But no—I accepted another job that is based ninety miles from home, requiring me to spend the early and late hours of the day driving back and forth. I still get up at 4:30 A.M., sometimes earlier (in part so that I can write this book on character!).

I have been around many workaholics in my time, and partly by seeing myself reflected in them, I have learned how we think. We justify our obsessive habit (of course we don't call it a *vice* or a *sin*) by saying that all our hard work is "for the company" or "for the community" or even "for God" and so it must be okay. It is not easy to acknowledge that we work so hard because selfishly we need affirmation through our achievement.

But I have to ask myself some hard questions. I tell myself that my hard work has been an act of self-denial, but is it not true that my wife and children are the ones who have been denied all these years, because I have so often been absent in attention if not in fact? What debt have I left unpaid to those closest to me as I have striven to achieve for selfish purposes and rewards?

Justice is about loyalty, faithfulness, fairness, honesty, integrity, keeping promises, courtesy, respect, attentiveness, quality, and excellence—and what gets in the way of these qualities more than selfishness? Justice, it seems, needs self-denial most as its supporting virtue. We have to learn to take our own self-interest out of the equation.

How to Neutralize Self-interest

When a judge has a stake in the outcome of a court case, he steps aside because self-interest is likely to get in the way of a just decision. But almost always, in our personal lives, we do not have the luxury of not participating when self-interest might mar our judgment. In marriages, we have a personal interest in how we structure the family budget, what we choose to do on the weekend, where we go to church, and so on. For our children, we have an interest in the grades that teachers give them and the decisions that coaches make in who plays. So also in business—in making sales, forming partnerships, filling out expense reports, and so on—we will profit if we do things one way rather than another. Much as we might seek objectivity, we cannot be truly impartial.

What is the solution here? Where we have an interest, how can we be just? First, we must continuously seek the Lord in prayer and through His Word. The Bible teaches,

Evil men do not understand justice,
> but those who seek the LORD understand it
> completely (Proverbs 28:5).

175

The Holy Spirit will make our consciences sensitive to what is just and right in decisions (those we make and those we receive).

Second, we must listen with an open mind to those who have a competing interest in the issue—our spouse, our children, those who report to us in business, whomever. Every just decision requires knowledge of the truth. That is the purpose of legal proceedings. The rules of evidence and trial procedure are intended to allow judges and juries to know the truth before a decision is rendered. So must we. And we will not understand until we have listened.

But still we are too easily misled by our self-centeredness. And so, third, we must seek advice from someone we trust—someone who will be candid and who has no self-interest in the outcome.

> Without counsel plans fail,
>> but with many advisers they succeed
>> (Proverbs 15:22).

This is the reason why, in business, we have bosses and committees and why CEOs have boards of directors. We all have pastors and we all need prayer partners and others who can help us both understand our selfishness and probe the mind of the Lord.

These, then, are the habits that undergird personal justice—seeking the Lord for a godly conscience and wisdom, listening to all concerned to understand the truth, and seeking advice. The wise person has habituated such a process. It is second nature to him, and he is likely to be just.

Halting for Justice

In the 2001 Tour de France bicycle race, Jan Ullrich of Germany was in the lead during the thirteenth stage, with the American champ Lance Armstrong close behind. Suddenly Ullrich, making a minute misjudgment, ran off the road and vaulted over his handlebars. What did Armstrong do then? Did he zoom past Ullrich, pleased with this opportunity to take the lead? No, he stopped, halting the race until Ullrich could recover from his spill and resume the race.

Two years later the situation was reversed. Armstrong was in the lead, pursuing a fifth straight victory, when his handlebars hooked in the bag of a fan leaning across the barrier to get a better view. Armstrong tumbled to the street. This time Ullrich stopped and halted the competition while Armstrong picked himself up and remounted.

It is true that bicycle racing etiquette demands that following racers stop if the lead racer takes a spill. But etiquette is not regulation. Ullrich and Armstrong each could have taken advantage of the other if he had chosen. But in these cases, the athletes practiced the Golden Rule in perfect reciprocal fashion. Even in the heat of competition they overcame their motivation of self-interest to treat each other with justice.

Fair Play

So far, we have discussed the duty of each of us as individuals to give others their due. But there is another aspect to justice, and that is ensuring that the conditions are right for others to receive justice. You might think of it as acting like a referee to assure fair play in the game of life. Not only judges such as myself, but everyone in some position of authority— parents, teachers, coaches, managers, and police, to name a few—are responsible for ensuring that the conditions are right for others to be treated justly.

Fair play is certainly one of the laws that is "written on our hearts" (see Psalm 40:8; Romans 2:15). Every child, from early on, has a sense of fair play—witness the frequent playground refrain "That's not fair!" Instinctively, we all realize that every group needs rules of order by which fairness might be maintained.

Favoritism by one in authority inevitably creates envy and resentment. Joseph was sold into slavery because his brothers saw him to be his father's favorite (Genesis 37). Fans of a team become irate to the point of rioting when they believe the referees are biased for the other team.

A level playing field is essential for freedom and is critical for character formation. Where there is no level playing field, there must be coercive power to back up the unfairness. Slavery, for example, always takes harsh laws and a strong police force—public or vigilante. So do all other forms of tyranny.

The virtue of justice calls for everyone in authority to establish rules that are fair, to administer them impartially, and to personally submit to them. Taking this approach releases enormous energy in any organization or group, whereas failure to do so depresses energy.

Students work harder when they know grades will be based strictly on merit and not on teacher favoritism. If an A will be given to the undeserving and a C to the best student, why bother to study hard? The same is true in any company, relating to how pay and promotions are determined. Bureaucratic rules develop in businesses because decision makers are not trusted to be just, with the result that factors other than merit control pay and promotion—and morale and effort suffer as a consequence.

People will not give their best effort for a boss or organization that will not treat them fairly. Even those *favored* by discrimination will give less than their best because they know they will be rewarded when they do not deserve it.

The result in an unfair situation like this is that character fails to develop. Perseverance in the face of adversity is not engendered; instead, laziness is.

Each of us would do well to consider where we have authority to influence rules of fair play. Are we parents? We must treat each of our children even-handedly. Are we bosses? We should let our employees earn rewards based on merit.

One area where all of us can help to even the playing field is by giving justice to the least favored among us: the poor and needy.

An Open Hand for the Poor

One of the most persistent themes in all of Scripture is the requirement of God to treat the poor justly. For example, the Law demanded equal rights for the poor at the bar of justice (Exodus 23:6). Leaders were expected to take up the cause of the poor and needy (Proverbs 31:8-9). Prophets and teachers denounced the powerful who grew wealthy through oppression of the poor (Proverbs 22:22-23; Amos 5:11-12).

This theme is especially well developed in Deuteronomy, where we read Moses' words to the Israelites about taking care of the poor.

> If among you, one of your brothers should become poor, in any of your towns within your land that the LORD your God is giving you, you shall not harden your heart or shut your hand against your poor brother, but you shall open your hand to him and lend him sufficient for his need, whatever it may be. Take care lest there be an unworthy thought in your heart and you say, "The seventh year, the year of release is near," and your eye look grudgingly on your poor brother, and you give him nothing, and he cry to the LORD against you, and you be guilty of sin. You shall give to him freely, and your heart shall not be grudging when you give to him, because for this the LORD your God will bless you in all your work and in all that you undertake. For there will never cease to be poor in the land. Therefore I command you, "You shall open wide your hand to your brother, to the needy and to the poor, in your land" (Deuteronomy 15:7-11).[5]

The lawgiver's emphasis upon both a generous *act* and a generous *attitude* is one that we could well emulate.

Of course, we might say that it is up to government to establish justice for the poor; our work as Christians is evangelism.

179

But that is a misconception. True social justice in every community is the liberation of each person, under God, to be the best that is in him. This basic obligation of justice starts in our families but it also applies to our work units, to the charitable agencies in our communities, to our municipal and county governments, to our states, to the nation, and to the world. Justice is a part of our duty to God and the men and women created in His image.

I need to add here that the democratic system in the United States, together with a people who on the whole have a heart for the poor, have made great progress in establishing justice for the poor. Though not perfectly, our judicial systems, as well as any the world has known, provide equal justice for all. Public education and Medicaid programs extend learning and health care to the least of our young brothers and sisters. Through our charitable donations, many of which reach the poor and afflicted, we are by any measure the most generous nation in the world. Despite shortcomings, programs administered by the government and offerings of private charity commingle in a way that certainly pleases God.

But there is one area where America is failing a category of the needy. I am speaking about the travesty of abortion.

Justice for the Unborn

Our laws are the most permissive in the developed world in allowing parents to take the life of their unborn children. Meanwhile, abortion is a denial of biblical justice. In the most basic way—by denying the right to life—abortion fails to give what is due to another. The original abortion decision of *Roe v. Wade* ranks with the 1857 Dred Scott decision, which declared that slaves had no rights as U.S. citizens, as the worst a court can do.

It is worth recalling the immortal words of Justice McLean, dissenting in *Dred Scott v. Sandford*: "A slave is not a mere chattel. He bears the impress of his Maker, and is amenable to the laws of God and man; and he is destined to an endless existence."[6] This is straight biblical morality, and it applies with equal rigor to every unborn child. They bear the impress of their Maker and they deserve justice.

The day after *Roe v. Wade* was decided in 1973, the *New York Times* declared that the U.S. Supreme Court had put the abortion matter to rest. Certain editors of that newspaper no doubt hoped that our collective conscience would soon become seared to the unheard cry of the unborn. Now, more than thirty years later, we know that in a democracy that trusts in God such blatant injustice, no more than slavery, can be put to rest.[7] The Dred Scott decision, in God's time, was abolished, and so will be *Roe v. Wade*.

What Will We Do?

A cartoon pictures two turtles. One turtle says, "Sometimes I'd like to ask God why He allows poverty, famine, and injustice when He could do something about it." The other replies, "I'm afraid God might ask me the same question."

Just as acting justly honors God, so the failure to act justly dishonors Him. And beyond that, because justice always involves someone else beside ourselves, that other person is always hurt as well. If we succeed at the root virtues and at the trunk and branch virtues, yet fail with the fruit of justice, we have still fallen short in our character.

Certainly God sees our every act of injustice. And we should not suppose that others do not notice our injustice as well. They not only notice; they carefully remember.

I have a good friend who has resisted entering into a deeper relationship with Christ. In conversations it is clear to me that he has in his mind a scrapbook of Christian injustice—not necessarily injustices done to him personally but injustices done to others. And wherever he has noted such failure on the part of a Christian, he has committed it to memory. It is a very effective defense against my urgings to follow Christ.

Others such as Benjamin Franklin (see pages 41-42) are watching our practice of personal justice, and they are right to do so. We honor or dishonor God by what we do measured by biblical standards of justice. If we are to glorify God, justice is the minimum.

Are we honoring our just God by behaving justly? Let us practice the "elementary love" of justice by giving others their due, just as we would like them to do to us. Wherever we can, let us help to create conditions where others can enjoy justice, especially empowering the poorest and neediest among us to be all they can be.

With justice as a beginning point in our character's fruit bearing, we can go on to produce the fruit that is the pinnacle of achievement in character: love.

Character Questions

1. Do you agree with Benjamin Rush that "the world is more in need of justice than love"? Why or why not?

2. Let's say you're the second turtle in the cartoon and God really does ask you why you haven't done more about the injustice in this world. What would you answer?

3. Is there any habitual injustice in your life? If so, how can you replace it with habitual justice?

11

Love: Seeking the Best for Others

Robertson McQuilkin was president of Columbia Bible College and Seminary (now Columbia International University) in Columbia, South Carolina, when his wife, Muriel, began exhibiting symptoms of Alzheimer's disease. For a number of years, he was able to balance his professional responsibilities with care for his wife. Finally, though, in 1990, he made the decision to leave his job for Muriel's sake.

In a letter explaining his resignation, McQuilkin wrote the following:

> My dear wife, Muriel, has been in failing health for about 12 years. So far I have been able to carry both her ever-growing needs and my leadership responsibility at Columbia. But recently it has become apparent that Muriel is contented most of the time she is with me and almost none of the time I am away from her. It is not just "discontent." She is filled with fear—even terror—that she has lost me and always goes in search of me when I leave home. So it is clear to me that she needs me now, full-time.
>
> The decision was made, in a way, 42 years ago when I promised to care for Muriel "in sickness and in health ... till death do us part." So ... as a man of my word, integrity has something to do with it. But so does fairness. She has cared for me fully and sacrificially all these years; if I cared for her for the next 40 years I would not be out of her debt. Duty, however, can be grim and stoic. But there is more: I love Muriel. She is a delight to me— her childlike dependence and confidence in me, her warm love, occasional flashes of wit I used to relish so, her happy spirit and tough resilience in the face of her

continual depressing frustration. I don't *have* to care for her. I *get* to! It is a high honor to care for so wonderful a person.[1]

Here is real love. Love as a feeling *and* love as doing. Love that lasts and that does not count the cost. Love as the supreme virtue.

Some may object to calling love a virtue. In our culture, we're accustomed to viewing love as an emotion, one we express in a Hallmark card manner to family and friends. And as we see with the McQuilkins, that is part of it. But make no mistake: Love is more than just a sentiment.

If we view love only as a feeling, checking our love at the door when we enter the workplace, the playing field, or other competitive arenas, we will not live into our ultimate purpose. Like the abundant fruit of a healthy tree, love is the crowning glory of a character that allows us to glorify God and enjoy Him forever.

Again and again, the Bible proclaims this message. In Matthew we read: "You shall love the Lord your God with all your heart and with all your soul and with all your mind. This is the great and first commandment. And a second is like it: You shall love your neighbor as yourself. On these two commandments depend all the Law and the Prophets" (22:37-40). Paul declares that faith expressing itself through love is "the only thing that counts" (Galatians 5:6 NIV).

As the theologian Jonathan Edwards put it, love is "the sum of Christianity."

Love Among the Virtues

It is important to understand love's relationship with the other virtues that are the subject of this book. Three points are crucial.

First, love depends on the other virtues for its full expression. Humility, faith, and hope open us to the flow of God's grace and sustain that grace within us. Wisdom, courage, and self-control strengthen us. Justice, which we have called "elementary love," provides love's foundation and is completed by it. With all these virtues worked into our character, love achieves its full potential. Love is the ultimate fruit of the tree of virtue. All other parts of the tree exist to produce it.

Second, love engenders and mobilizes the other virtues. Edwards calls it "the spring and root of all virtue." We are able to love because we are courageous and self-controlled, but we become courageous and self-controlled because we love. When a couple has a child, for example, love prompts the parents to exercise faith and hope in God's provident love for the child, courage to protect the child, and wisdom and self-control to be worthy parents.

Third, love unifies the other virtues. In Colossians, Paul teaches that we are to "put to death" earthly passions and desires and "put on" compassion, kindness, humility, meekness, patience, tolerance, and forgiveness. He then says, "Above all these put on love, which binds everything together in perfect harmony" (Colossians 3:5,12,14).

In sum, love is the executive center of our character, organizing and coordinating each of the other virtues as we seek to glorify God in all we do. The story of Paul Rusesabagina provides a vivid example of how love draws on all aspects of our character.

Rusesabagina, whose story is told in the movie *Hotel Rwanda*, was manager of Rwanda's finest hotel in 1994 when the majority Hutu tribe began a campaign of genocide against the smaller Tutsi tribe. Rusesabagina, a Hutu who was married to a Tutsi, initially sheltered only friends and family members in his hotel. But as the violence escalated, he courageously took in strangers, so that the Hotel Mille Collines ultimately became a refugee camp for more than a thousand people, most of them Tutsis. Rusesabagina used all of his practical wisdom and contacts to hold off the deadly threat to the Tutsis, despite the grave risk to himself and his family. Hope of restored justice sustained him. In the end, though almost a million people were slaughtered during the bloodshed, Rusesabagina saved the lives of nearly all who had come to him for shelter.

Rusesabagina's courage illustrates the principle that, when we act in a loving way, love both calls on the other virtues within our character and strengthens and enriches those virtues so that our efforts to love are successful. What this means for us as students of character is that if we get love right, we get it all right. Our other virtues will be bound together in perfect harmony. If we get love wrong, our characters will be destabilized and our souls will be conflicted.

As Stephen Covey says, "The main thing is to keep the main thing the main thing." Love is the main thing.

Prepared to Love

Love is a gift from God. We don't create it; rather, we receive it and pass it on. As we gain access to God's grace through faith, He pours His love into our hearts through the Holy Spirit (Romans 5:5). Thus, if love is to be the fruit of our lives, the first thing we must do is pray Paul's injunction that we "be filled with the Spirit" (Ephesians 5:18).

But to receive this gift of love by way of the Holy Spirit, we must prepare ourselves. Paul writes to Timothy that "the aim of our charge [the purpose of our ministry] is love that issues from a pure heart and a good conscience and a sincere faith" (1 Timothy 1:5). Love does not abide where filth, deceit, and sin reside. Thus David cries out after he had committed adultery with Bathsheba and had Uriah murdered:

> Create in me a clean heart, O God,
>   and renew a right spirit within me.
> Cast me not away from your presence,
>   and take not your Holy Spirit from me
>   (Psalm 51:10-11).

In other words, without repentance, confession, and cleansing, we cannot receive God's love.

There may be no better model than the twelve steps of Alcoholics Anonymous to help us develop a pure heart, a good conscience, and a sincere faith from which love emanates. Though intended to help alcoholics recover from their addiction, the twelve steps can help all of us prepare ourselves to receive God's love.[2]

AA's first step calls for the admission of powerlessness, which in spiritual terms marks the shift of mind that is the beginning of repentance. This is the concept we discussed in chapter four. Steps two and three call for us to turn to a "Power greater than ourselves" and to "turn our will and our lives over to the care of God." In spiritual terms, this is surrender to God's will—also part of humility. In the Christian context, these three steps lead the believer to the sincere faith of which 1 Timothy 1:5 speaks.

The next steps of the program lead to a pure heart and a good conscience. They require us continually to make a "searching and fearless moral inventory," to confess our sins to God and another, and to humbly ask God to remove our shortcomings. Subsequent steps require us to seek forgiveness from those we have harmed and to make amends to those people. The final step involves reaching out to others in need of help—in other words, love. This fruit of love is based on the preceding eleven steps.

Just as we have seen in our tree illustration, love does not sprout out of nowhere. It issues from other virtues and from preparation to receive it as a gift.

Selfless Love

In addition to making our hearts, consciences, and faith ready, there is a second essential condition for the reception and expression of love in our lives. As is the case with all virtue, we must deny ourselves. We must lose our lives for Jesus' sake if we are to bring glory to God through love.

Before the New Testament was written, the most common Greek word for love was *eros*. This term conveyed the notion that the object or person loved was esteemed because of its value—a woman because she was beautiful, a diamond because it was worth a lot of money, a big house because it enhanced its owner's reputation. *Eros* sought a return on its investment. I invite you to dinner; I expect a dinner invitation (or maybe tickets to a sold-out game) from you. If *eros* provided some benefit for the less fortunate, it did so prominently and publicly, so the person who bestowed the benefit could be honored in others' admiration for his noble deed. *Eros* was essentially self-centered.

But Jesus proclaims that God's love is the opposite of *eros* (a radically new concept). Thus, the New Testament uses the term *agape* for love, connoting selfless love instead of *eros*.

The culture in Jesus' day insisted that God's love was for those who had earned it by obedience to the law. But Jesus declares, "I have not come to call the righteous but sinners to repentance" (Luke 5:32), shattering the prevailing conception of God's love for man. The Son of God ate with tax collectors and sinners. In His parable of the prodigal son, it is the sinful son who is given the feast. The love ethic of Jesus calls us to ask to a banquet those who cannot repay, to bind up the wounds of a stranger with no thought of return, to pray for our enemies, to bless those who persecute us, to give in secret.

Brennan Manning, in his *Ragamuffin Gospel*, says,

> Jesus spent a disproportionate amount of time with people described in the Gospels as the poor, the blind, the lame, the lepers, the hungry, sinners, prostitutes, tax collectors, the persecuted, the downtrodden, the captives, those possessed by unclean spirits, all who labor and are heavy burdened, the rabble who know nothing of the law, the crowds, the little ones, the least, the last, and the lost sheep of the house of Israel.

In short, Jesus hung out with ragamuffins.[3]

Nothing like this had ever been conceived of. And the most mind-blowing thing of all about Christianity was that Jesus Christ—who was truly God, through whom all things were made and in whom resided all authority in heaven and on earth—would die to save and give eternal life to, not just the righteous, but the lowliest sinners on earth, including even a condemned man crucified with Him and you and me.

Jesus and His apostles taught that our love for others is to be spontaneous, not to be motivated by any thought of return. Instead, loving as Jesus did, we are to meet needs wherever we find them, naturally, anonymously, and lavishly. In love, we are to be conduits of God's love. Freely, freely we have received this love. Freely, freely we are to give it.

One who reached a place of loving self-denial is Rudy Tomjanovich, who coached the gold-medal-winning U.S. Men's Olympic basketball team in 2000 and, as head coach of the Houston Rockets, has won two NBA titles. In 1977, Tomjanovich, then an all-star player for the Rockets, nearly died when Kermit Washington, a player for the Los Angeles Lakers, punched him as Tomjanovich attempted to break up a fight during a game. The punch dislodged part of Tomjanovich's skull and resulted in the need for five surgeries.

A lesser man might have felt justified in hating Washington, yet Tomjanovich has forgiven Washington. "I knew that to recover," Tomjanovich said of Washington, "I couldn't afford to hate him, that if I did, it would be like taking poison and hoping someone else would die from it." Tomjanovich told author John Feinstein that he wishes only the best for Washington. When Feinstein asked why, Tomjanovich replied, "Because we're brothers."[4]

As Tomjanovich's example shows, the self-denial that undergirds love in no way means that we have to drop out of life. One who seeks to deny himself can still excel as an athlete or in business. Every coach hopes to instill self-denial in his athletes, for a self-denying athlete is a great team player. And a self-denying businessperson who is called upon to act as a steward or servant for others can act tenaciously to protect their interests and will almost certainly have greater authority in doing so than one who acts from self-interest.

In fact, all of us can point to marriages, businesses, and teams that have failed because the people involved thought first of themselves. But such self-seeking behavior is, to use Tomjanovich's words, "poison." Thus, self-denial is not a prescription for failure. Quite the contrary: it is a secret of success and a necessary condition of love.

Longing and Acting

Thus far we have seen that love is a gift from God, that it is the beginning and end of all other virtues, that it proceeds from a pure heart, that it reaches out without regard to value, and that it denies self. Let's now turn our attention to say what love really is. A good definition is that *love both longs and acts for the good of another*.

Certainly love involves feeling. It desires deeply. We see examples of this all around us—in the love of a mother for her child, for example. And no mother and child better illustrate this feeling than St. Augustine and his mother, Monica.

Until his conversion at thirty-two, Augustine lived a rebellious life, far from the faith. As so many mothers do (including mine), Monica prayed her son into the kingdom. In his famous *Confessions*, Augustine recalled his mother's love and prayers: "Night and day my mother poured out her tears ... and offered her heart-blood in sacrifice for me ... Words cannot describe how dearly she loved me or how much greater was the anxiety she suffered for my spiritual birth than the physical pain she had endured in bringing me into the world.... She asked not for gold or silver or any fleeting, short-lived favor, but that the soul of her son might be saved."[5]

This longing for the good of others also appeared when Jesus looked out over Jerusalem and said, "O Jerusalem,

Jerusalem ... How often would I have gathered your children together as a hen gathers her brood under wings, and you would not!" (Matthew 23:37).

But while love longs for and greatly desires the good of others, even more importantly, it *acts* for the good of others. The Bible teaches us to love not just in thought and word but "in deed and in truth" (1 John 3:18). Robertson McQuilkin, in caring for his ailing wife, both longed for the good of Muriel and acted in pursuit of it.

The purest expression of acting for the good of others was Jesus' becoming obedient even unto death on a cross for our salvation. Paul taught that "God shows his love for us in that while we were still sinners, Christ died for us" (Romans 5:8). Would we die for someone who had made himself our enemy? Yet that is what Jesus did for us, showing His love.

To continue, what does it mean to act "for" another?

Sacrificial Love

The word "for" is a fundamental one in Christian life. Though we may not think of it this way, it has two meanings.

Each of us knows what it is to long "for" something, whether it is the happiness of our spouse or children, a winning season for our favorite sports team, or something similar. When we are "for" something in this way, we urgently desire its good. We rejoice in its every success. Threats against it upset us, and we suffer when it suffers. Certainly love includes this dimension of the word "for."

But there is another, more profound meaning of "for," which goes to the essence of Christian love as action. When the Bible says that Jesus died "for" us, it does not mean merely that He is rooting for us or is on our side (though He is). It means that He sacrificed Himself in our place. Isaiah 53 says:

> Surely he has borne our griefs
> and carried our sorrows....

> He was wounded for our transgressions;
>   he was crushed for our iniquities;
> upon him was the chastisement that brought us peace,
>   and with his stripes we are healed (Isaiah 53:4-5).

In other words, Jesus suffered "for" us by taking punishment in our stead.

This is sacrificial love, the highest expression of love. Paul expressed such love for his Jewish brothers and sisters when he said, "I am speaking the truth in Christ ... that I have great sorrow and unceasing anguish in my heart. For I could wish that I myself were accursed and cut off from Christ for the sake of my brothers, my kinsmen according to the flesh" (Romans 9:1-3). Moses had the same love for his people, saying to the Lord, "Alas, this people have sinned a great sin. They have made for themselves gods of gold. But now, if you will forgive their sin—but if not [as an atonement for them], please blot me out of your book that you have written" (Exodus 32:31-32).

In smaller or larger ways, sacrificial love goes on all around us. Our love for our spouses and children, for example, is often sacrificial love. And throughout our nation's history, our armed forces have risked and given their own lives on our behalf. Every day, law enforcement personnel do the same.

Perhaps no other group in modern life more clearly epitomizes the virtue of sacrificial love than the 343 New York City firefighters who died as they fought to rescue the victims of the September 11, 2001, terrorist attacks. These brave individuals did not act from self-interest; the people they sought to rescue were complete strangers to them. "Greater love has no one than this, that someone lays down his life for his friends" (John 15:13).

To act "for" another, in its highest sense, is to sacrifice on his behalf. But love also acts for "the good of another." What does that mean?

Fulfilled Potential

We act for the good of another when we identify that individual's legitimate needs and extend ourselves to help him meet those needs. This includes helping the other to achieve his full potential, so that he becomes all God intended him to be. Thus, the first thing love asks us to do for the good of another is to seek that person's salvation. Just as Monica prayed for Augustine, so we do not rest until those we love have come to a saving knowledge of Christ. We also work to provide the individual's basic needs for such things as food, clothing, and shelter as well as health care and education. And, since (after salvation) the most critical need of all humans is that they live into their ultimate purpose, the most important manifestation of our love is contributing to the development of another's character, so that he can glorify God and enjoy Him forever.

Not long after Rwanda's period of violence in 1994 (the time when Rusesabagina saved the refugees at his hotel), I visited that African nation. One afternoon, I saw a young Tutsi man, who was a Christian, leave his home with several books. When I asked where he was headed, he told me he was going to a prison to teach Hutus imprisoned there for their part in the genocide. This man was seeking to help the Hutu prisoners attain their ultimate purpose. He was acting selflessly for the good of others.

If love seeks to enable another to achieve his full potential, then on many occasions love must be tough. A mother shows love for a child when she insists the child study for the geometry exam instead of going to the movies. A drill sergeant shows love for the troops he is training when he is tough enough to prepare them for the rigors they will face in combat. Vince Lombardi loved his players, though he was probably the toughest coach in the National Football League.

The same goes for Bear Bryant, legendary coach of the Alabama Crimson Tide. Hundreds of young men who played on his teams achieved their potential, not just on the football field but also in their lives, because Bryant loved them enough to demand the best of them. When Sylvester Croom, an All-American center on one of Bryant's teams, was asked to comment on the Bear, he teared up and said, "He taught me to be a man."

In the same vein, sometimes we act for the good of another by withholding what that person most wants. And sometimes, like the father of the prodigal son, we act for the good of our children when we give them freedom, knowing that thereafter, at least for a season, all we can do is pray for them to repent and come home.

All of us have limited time and many responsibilities, and our spheres of influence are small. But in all our roles— husband or wife, mother or father, employer or employee, and all the other ways in which we move through the world—our primary attention should be toward longing and acting for the good of others. And where we cannot reach others with what we do in a physical way, we can pray for them as God lays their needs on our hearts.

I've already mentioned Vince Lombardi and Bear Bryant, but permit me to mention a couple of other football greats. If love, as we have defined it, applies in the rough and competitive world of football, then it can apply everywhere else.

Love and Football

Having a shouting ritual before a game is nothing unusual for a high school football team. But what *is* unusual about the ritual before the Greyhounds of Gilman School (Baltimore, Maryland) head out to the field to play is what the coach and players say to each other.

Coach Joe Ehrmann shouts, "What is our job as coaches?"

"To love us!" the Gilman boys yell back.

Ehrmann shouts a second time, "What is your job?"

"To love each other!" the boys respond.

Ehrmann, a former all-pro player for the Baltimore Colts, is not only coach of one of the winningest high school football programs in the state; he is also pastor of a large church and the founder or a leader of more than one nonprofit ministry. He is the one who came up with love as the basis for the Gilman football program.

Ehrmann got involved with coaching because he wants to teach boys how to become men. "Masculinity, first and foremost, ought to be defined in terms of relationships," he says. "It ought to be taught in terms of the capacity to love and to be loved."

This philosophy might sound unrealistic, but Ehrmann and his fellow coaches make it practical by teaching that Gilman football is all about living in a community. It is about serving others and seeking justice on behalf of others.

"I was blown away at first," said Sean Price, one of the players. "All the stuff about love and relationships—I didn't really understand why it was part of football. After a while, though, getting to know some of the older guys on the team, it was the first time I've ever been around friends who really cared about me."[6]

Similarly, it should come as no surprise that Auburn coach Ralph "Shug" Jordan attributed Auburn's 1957 national championship not to the toughness of his team (though it was certainly there) or even to their ability but rather to the spiritual dimension. "There are countless intangibles and unusual circumstances that lead to success or failure in almost every endeavor.... I'm convinced that the underlying reason why Auburn attained the national football championship in 1957 was a spiritual one."[7]

Love as a Habit

We have already discussed how other virtues grow as they become habits engraved into our character by practice. The same holds true for love. Love becomes more deeply carved into our souls as we repeatedly put it into action.

John teaches that "if we love one another, God abides in us and His love is perfected in us" (1 John 4:12). These words describe how the habit of love is engraved in our character. Each of us has experienced the circular process John described. God gives us His love, and as we use it to love one another, not just in thought but also in deed, then God abides with us and our fellowship with Him deepens. And as we feel profound joy and affirmation, we are motivated to love even more. This virtuous cycle "perfects" God's love within us.

Interestingly, we can enter into this reinforcing cycle of love at any of its stages. Tony Campolo, professor emeritus of sociology at Eastern University, says that he advises couples in marital counseling to do ten things each day that they would do if they were first "in love" with each other. If the couples commit to this practice, Campolo says, soon they will feel love toward each other again. "Love is what one wills *to do* to make the other person happy and fulfilled," he writes. "Doing these things generates the feelings which are associated with 'being in love.' "[8]

The same approach can work in any type of relationship. C. S. Lewis advises, "Do not waste time bothering whether you 'love' your neighbour; act as if you did…. When you are behaving as if you loved someone, you will presently come to love him."[9] Oswald Chambers says, "Love is spontaneous, but it has to be maintained by discipline."[10]

Love for God

Thus far we have talked primarily of love for our neighbor. But the love of God comes first.

In some respects, our love of God differs from our love for our neighbor. God has no needs for us to meet; there is no good of His that we can supply. And we need Him, because there is a God-shaped emptiness in our souls that only He can fill. Thus, our love for God is self-seeking.

We are commanded to love God with all our heart, soul, mind, and strength (Mark 12:30). This means that we are to leave nothing out—we must love God with everything we have. Because everything we as humans know or experience is essentially partial, this truth is hard for us to comprehend. But this is the meaning of 1 Corinthians 13:10, where Paul teaches the partial will one day pass away. When the perfect comes, it will be clear that every human was created to love God with all our hearts.

God's grace covers the totality of our lives. Likewise, our love for God is to consume the totality of our lives, so that "in all things at all times" whatever we do, whether in word or deed, we do in love for God and His glory (2 Corinthians 9:8).

Loving in All We Do

How do we put love into practice? How, in God's grace, can we habituate the most excellent of all virtues? Though working love into our souls is a lifetime process filled with failures, some agonizing, Paul has given us a simple checklist, easily memorized, to serve as our exercise chart. It is in 1 Corinthians 13:4-8 (here quoted in the *Message* paraphrase and the *English Standard Version*):

Love never gives up.
Love cares more for others than for self.
Love doesn't want what it doesn't have.
Love doesn't strut,
Doesn't have a swelled head,
Doesn't force itself on others,
Isn't always "me first,"
Doesn't fly off the handle,
Doesn't keep score of the sins of others,
Doesn't revel when others grovel,
Takes pleasure in the flowering of truth,

197

Puts up with anything,
Trusts God always,
Always looks for the best,
Never looks back,
But keeps going to the end.

Love is patient and kind; love does not envy or
boast; it is not arrogant or rude. It does not insist on its
own way; it is not irritable or resentful; it does not
rejoice at wrongdoing, but rejoices with the truth. Love
bears all things, believes all things, hopes all things,
endures all things.
Love never ends.

These words should guide our lives. They tell us how we are
to live into our ultimate purpose. They tell us how we glorify
God in what we do.

I know we don't do all these things consistently (at least I
don't), but we need to be disgusted with ourselves when we fail
anywhere on the love checklist. We need to ask forgiveness
from others and God, and we need to keep on practicing and
praying. As we do, then in God's grace we will become more
loving, not just in doing, but in our inner being and hearts as
well. Exercising love for God's glory is life's destiny. Without
such love worked into our lives, nothing else in the world
matters.

We may be tempted to say that this description of love sets
the bar too high, that no one can wholeheartedly attend to love
every moment, and if we did, our lives would become unbal-
anced. But we need to understand that neither love for God nor
love for neighbor should unbalance our lives. This is because—
as we saw earlier—love is a unifier of all virtue. In the core of
our souls, love balances and harmonizes all other virtues.

This does not mean that we cannot concentrate on singular
objectives. God often calls us to passionate commitments. Jesus
was committed that way. He set His face like flint as He

headed toward the cross. Likewise, Paul was singularly committed to fulfilling the commission Jesus gave him on the road to Damascus. But as Jesus and Paul pursued their missions, they did so with a harmony in their souls produced by total love of God and a deep love for their fellowman.

One of the twentieth century's great psychiatrists was Karl Menninger, who believed balance in the soul was the critical need of his psychiatric patients. Menninger counseled depressed patients that working to help the poor and oppressed would contribute to lifting their depression. I do not know how Menninger described this from a psychiatric point of view, but from a biblical perspective, we know that loving creates order and peace within our souls. We have all experienced this; making a material contribution to the quality of the lives of those in need feeds our souls.

Certainly, we will all fall short of the ideal of love that the New Testament describes. Nevertheless, all who follow Christ should seek to let God's love give expression and energy to all we do. Because we are commanded to love as our highest and best purpose, love is not just for romance, for our families, or for after work. Like the beating of our hearts, love is not to be turned on and off at will but is to be a constant function of our lives.

The task is not an easy one, but God has equipped us for it with His loving grace. G. K. Chesterton had it right when he said, "Christianity has not been tried and found wanting. It has been found difficult and not tried."[11] When it is tried it is never wanting. The burden of love and all virtue is indeed a light one. With the Spirit working within us and our putting the virtues into practice, they become more and more natural and our lives infinitely more abundant.

Character Questions

1. In your opinion, how are worldly conceptions of love off base, when compared with the biblical perspective?

2. C. S. Lewis says, "When you are behaving as if you loved someone, you will presently come to love him." When have you seen that to be true?

3. What typical ways of acting must you change to become more loving?

4. How do the means of grace relate to love in all you do?

Part 3

Character in the Real World

The Lord is the Spirit, and where the Spirit of the Lord is, there is freedom.

—2 Corinthians 3:17

Introduction to Part 3

Following the American Civil War, General Robert E. Lee became president of Washington College (later renamed Washington and Lee University) in Lexington, Virginia. He began to run things differently, in a way that may have seemed only slightly less strange in its time than it seems today. One biographer described it this way:

> General Lee initiated the honor system very soon after he came to Lexington, and made it the basis on which all students were received. Faculty visitation of dormitories and all forms of espionage were abolished. If any breach of discipline occurred or any injury was done to college property, he expected the students who were involved in it to report to him. "We have no printed rules," Lee told a new matriculate who asked for a copy. "We have but one rule here, and it is that every student must be a gentleman." The first and the final appeal was to a student's sense of honor. "As a general principle," he told a young professor, "you should not force young men to do their duty, but let them do it voluntarily and thereby develop their characters." The code of the college, as Lee developed it, was positive though unprinted.[1]

By asking the male students of the day to behave as "gentlemen," Lee was in effect relying upon their character. If they behaved according to enlightened conscience, they would be doing as they ought, even though no external regulations or authority was constraining them. Lee's appeal was to discipline ordered not from the outside but from the inside. The point we cannot miss is this: Because the students were guided by their character, they had a maximum of freedom.

Edmund Burke (1729-97), British political philosopher, once stated, "Society cannot exist, unless a controlling power upon will and appetite be placed somewhere; and the less of it there is within, the more there must be without. It is ordained in the eternal constitution of things, that men of intemperate minds cannot be free."[2] In other words, proper behavior in society can come from one of only two sources: internal character or external coercion. A nation can get by with fewer laws, fewer court cases, and less police enforcement if its citizens are people with good character. These people can then enjoy maximum freedom.

William Golding's classic novel, *The Lord of the Flies*, is a stark reminder of the need for character in freedom. The story unfolds after a group of young boys are stranded on a desert island. With total freedom, but without mature virtues to steer their efforts to shape an ethical society on the island, the boys fall into an abyss of evil, anarchy, and savage violence. It's a clear demonstration of how the moral character of each individual in society stands in the gap between love and malice, between peace and war.

Moving from fiction to an observation from one with keen insight into our societal challenges, "Societies are tragically vulnerable when the men and women who compose them lack character," declares Charles Colson. "A nation or a culture cannot endure for long unless it is undergirded by common values such as valor, public-spiritedness, respect for others and for the law; it cannot stand unless it is populated by people who will act on motives superior to their own immediate interest."[3]

Possibly the single most important point to consider in understanding why character counts is the relationship of character to freedom. We must have virtue in order to be free. Without virtue, we will lose our freedom politically, economically, morally, and spiritually. And such freedom is what God desires for us to have.

Jesus and Freedom

After Jesus was baptized by John, He was led by the Holy Spirit into the wilderness, where He fasted and prayed for forty days. During these forty days, Jesus was tempted three times by the devil (Luke 4:1-13). All of these temptations related to our freedom: Would we be free to choose or refuse Him? Free to choose to do evil rather than good? Free to love God and our neighbors (for if love is coerced, it is not love)? Satan offered Jesus alternatives that would allow Him to control His people, because Satan desired that our commitment to and trust in Jesus be based on something other than faith and love freely given.

The first temptation was for Christ to draw people to God by using bread evoked magically from stones rather than from human enterprise and labor.

Now, if God decided to meet the physical needs of mankind apart from the sweat of our brow, we would flock to the church. I am in government and I like to look at the metaphor of bread as what elected officials call "pork," a project given to one community but paid for by others. Elected officials clamor for pork because they know pork means votes. If Jesus had relented to this temptation, He could have used all kinds of pork to create a giant welfare state and draw men to Himself. But no longer would we have been truly free to choose Him. We would respond, not in love based in freedom, but rather to fill our stomachs with bread. In effect, our choice, our obedience, and our love for Him would be bought. Having been bought, whatever fruit we produced would hardly be glorifying to God. Jesus' decision was to leave us free and to draw us to Himself by being high and lifted up on a cross.

The second temptation was for Jesus to grab governmental power.

One thing the Bible makes clear is that all authority in heaven and earth has been given to Jesus for eternity. It would have been easy for Jesus to have decided to exercise governmental power to be sure we obeyed and worshiped Him. He could have come to us as emperor or Caesar—worldwide, war could have been outlawed forever, likewise abortion, drugs, pornography, and prostitution. Jesus could have forced His teaching upon us. All schools would be religious. Church attendance would be mandatory. Heresy would be outlawed.

Children would obey their parents, and wives would submit to their husbands, under threat of criminal law. It is hard to imagine such a world, and certainly God would not be glorified in it. We got a taste of it when the Taliban regime of Afghanistan was in the news. So to this temptation Jesus said no. We were to be free.

The third temptation was that Jesus climb to the top of the temple and jump off spectacularly, drawing on God's miraculous power to save Him.

We can relate the third temptation to magic. The world loves the mystery of magic and power to change the laws of nature. If the Church and its ministers and priests could perform miracles on command to enhance popularity, churches would overflow with believers. Soon, however, we would be like Simon, a Samaritan magician who, upon witnessing the miracles performed by Peter as recorded in Acts 8, asked how he could acquire such power. Peter rebuked Simon. For though there were and are miracles in the Church through the power of the Holy Spirit, they are not to be presumed upon nor commanded as the devil would have it. Jesus wanted no cult and no magic. He left us free.

It is hard to imagine the magnitude of the importance of this decision.

After Jesus completed His fasting, prayer, and communion with God in the wilderness, He commenced His ministry with a sermon that had freedom as its keynote. Jesus was in the synagogue in Nazareth, and opening the Scripture to Isaiah 61, He read from it this prophecy of the Messiah:

> The Spirit of the Lord GOD is upon me,
>> because the LORD has anointed me
> to bring good news to the poor;
>> he has sent me to bind up the brokenhearted,
> to proclaim liberty to the captives,
>> and the opening of the prison to those who are
>> bound (Isaiah 61:1).

Speaking of Himself and His kingdom, Jesus added, "Today this Scripture has been fulfilled in your hearing" (Luke 4:21).

From this opening shot, delivered after the struggle in the wilderness where alternatives to freedom were rejected, it is clear that at the core of Jesus' kingdom would be the importance of liberty. Freedom, then, is our birthright. But we have to make sure we understand what kind of freedom Jesus has given us.

A Law Unto Oneself

Secular persons in our society have created a philosophy of freedom based on autonomy, or the idea that we are a law unto ourselves (*auto* = "self"; *nomos* = "law"). Essentially, this mindset says that freedom is creating our own lives as we wish, apart from any permanent moral norms.

The autonomous self lives in conflict with the denied self. It was a desire to be autonomous of God, and be legislators of their own law, that caused Adam and Eve to eat the forbidden fruit, which signified "the knowledge of good and evil" (Genesis 2:17). Thus, taking responsibility for defining good and evil was mankind's primal sin.

The defiant, autonomous self today asserts exactly what Adam and Eve wanted—the right to decide what is good and evil apart from God's decrees. The autonomous self proclaims freedom to ignore the transcendent moral norms handed to us in biblical revelation. This right to define our own morality might reasonably be called the first canon of secularism.

While the confusion of biblical liberty with autonomy is a perennial human problem, it has perhaps become worse than ever in the last few centuries, dating back to the Enlightenment of the seventeenth and eighteenth centuries. Beginning from that time, strong forces in Western society have attempted to throw off the beliefs of the Judeo-Christian tradition. We are being poisoned by the bitter fruits of such secularism still today.

Where it has been incorporated in government, the autonomous mind-set has created tyranny and disaster. Let's take as an example Communism, whose goal was to depart from biblical truth and create a godless society. What was its result? An environment in which there flourished ruthless dictatorships and purges that claimed the lives of tens of millions of people.

A pure expression of freedom as autonomy was expressed by several justices in the U.S. Supreme Court in *Planned Parenthood v. Casey*, the landmark abortion decision in 1992 that upheld abortion rights established in *Roe v. Wade*. Here the main opinion stated, "At the heart of liberty is the right to define one's own concept of existence, of meaning, of the universe and of the mystery of human life."[4]

In simplest terms, this opinion is an endorsement of the view that it is our right to eat of the fruit of the tree of the knowledge of good and evil and, in the words of Satan, to "be like God" (Genesis 3:5). And, of course, in the context of abortion, what the justices were saying was that liberty includes the right to define one's own concept of existence even to the point of killing unborn human life.

This concept of freedom to define our own concepts of existence and meaning is accepted as "gospel" in American secular culture. But as the wreckage of millions of lives in our country tells us, this idea of freedom is a recipe for disaster and a prescription for bondage to all the pathologies of mankind— whether it be in a life sentence in the penitentiary or in bondage through drugs or through failed or frustrated careers, marriages, or parenting.

Twentieth-century journalist Walter Lippman says of people who have given up on biblical morality and tried to construct their own ethics, "They are deeply perplexed. They have learned that the absence of belief is vacancy; they know, from disillusionment and anxiety, that there is no freedom in mere freedom."[5] So-called freedom, under the secular view, ends up being no freedom at all.

We, as God's creatures, are free to obey or disobey His moral decrees, but we fool ourselves if we believe we will be free by insisting on the freedom to make our own rules.

Freedom *From* and Freedom *For*

True freedom always has two dimensions. First, it is freedom "from" some kind of bondage. Christ's freedom is first from the condemnation of the law. "There is ... no condemnation for those who are in Christ Jesus" (Romans 8:1). Through grace we are set free from any requirement that we must merit our acceptance by God. Our salvation has been bought by Christ and is freely given to us through faith.

In Christ we are also called to be free from the bondage to sin. "We know that our old self was crucified with [Christ] in order that the body of sin might be brought to nothing, so that we would no longer be enslaved to sin" (Romans 6:6). Living into this freedom as we throw off our sinful nature is a lifelong journey, and we accomplish it only as grace works through biblical virtue. This is the freedom that Paul announces when he writes, "For freedom Christ has set us free; stand firm therefore, and do not submit again to a yoke of slavery ... For you were called to freedom, brothers. Only do not use your freedom as an opportunity for the flesh" (Galatians 5:1,13).

Though we gain freedom *from* the condemnation and bondage of sin in Christ, we are created to use our freedom *for* the glory of God. Therefore, the law no longer condemns us but rather guides us to a glorifying life. We are now free to obey. This is what it means to be "free indeed" (John 8:36).

Biblical freedom, therefore, is a freedom that is subject to the objective moral principles taught in Scripture. This is almost impossible for us Americans to understand. Yet it is the wisdom of God given to us in Scripture.

This wisdom has been echoed in the voices of men and women of godly character throughout the ages. In the words of the fifth-century bishop Augustine, "Liberty is merely the good use of free choice." Early American theologian Jonathan Edwards stated, "Freedom is the ability to obey God's law." Britain's Lord Acton declares, "Freedom is to do what we ought and not what we wish." *The Book of Common Prayer* says that service to God "is perfect freedom" (p. 312).

The clearest statement of this principle is Jesus' teaching, "If you abide in my word, you are truly my disciples, and you will know the truth, and the truth will set you free" (John 8:31-32). True freedom exists only in relation to abiding in the Word. And "abide" does not mean a lick here and there. According to the dictionary, it means "to endure without yielding." Only when we are disciples of Jesus, following His teaching and ways, can we know the liberty of God's kingdom.

There is one other key to biblical freedom—this: "Where the Spirit of the Lord is, there is freedom" (2 Corinthians 3:17). The power to be free of bondage to sin and its various vices comes from Christ through His Holy Spirit. This is simply another expression of the importance of the third side of our triangle. If we are to be free to live a life that glorifies God, it will be through the grace of His Holy Spirit.

Freedom in Public Life

Freedom is one of the overarching truths of God's kingdom. It is also one of the great values of our country.

The United States of America is a beacon of freedom in the world. Our Declaration of Independence declares an "unalienable" right endowed by our Creator to "liberty." We pledge allegiance to a flag that stands for "liberty and justice" for all. Our government is based in freedom. So is our economic system.

How can we preserve our freedom, both spiritual and temporal? Only with strong character.

This book started out by mentioning the current risks to American character. We are facing the diminishment of the reserve of character in this great country. And the reason this loss matters is that without strong character we will slowly but inevitably lose our political, economic, moral, and spiritual freedom.

Burke is right. We will have order in society. We either will have it in freedom because we have the internal strength to do the right thing or we will have it by virtue of the coercion of law that will eliminate our freedom. Most law exists because of the default of virtue.

We turn now to a discussion of character in government.

12

Character in Government

Even before the American colonies declared their independence from England, there were signs that our nation was intended for a lofty destiny. "We must consider that we shall be as a city upon a hill," declared John Winthrop, the Puritan leader who set sail for America in 1630. "The eyes of all people are upon us."

Winthrop, of course, was echoing the Sermon on the Mount, where Jesus taught that we "are the light of the world. A city set on a hill cannot be hidden." (Matthew 5:14)—a teaching as applicable to Christian Americans today as it was to the Puritans in Winthrop's time. Winthrop predicted that as the Puritans loved God and one another and walked in His ways and His commandments, "the Lord our God [will] bless us in the land whither we go to possess it."[1]

Winthrop's words turned out to be prophetic indeed. God has bestowed tremendous blessings upon our land, the noblest nation on the face of the earth. Among the most significant of those blessings were the gifted, farsighted, and devout leaders who founded this country. Their vision was the driving force behind America's greatness.

These men were clear thinkers who believed that the country they were founding could achieve lofty purposes while allowing its citizens a level of freedom that had previously been unimaginable. The key to the success of such a venture, they believed, was the virtue of the American people.

Just as the character triangle provides a framework for understanding both individual and organizational character, so aspects of it can also shed light on the different aspects of our nation's character—both the critical role our forefathers

213

believed it would play in the American experiment and the pervasive threats that character faces today. In this chapter we'll explore the important role virtue has played in our nation's development as well as modern-day challenges to the vision our forefathers had for this great nation.

Our Nation's Noble Purpose

From the beginning, our Founding Fathers made clear that a primary purpose of the country they were establishing would be the protection of individual rights and freedoms. In the Declaration of Independence, these leaders declared that the new nation was dedicated to the proposition that "all men are created equal, that they are endowed by their Creator with certain unalienable Rights, [and] that among these are Life, Liberty, and the pursuit of Happiness." In the Preamble to the Constitution, the Founding Fathers spoke of the intent to "form a more perfect Union, establish Justice ... and secure the Blessings of Liberty to ourselves and our Posterity." Bold proclamations such as these made ours the first country in the Christian era whose government truly was by the people, of the people, and for the people.

Securing our rights to life and liberty may have been America's declared purpose, but in practice our nation has served another critical function as well. Since the first Puritans settled on our shores, America's mission has also been to provide a haven for the persecuted, particularly those oppressed because of their religion, and for poor but brave souls throughout the world "yearning to be free." The Statue of Liberty signals this purpose just as clearly as the Declaration and Constitution evidence the other.

For more than two hundred years, God has blessed the United States with the ability to achieve these purposes. Millions have come here from all over the world and found sanctuary from oppression. With the glaring exception of slavery, which the Constitution's Thirteenth Amendment eliminated, those fortunate enough to make this country their home also have been favored with a government and local communities that provide the greatest freedom and highest quality of life of any nation on earth. Ronald Reagan was correct when he reminded us in 1974 that we are still a "city on a hill."

Yet this tremendously successful government, which we are all too prone to take for granted, was a daring and bold experiment—and one that might have turned out differently had it not been for George Washington's character.

At the end of the Revolutionary War, George Washington's status was such that he could easily have seized control of the nation and made himself king. (This, essentially, is what Napoleon did after the French Revolution.) But Washington had no desire for such power. Like Cincinnatus, the Roman general who voluntarily gave up power at the end of a war to return to his farm, Washington returned to civilian life. He lent his moral authority to the Constitutional Convention and accepted two terms as president, but he always served at the will of the people. Speaking of Washington, Thomas Jefferson would later note that "the moderation and virtue of a single character probably prevented this Revolution from being closed, as most others have been, by a subversion of that liberty it was intended to establish."[2]

Washington's decision and the new government that resulted meant that sovereignty resided in the people, not in a monarch. Still, questions remained whether such a democratic union "can long endure" (as Abraham Lincoln put it eighty years later). Even such notable Founders as Benjamin Franklin expressed doubts about how the American experiment would fare over time. Asked at the conclusion of the Constitutional Convention whether the new government was a monarchy or a republic, Franklin replied, "A republic, if you can keep it."

Virtue, Religion and Free Government[3]

No generation of leaders has understood the philosophy and mechanics of free government better than did America's

Founders. Though a diverse lot, these leaders shared a conviction that virtue and religion were essential if America was to "keep" its republic. They believed both that a virtuous citizenry is necessary if free government is to succeed and that religion is necessary for the cultivation of that virtue. Therefore, they reasoned, religion is necessary for successful free government.[4]

Time and again, the leaders whose vision shaped and sustained our nation in its infancy emphasized the importance of religion-based virtue to the new government. To George Washington, for example, virtue wasn't merely advisable or beneficial for successful free government; it was essential. Thus, in his farewell address to those he had led as both general and president, Washington warned that we must "with caution indulge the supposition that morality can be maintained without religion."[5] For Washington, as for all the Founders, "morality" meant a virtuous life. Washington told the American people, "'Tis substantially true, that virtue or morality is a necessary spring of popular government. The rule indeed extends with more or less force to every species of free Government."[6]

John Adams was as convinced of the necessity of virtue as was his predecessor in the presidency. "Our Constitution was made only for a moral and religious people," he said. "It is wholly inadequate to the government of any other."[7] Elsewhere Adams counseled, "It is Religion and morality alone ... upon which Freedom can securely stand."

Other early American leaders shared the same sentiment. Benjamin Franklin believed that "only a virtuous people are capable of freedom."[9] James Madison declared that "We have staked the whole future of American civilization ... upon the capacity of all of us to govern ourselves according to the Ten Commandments of God."[10] As death approached, Thomas Jefferson advised his grandchildren simply to "pursue virtue."[11]

Church and State: Separate but Related

Given the Founders' conviction that religion was critically important to the new nation's destiny, the constitutional framework they designed was bold indeed, for it decoupled religion from national governmental support and control for the first time since the advent of Christianity. Though the Christian faith has freedom at its very soul, it took Western civilization eighteen hundred years before a nation prohibited established churches and guaranteed the free exercise of religion.

As we all know, a vast number of early immigrants to America were fleeing religious persecution by the British government. When America's Founders drafted the Constitution, the Baptists, who did not worship in the "established" Congregational, Presbyterian, or Anglican churches, insisted on an amendment guaranteeing the free exercise of religion. Because it appeared doubtful that the states would ratify the Constitution without such a provision, the Founders drafted the first clause of the First Amendment to the Constitution to provide that "Congress shall make no law respecting an establishment of religion, or prohibiting the free exercise thereof." The various denominations in America, especially the Baptists and Methodists, became ardent supporters of free government.

The experiment to abolish established churches and protect free worship in the United States has been stunningly successful. Though no longer "established," religion has marched in partnership with American government for more than two hundred years.

Shortly after America's founding, the Second Great Awakening birthed the evangelical churches as we know them today. The Second Awakening began on the Plains and swept through the Midwest and South. Before this fervent revival, 55 percent of America's churched were traditional Congregationalists, Presbyterians, and Episcopalians, with Baptists and Methodists only a tiny minority. After the Second Great Awakening, the evangelical Baptists and Methodists were 55 percent of a much larger American population, and fewer than 20 percent of Americans were members of traditional denominations.[12]

With this shift, the evangelical worldview, which was very patriotic, became the dominant national philosophy. Historian Mark Noll notes that "in comparative terms the United States possessed no alternative ideology that came anywhere close to the influence of evangelical Protestantism from the early years of the nineteenth century through the Civil War."[13] Though few Founders were evangelical Christians, their vision of a free government sustained by religion-based virtue fit perfectly with the evangelical mind-set of the nineteenth century.

Alexis de Tocqueville, a Frenchman who visited the United States toward the end of the Second Great Awakening, wrote *Democracy in America*, still one of the best studies of its kind. Even today most historians agree with two of his key observations about the American experiment.

First, de Tocqueville noted, the legal prohibition against church establishment ironically had produced a society where church and state worked in partnership to promote freedom. "Religion in America takes no direct part in the government of society, but it must be regarded as the first of their political institutions," de Tocqueville wrote. "I do not know whether all Americans have a sincere faith in their religion—but I am certain that they hold it to be indispensable to the maintenance of republican institutions."[14]

De Tocqueville also observed that the churches' support of biblical morality was essential to the maintenance of America's new freedom. "While the law permits the Americans to do what they please, religion prevents them from conceiving, and forbids them to commit, what is rash or unjust," he wrote. "Despotism may be able to do without faith, but freedom cannot.... How could society escape destruction if, when political ties are relaxed, moral ties are not tightened? And what can be done with a [free] people if [they] are not subject to God?"[15]

Much of the Bible indicates that religion and freedom are intended to be staunch allies. The Hebrew Scriptures teach that freedom would characterize the reign of the coming Messiah. Jesus taught that as we "abide" in His word we are "free indeed" (John 8:36). But the American experiment was the first time a government had recognized this intended alliance.

The linkage between biblical religion and freedom was adamantly opposed in the French Revolution, which began in 1789. There, the church was viewed as the enemy of freedom. Church leaders were guillotined; church lands were confiscated. A government committed to liberty but based on atheism took power. Instead of freedom, a murderous reign of terror ensued, and the French republic gave way to Napoleon's despotic rule.

Which of the two experiments in government—American or French—succeeded?

America's experiment with religious freedom continues to flourish. We are by far the most religious nation in the developed world. In 1939, when the Gallup poll started, 41 percent of adults in America said they attended church weekly. Sixty years later, in 1999, a similar number—43 percent of adults—said they had attended church in the past week.[16]

With religious material increasingly available through cable TV, a proliferation of Christian publishers, and the Internet, the reach of the Christian message in America is greater today than ever before. And since the September 11 terrorist attacks, the alliance between religion and patriotism has grown even stronger. "God Bless America" is now proudly sung across the nation, from baseball stadiums to the halls of Congress. In many parts of the country, including Alabama, evangelical Protestantism shows signs of revival not seen in a hundred years.

A Nation Under God

At least through the first century of American independence, there was wide acceptance of the idea that God was watching over our new nation and that only in His grace would it succeed. Our early leaders spoke freely of God's role in our nation's fate. The word our forefathers used was "providence," but the idea they espoused was that God's power and plan were guiding this country. To them, we were clearly a nation "under God," as our Pledge of Allegiance has it.

Thus, George Washington's first inaugural address was largely an expression of gratitude to God for His guiding power and wisdom in our Revolutionary War victory and the shaping of the new country. "No people can be bound to acknowledge and adore the Invisible Hand which conducts the affairs of men more than those of the United States," Washington reverently observed. "Every step by which they have advanced to the character of an independent nation seems to have been distinguished by some token of providential agency."[17] And in his second inaugural address, he called for "increasing vows that heaven may continue to [the American people] be the covering of its beneficence and that our free government will in God's grace forever be sacredly maintained."[18]

Calling for prayer at the Constitutional Convention, Benjamin Franklin scolded his peers for forgetting the "powerful friend" whose hand guided America to victory in the war with Britain. "The longer I live," Franklin declares, "the more convincing proofs I see of this truth—that God governs in the affairs of men."[19]

Aside from Washington, the president most keenly aware of God's role in shaping America's destiny was Abraham Lincoln. At the time of the Civil War, of course, the understanding of a nation "under God" had a much more sober meaning. As Lincoln agonized over the bloodshed of the war, he wrote, "The will of God prevails.... By his mere quiet power, on the minds of the now contestants, He could have either *saved* or *destroyed* the Union without a human contest. Yet the contest began. And having begun He could give final victory to either side any day. Yet the contest proceeds."[20]

In his second inaugural address, which he delivered shortly before his assassination and the end of the war, Lincoln reaffirmed his conviction that God was in control of this nation's journey. "The Almighty has His own purposes," he declared. "The judgments of the Lord are true and righteous altogether."[21]

A Nation Divided

Fueled by evangelicalism and its dreams of widespread conversion, Americans remained in remarkable agreement at least through the Civil War as to our national purpose, the importance of virtue to freedom, and God's guiding role in our country's success. But following the war, this harmony—as well as the mutually supportive relationship in the United States between evangelical religion and government—began to break down.

It is beyond the scope of this book to comprehensively explore the causes of these changes. But we can note briefly two developments that led to the increased influence of secularism and an open hostility among elites to orthodox, or evangelical, religion. One such development was the 1859 publication of *Origin of Species*, in which Charles Darwin purported to give a scientific and wholly materialistic alternative to the supernatural foundation of the biblical story. The second was the importation from Europe of philosophies holding that man is essentially good and that the solution to humanity's problems is to be found in psychology and social engineering, not in repentance and virtue.

In the wake of these developments, our universities, the national media, the entertainment industry, and certain feminist groups have grown increasingly secular over the past century, even stridently so. As a result, there is now a deep divide in our nation between orthodox religion and powerful opinion leaders on such issues as the meaning of freedom, the rules we are to play by, and the importance of virtue. Many now question whether God is needed, whether His will prevails in national affairs, and whether He even exists. This divide has produced the culture wars.

We can and do debate these issues, but on one point there can be no disagreement. Our Founders would be dismayed to learn that virtue and biblical religion, the foundation upon which they were certain free government must rest, are under assault by our nation's opinion leaders.

To those who attack the foundation, freedom does not refer to ordered society wherein virtuous people live according to traditional morality and manners. To these attackers, freedom means individual autonomy, free of all bounds except coercive ones created by law. There have been various efforts to construct a secular morality on principles that are widely accepted, but these projects have all failed. According to a famous critique, all such attempts ultimately boil down to the same question: "Sez who?"[22] Whereas in traditional morality God ultimately decides, secular morality has no authority except a mere mortal who "sez" something is right or wrong, good or evil.

In our divided land, those of us who defend the foundation find ourselves under attack. We are labeled fundamentalists and called "intolerant," "narrow-minded," even "dumb" and "backward." As Senator Joseph Lieberman has said, the attackers have made "religion one of the few remaining socially acceptable targets of intolerance."[23] Interestingly, evangelicals and conservative Catholics have not changed their positions on the culture-war issues in any material respect in the last fifty years. What has changed has been the views of the attackers, who espouse positions on such issues as divorce on demand, abortion, gay rights, gambling, and pornography that were unimaginable a half century ago.

Legislation from the Courts

Particularly unacceptable to evangelicals and conservative Catholics is that controversial social issues have largely been removed from the democratic process, where a majority of Americans stand ready to defend the traditional foundation. Instead, the culture wars are being decided by as few as five United States Supreme Court justices who, because of their lifetime appointments, are not subject to the democratic process. According to the court's own late chief justice, William Rehnquist, a majority of the justices "bristle with hostility to all things religious in public life."[24] That position is far removed from the wisdom of those who birthed this nation.

Our nation's Founders certainly never intended that a Supreme Court made up of judges who cannot be voted out of office would decide such critical policy issues as those relating to abortion. Our early leaders considered the Supreme Court the least dangerous branch of the federal government because it was there only to interpret the Constitution and the laws of the United States, not to override the democratically elected state legislatures on policy issues on which the Constitution is silent.

Pitted against religious groups seeking to defend traditional morality and virtue in the culture wars are secular groups who assert an ever-growing array of "rights" and a Supreme Court searching for opportunities (including the use of European judicial opinions) to advance a rights agenda.

This nation has always held rights in high esteem. Our Declaration of Independence holds the rights to life, liberty, and the pursuit of happiness to be unalienable. Our Bill of Rights is one of history's greatest charters protecting citizens from governmental abuse. Beginning in the 1950s, the civil rights movement completed the achievement of equal rights for African-Americans who had been denied them for centuries.

We must never forget, however, that with every right comes responsibility and with precious rights come solemn responsibilities. The Declaration concludes with words as noble as those with which it begins: "And for the support of this Declaration, with a firm reliance on the protection of divine Providence, we mutually pledge to each other our Lives, our Fortunes, and our sacred Honor."

Those of us who defend traditional morality and virtue are not against rights. Instead, our position is that rights protected by the Constitution should be interpreted in accordance with the plain meaning of the words as originally intended. Enlargement or restriction of rights is the province of the legislatures and the democratic process, not of modern judges who seek to create new rights, modify constitutional protections, and import European law to suit their particular sensibilities.

A Nation in Need of Prayer

For those of us who ask how America's Judeo-Christian ideals can be preserved against the secular onslaught, the answer is that prayer comes first. The continued renewal of America's foundation has always depended upon religious revivals. And revivals are the product of prayer, repentance, and God's grace.

Our national history illustrates the critical importance of periodic religious revivals. For example, the noted historian Paul Johnson has called the First Great Awakening, which ran from about 1720 to 1750, "the formative event in the history of the United States, preceding the movement for independence and making it possible."[25]

The connection between that revival and America's break from Great Britain can be found in the great evangelist of that awakening, George Whitefield. Comparable to Billy Graham in today's world, Whitefield preached to the masses outside the confines of the established churches and had an enormous popular following. His personal evangelism, which represented a rebuke to established authority, birthed a spirit of independence in the average American. As a result of Whitefield's preaching and the First Awakening, the language and spirit of popular Christianity merged with the fledgling democratic political movement, providing the energy and fervor that made American independence possible and the American Revolution successful.[26]

Through the years, religious revivals have provided continual renewal of the beliefs upon which the American experiment was based. As we have already noted, the Second Great Awakening profoundly influenced American life through the first half of the nineteenth century. And the Pentecostal Awakening of the early twentieth century continues to shape American life. With its emphasis on "baptism in the Holy Spirit" and the power of the Spirit in daily life, the movement has added millions of Americans to our nation's evangelical base. That base is becoming increasingly influential in shaping national policy and in fact swung the 2004 presidential election to George W. Bush. And though historians have noted only the sweeping ones, smaller revivals go on in our communities on a regular basis.

It is to this continuous renewal of the church through revival that Christians who worry about our nation's future should first turn. Without a fresh outpouring of the Holy Spirit, the religious core of this land will atrophy as it has throughout much of Europe. Political activism cannot supplant our national need for repentance and for united prayer for revival. Just as our personal virtues can grow only if they are rooted in humility, so our political strategies must be planted in similar soil.

As we earlier noted, Russell Kirk, a keen observer of American trends, writes that we need to be concerned first of all with the "regeneration of spirit and character—with the perennial problem of the inner order of the soul, the restoration of the ethical understanding and the religious sanction upon which any life worth living is founded."[27] For that regeneration to occur, we must repent and pray.

For almost four hundred years, it has been our country's blessing and responsibility to be as a city on a hill—a glowing recipient of our Father's favor as we remain a nation under God. Though "under God" means we are blessed, the words also mean we are accountable. We are as subject to God's judgment as we are to His benediction.[28]

We do well to remember God's words to His chosen people in 2 Chronicles 7:14. "If my people who are called by my name will humble themselves, and pray and seek my face and turn from their wicked ways, then I will hear from heaven and will forgive their sin and heal their land."

And we must not forget John Winthrop's counsel that we will be blessed only as we bear fruit for the glory of God. Thus, to strengthen the nation we so dearly love, we must focus on our hearts, our families, our communities, and our churches. As they are spiritually strong, so too—by the blessing of God—

will our nation be strong. We turn now to the arena in our communities where most adults spend a majority of their daylight hours.

Character Questions

1. In your opinion, should faith and politics mix? If so, how?

2. What would you say is the state of the culture wars today? Who's winning? Where have been the retreats and advances?

3. Not all of us are government officials, but all of us can help elect government officials, express our opinions to them, and pray for them. What actions will you take to help ensure that America remains a nation under God?

13

Character in Business

If the ultimate purpose of our lives is to bring glory to God, then how can what we do for a living be unrelated to that purpose? The answer, of course, is that it can't. If we are to glorify God, all parts of our lives must point toward that goal, including those parts for which we receive a paycheck.

We too often think, however, that our best energies are meant for church work and other clearly spiritual tasks, not for the marketplace. This attitude is misguided. If we are to fulfill our ultimate purpose, then those of us who make our living in the business world must work to the honor of God, not just in church on Sunday, but Monday through Friday, on the factory floor, at the sales meeting, and in the boardroom.

Fortunately, today's business climate offers far greater opportunities than were once available for both business organizations and the people in them to bring glory to God through work. The idea that business has the capacity to develop our character and allow us to attain our ultimate purpose will, of course, seem implausible to those who consider the free market system immoral—a group that numbers many Christians among its members. But I believe our economic system has great moral potential.

In this chapter we will see that the best of our businesses operate in the context of the same character triangle that applies to us as individuals. We'll look first at the moral foundation of our free market system. Next, we'll examine ways in which many American businesses have come to focus on noble purposes and principles, thereby aligning their goals more closely with spiritual values. Finally, we'll look at the role of virtue and character in business and how we can aim our lives toward our ultimate purpose even in the heat of marketplace competition.

Overcoming Poverty

In *The Wealth of Nations*—one of the most influential books ever written—social philosopher Adam Smith demonstrated that overall wealth increases when individuals are free to pursue their enlightened economic self-interest. Smith advocated a minimal role for government in its citizens' economic lives, the protection of private property, the enforcement of private contracts, and the provision of widespread access to the benefits of commercial activity. Smith's book led to the spread of free markets and capitalism throughout the world.[1]

Before Smith wrote *The Wealth of Nations*, most people in even the most advanced nations had lived in abject poverty for centuries. Michael Novak has written of the widespread misery people endured before the advent of capitalism. During this period, Novak writes, "A simple life just above a bare minimum was considered something of a blessing. There was enormous misery, and great bands of beggars and the indigent wandered about, at times breaking out in wild and furious rebellions as the centuries advanced. In France itself, near the end of the eighteenth century, 90 percent of the population ... [spent] 80 percent of its income for bread alone."[2]

The rise of the free market system marked the beginning of the end of such conditions. Standards of living for the masses slowly rose to the point where food, shelter, and clothing became available to nearly all. Today even our nation's working poor live more comfortably than all but the richest prior to Adam Smith's time.

As we saw in the introduction to part three, Jesus began His ministry by preaching from Isaiah 61. That text speaks of oppressed people, declaring,

> They shall build up the ancient ruins;
> they shall raise up the former devastations;

they shall repair the ruined cities,
> the devastations of many generations
> (Isaiah 61:4).

This messianic prophecy reflects a concern with the material well-being of God's people. The last two hundred years have seen the free market system build up, raise up, and repair the devastation of many generations, releasing hundreds of millions of people from the bondage of poverty and offering them a degree of economic freedom unimaginable before capitalism. The free market system is no Messiah, but its result in freeing millions from the scourge of poverty is consistent with the heart of God.

Nevertheless, the free market system is still strongly criticized, and even condemned, both inside and outside the Christian community.

Self-interest

The free market system receives criticism because it is based on the pursuit of self-interest. Both *self* and *interest* are negative words for moralists. Thus, many see the free market system as at best a necessary evil. To be sure, they allow, it lifts the poor out of poverty, but along the way it fosters self-interest and greed and therefore is, at its core, immoral.

Such criticisms are misguided. Though the free market system is far from perfect, it is morally worthy. One reason for capitalism's success is its recognition of an essential fact of life: All mankind is fallen. Even the most saintly among us act in accordance with self-interest. Capitalism controls self-interest and channels it into productive enterprises that help other people. This is certainly not a morally offensive objective. If we were morally spotless, we could design a better system. But defining reality as it is, not as we wish it to be, is where the design of every effective system must begin.

Novak gives the free enterprise system a grade of two stars on a three-star scale because of the greed it engenders. I won't quarrel with him; certainly the system is not perfect. But no other economic system is as good at lifting the poor out of poverty, raising standards of living, and providing health care and education to citizens of all economic classes. The once-competing theory of socialism has been so thoroughly defeated that no thinking person can any longer argue that a centrally managed economy works as well as a free one.

By restraining self-interest with competition, the free market system makes it impossible for one company to gouge consumers with higher prices and remain successful. Why? Because another company, acting out of self-interest, will drive prices down and gain new customers. If a company oppresses its workers with low wages, then a competitor—acting out of self-interest—will lure the best of those workers away with higher pay. If greedy managers mistreat the owners for whom they work, then the owners will act to protect their self-interest, investing their capital elsewhere. In all cases, in order to stay in the free market game, business must produce a product or service that consumers exercising free choice will buy. This fact assures that self-interest ultimately creates value for consumers.

A review of the development of business practices in America suggests that business is becoming more conducive to the formation of a good character than it has ever been.

The Moral Climate of American Business

A century ago, America was building a powerful industrial and manufacturing base, founded in large part on cheap immigrant labor. Education meant little. In fact, to the barons of business, an uneducated workforce was desirable. What mattered was the work of the hands and the sweat of the brow. Even Henry Ford, one of the most progressive of the industrialists, said of his workers, "Why is it that I always get a whole person when what I really want is a pair of hands?"

The economics of the typical industrial company were viewed largely as a win-lose game. Trust, communication, and teamwork were not valued. Whatever was paid to workers was seen as having been taken away from owners. In such an environment, Communism gained a foothold in Europe and captured control of Russia.

In America, business decisions were scientifically driven. Engineers, accountants, and business-school graduates in the back office were the ones who decided how production workers could be most efficient. The workers themselves were viewed as little more than human machines and units of production. Commands "came down." Virtually no input from the worker on the factory floor was sought or considered.

Not all was bad with the system. Though the Depression caused economic misery, following World War II, the standard of living in this country grew steadily. Housing and transportation proliferated. The manufacturing economy slowly shifted to one based more on service and technology. With increased wealth to pay for schools, Americans' educational level steadily increased. More and more workers became literate and many were able to obtain a college education.

Around mid-century, two other critical developments took place that were positive for profits, good for the workforce, and aligned with a biblical understanding of the worker. One was a shift in understanding business's purpose and values. The other was a heightened recognition of the importance of the worker.

The Purpose of Business

In much the same way that individuals do, businesses have a character. Every business pursues a purpose, whether or not it is formally recognized. The purpose may simply be to make money, but in a growing number of companies, it is something nobler. Businesses also have principles, or values, that shape their conduct. The values may be strictly economic, but often they are loftier. And businesses have a power source—the motivation of the workers, which is related to the business's purpose and principles.

Whereas the prevailing view had been that business was solely concerned with production and profits, at mid-century an understanding arose—first within a few companies but ultimately within many—that companies did not live by bread alone. An early proponent of this new way of looking at business was Peter Drucker, currently Clarke Professor of Social Sciences at Claremont Graduate University and the most influential student of business management of the last fifty years.

In an enormously influential book called *The Practice of Management*, Drucker reflected on the purpose of business. Contrary to the conventional wisdom of his day—that business's first priority was to turn a profit—Drucker believed the purpose of business was to "create a customer." After all, it was the customer's payment for a product or service that allowed business to make money. "The customer is the foundation of a business and keeps it in existence," Drucker wrote. "He alone gives employment. And it is to supply the consumer that society entrusts wealth-producing resources to the business enterprise."[3]

Drucker recognized the importance of profit; in his understanding, it was critical, both as a measure of performance and as an ingredient for the business's growth. But he believed people, not profit, were the reason for business's existence.

The publication of Drucker's book in 1954 signaled a trend. Many of America's most successful businesses began to reflect seriously upon their purpose. And like Drucker, many companies defined their purpose as something deeper than mere profit and production.

At the same time, business leaders began to recognize the importance of conducting their operations according to shared values and principles. IBM was a leader in this development.

The Values of Business

When Drucker wrote *The Practice of Management*, IBM was the dominant technology business in America. Its CEO, Thomas

Watson Jr., was to American business then what Bill Gates is today. If Drucker redirected the American understanding of the purpose of business, Watson illuminated the importance of a business's values, which he called "beliefs."

In a series of lectures at the Columbia University Business School, Watson declared, "I firmly believe that any organization, in order to survive and achieve success, must have a sound set of beliefs on which it premises all its policies and actions."[4] In character terms, Watson was talking about the principle point of the character triangle—the guidelines a business most values in pursuing its purpose.

For Watson, IBM's rise to become the world's most successful technological company hinged on far more than just man and machine. "The most important single factor in corporate success," he says, "is faithful adherence to these beliefs." Though everything else about a business might change over time, Watson says, a business's core beliefs, just like other transcendent moral principles, should not.[5]

IBM's core beliefs were showing respect for the individual, offering the world's best customer service, and pursuing excellence in all tasks. These principles became engraved in IBM's character.

Watson was one of the first executives to highlight the importance of core values to business success, but many successful companies have characters centered on their basic beliefs. In researching *Built to Last*, a study of some of America's greatest companies, authors Jim Collins and Jerry Porras found that almost all of those companies that had outperformed the competition for seventy years had a "core ideology," that is, a set of values as well as a statement of purpose that were communicated both inside and outside the company and that determined how it conducted its business.

The core ideology of Johnson & Johnson, which has guided it since 1943, provides an excellent example of the principled focus of a great American business. Johnson & Johnson's core ideology stated that its primary responsibility was to doctors, nurses, and hospitals. Next came responsibilities to employees, then to management, then to the community. Finally, "our fifth and last responsibility is to our stockholders. Business must make a sound profit.... The stockholder should receive a fair return."[6]

Certainly, statements such as Johnson & Johnson's core ideology are aspirational. They stand above the capabilities of fallen human beings to fully obtain. America's greatest companies have had, and will continue to have, moral lapses, some of them grave. But the recognition that business has a higher purpose than mere profit generation and that the values of a business matter means that, while the bottom line is still critical in American business, the soul of many organizations is now also important.

As a result, just like Johnson & Johnson, many businesses today are moving beyond a technical approach to success. For instance, Protective Life, the company where I worked for many years, has three core values: quality, serving people, and growth. Integrity is identified as the "heart" of quality.[7] We had Five Cardinal Principles for Building Quality which came straight from the teaching of Edwards Deming[8] which I discuss in the next section. I talked about the Values and Principles with employees whenever I got a chance, employing biblical precepts but not biblical references. At first I worried that they would get bored with the subject and start to tune it out. But the opposite seemed to be true: Workers loved hearing about our values, and these values motivated them. The fact is, people want their work to mean more than just money; company values, faithfully adhered to, are how they know it does.

Lord Griffiths, an Englishman who has served as an economic adviser to Prime Minister Margaret Thatcher, a professor at the London School of Economics, and an international banker, has noted that shared values based on honesty, trust, and employee satisfaction have turned out to be "the most critical factor in explaining the superior performance of excellent companies."[9]

In a speech made at the Drucker Institute of Management in 1996, Griffiths noted that the Judeo-Christian foundation of the United States, which "starts with God as creator of the world, with people made in his image with the divine mandate to take responsibility for the earth and make it productive," has resulted in a respect for people and a moral basis for work and wealth creation.[10] The three shared values that Griffiths found to be most relied upon in business—respect for the individual, recognition of the importance of truth, and acknowledgement of obligation to those outside the company—all arise from this Judeo-Christian foundation.[11] Far more than a "superficial gimmick," Griffiths says, a corporate value system is "something which goes to the roots of our cultural heritage and of what it means to be human."[12]

Along with recognizing a business's purpose and values, a second development of the mid-twentieth century was just as important to broadening America's understanding of what business was all about.

The Importance of the Worker

With its strong manufacturing base still intact after World War II (unlike some countries that faced an enormous burden restructuring theirs), the United States dominated the world's production in the period immediately following the war. But by the 1960s, we were startled to see cars and television sets come into this country from Japan that were of a much higher quality than those we were producing. We had vanquished Japan in the war; its manufacturing base had been decimated. How had Japan, in just twenty years, come to create products that were better than ours?

The answer was that Japanese businesses looked at their workers in a new light. Ironically, the most important individual contributor to this phenomenon was an American statistician, Edwards Deming. The government of Japan had retained Deming following World War II to help conduct a national census. Aware that successfully competing against America's business power would be no easy task, Japan's business leaders also sought Deming's advice on how to build quality into their products.[13]

The heart of the "Deming System," which companies such as Sony, Toyota, and Honda implemented, was simple: Involve the worker. While Deming shared Drucker's belief that the customer was important, Deming also stressed that management needed to liberate, empower, and equip all workers within the organization, trusting their ability to serve as both architects and managers of the company's production quality. Deming believed the blue-collar people on the factory floor knew more about quality than any CEO, VP, engineer, mathematician, or business-school grad. Compared to American management philosophy at the time, this was revolutionary.

American companies were late in catching on, but by the 1980s the concept of equipping and empowering all workers to contribute to the quality of a company's products and services was widespread in this country. These trends continue today. Certainly, plenty of tough manufacturing jobs still exist, particularly in developing countries where working conditions are poor and wages are low. But with technological advances in manufacturing and the growing number of service and high-tech jobs around the world, conflicts between owner and worker are diminishing and the benefits of teamwork among people of virtue are increasingly recognized.

The Free Market System and Character

Because of these developments, at the dawn of the twenty-first century, American business has the potential to become more morally sound than ever before. If, as Lord Griffiths noted, we have all been created in God's image and given the mandate to take dominion over this earth and make it productive, then now more than ever we have recognized the importance of allowing individual workers to participate in the fulfillment of this commission. We have begun to aim our businesses toward loftier goals than the mere making of money and to conduct those businesses according to carefully considered values and principles. We have come to see that incorporating these purposes and values into the daily life of business makes it more productive and more successful in marketplace competition.

This changed world of business provides fertile ground for the strengthening of character. Because communication, trust, and teamwork in the heat of competition are what make a business successful, it is the virtuous worker who, over time, will be the most important contributor to a business team's success. A workforce of people with strong character is the most important strength for attaining the business's purpose in accordance with its values.

To understand this, it's important to understand the nature of competition. Competition is part and parcel of the free market system. And for better or worse, competition always shapes character. By the same token, the character of competitors also shapes the competition.

Whether in business, sports, or war, competition involves two dynamics: a win-lose dynamic between competitors and a win-win dynamic among members of a team.

It is the nature of the win-lose dynamic that what is good for one is equally bad for another. A touchdown, for example, inevitably means a six-point advantage for one football team and a six-point deficit for the other. The same holds true in business: when one company makes a sale, another company has lost that sale.

This win-lose competition shapes the character of both winners and losers. Winning may lead to a rededication to winning again or to vices such as pride and complacency. Losing may prompt the loser to study the loss and improve or to lose hope and give up. Thus, whether we win or lose, competition engraves virtues or vices into our character.

In any win-lose game we prepare and play our hardest to win. The outcome is in God's hands. It is our role to play by the rules and honorably, in accordance with the Golden Rule. Where the competition is hard-nosed, there is nothing in love or justice that prevents us from being tough.

The second dynamic at work in free market competition is what goes on within the team. The minimum requirements for a consistently winning team are trust, good communication, and a commitment to truth and excellence. If the intra-team dynamic is weak in any of these areas, the team will be weak. And, over time, weak teams don't prevail in win-lose competition.

This dynamic within the team is a critical point where the virtues come into play in business, with its never-ending series of win-lose competitions. Consistent business success in our free market system requires great teamwork, sometimes among thousands of people spread across several continents. And virtuous people make great team players. Why? Because they can be trusted. They tell the truth. And they are committed to excellence.

Trust is particularly important to effective teams. The stronger the bonds of trust within a company, the more effectively it can compete. If team members don't trust each other, they cannot work together to attain the benefits that outweigh what any one of them working alone could achieve. First Corinthians 13 teaches that love "always trusts" (v. 7 NIV). Because of the relationship between trust and love, the individual upon whose character the virtue of love has been engraved is an asset to any team lucky enough to have him or her as a member.

But the competitive team also benefits when its leaders and members have the humility to deny themselves, the optimism generated by hope, the confidence fostered by faith, and the long-suffering patience that grows from love. In successful teams and companies, these qualities, particularly the willingness to deny self, lead to bonds of affection among teammates, strengthening the team and thus improving its chances in win-lose competition. This is the reason biblical people often make great team members, both in business and sports; why most professional sports teams now have a chaplain; and why there is a growing recognition of the need for spiritual leadership in college athletics. Whatever the competitive arena, team members with these virtues engraved in their character are almost always admired and favored within the team and by the coach.

But despite our free market system's enormous potential to develop virtue, we must never forget that it can also be a veritable machine in generating vice—not just in businesses but in us as individuals as well.

Risky Business

Why is the free market system potentially risky to us as individuals? The answer lies in the fact that we spend approximately half our waking hours, five days a week, on the job, where the pressures of our responsibilities are constantly on our mind. We worry about the economic well-being of our families. Economic issues—employment, taxes, Social Security, the cost of health care—dominate our elections. With such concerns continually demanding our attention, the temptation to make money a god is intense.

As mentioned at the beginning of this chapter, the win-lose competition inherent in our free market system helps to contain self-interest. Yet the dynamic within competitive teams also has tremendous moral power, for good *or* bad. The culture at companies such as Johnson & Johnson is an altogether different moral force than that of some companies now embroiled in accounting scandals. We should never underestimate the fragility of corporate cultures nor their vulnerability to the destructive forces of greed.

The vulnerability to greed is built into all of us. Beyond market forces, only two forces can control this greed. One is external: the coercive force of law, imposed either by the government or by a company's rules. The other is character.

Yet, our nation's primary ethical focus, including that in our business and law schools, has for some time now been on what is right and wrong in particular situations. We have almost totally lost a focus on the importance of developing virtue and character that allow us to develop into individuals who can handle our moral freedom responsibly in a business context.

The future success of American business depends on the ability of our nation—and more importantly, of our families, churches, schools, and communities—to develop virtue in those who enter into business. Continued success will also depend upon management's ability to convert virtue in its workers into better products and services for customers. We need to recognize that character issues are as important to our national economic success as factors such as education. Laws such as the recently enacted Sarbanes-Oxley (intended to strengthen corporate governance and restore investor confidence), though regrettably sometimes necessary, restrict our freedom and are expensive for companies to comply with. What our nation's business community needs even more than a coercive legal response to the problem of greed is a moral response that focuses on the purpose and values of companies and the potential of their cultures to promote virtue and character development.

This is not pie-in-the-sky moralism. It's just good business.

Character Questions

1. The author makes the controversial claim that the free market system is the most moral economic option available today. Do you agree or disagree, and why?

2. What is your business's purpose? How, if at all, does it help to fulfill the ultimate purpose of bringing glory to God? What are your business' values? How do these values line up (or not line up) with biblical principles?

3. Within your professional sphere, what can you do to help business have a "character," or moral quality, that is more pleasing to God?

14

Character in Leadership

John Maxwell, a Christian writer and leadership expert, defines leadership as "the ability to influence, pure and simple."[1] In my view, that "pure and simple" definition is a bit *too* simple. After all, bribes influence, but the ability to bribe is certainly not leadership.

To understand leadership, we have to understand what organizations are all about. In the most fundamental sense, whether the group is a business, a family, a church, a sports team, or a community, *people* are its reason for being. Organizations exist for the good of people, both inside and outside the group; therefore, leadership is about bringing out the best in people and enhancing the quality of their lives. For Christians, that means the ultimate purpose of leadership is to help others attain their ultimate purpose.

The ways in which a leader helps those he leads to glorify God varies tremendously, depending on the group's mission. The head of a Habitat for Humanity building crew focuses on an entirely different set of concerns than does a mother chaperoning a school field trip or a CEO steering a Fortune 500 company through troubled waters. But for all leaders, the essence of the task is the same. No matter the context, the good leader creates an environment where all group members are freed and empowered to the greatest extent possible to glorify God. And by helping those within the organization achieve *their* ultimate purpose, in God's grace the leader fulfills his *own*.

A Leader's Character

No matter the organization, character is the most important attribute of its leader. It's even more important than talent or competence.

This is true because leadership necessarily involves power, and as Lord Acton noted, power corrupts and absolute power corrupts absolutely. Power, without character, is a curse, not a blessing. Whether it is in the hands of a foreman, a CEO, a judge, a teacher, or a policeman it tends to corrupt the person who has it and poisons the system in which it is possessed. Only when combined with strong character in a leader can power be converted into creative enterprise.

Also, in America people are free to walk away from virtually all organizations and groups they are a part of. So, what is to make people follow? The character of the leader. A primary responsibility of the leader is to bring strong character to the job so that he is a person whom members of the group will choose to follow.

Good character, therefore, is what a business must first look for in its managers, what men and women who hope to raise a family should first seek in their spouses, what churches should first expect in their ministers, and what citizens should first demand of the politicians they elect. Certainly, competence is essential, but where a leader with good character discovers he is in over his head, the organization likely will survive because his character will prompt him to seek competent advisers to assist him. When the leader's character is bad, however, no matter what his competence level, the organization's strength eventually will dissipate as good people leave, resources are squandered, and morale diminishes on his watch.

As we saw in the introduction to part two, the theological virtues are said to produce "saints" and the cardinal virtues produce "heroes." Many people think that a leader needs the cardinal virtues but that, if anything, the theological virtues get in the way of effective leadership. But this is not so. A leader who combines "sainthood" and "heroism," as we have characterized them in relation to virtue, is poised to be a great leader.

Because we as Christians are to be conformed to the image of Jesus Christ, and therefore to lead in that image, we must look to Him as our model as we seek God's grace to lead. Jesus was profoundly successful as a leader based on four fundamental pillars: authority, humility, love, and stewardship. Let's look at each of those characteristics.

Leading with Authority

In leadership terms, we need to recognize a difference between authority and power. We can define authority as the ability to lead someone to willing participation. (This is not the common meaning of authority but one that specialists use in discussing this subject.)[2]

People follow a leader with authority because they respect both him and his program. Such leaders persuade their followers that the desired course of action makes sense. Power, on the other hand, is the use of raw force to coerce someone into following. Authority and power are inversely related; the more authority a leader has, the less power he must use to coerce compliance, and vice versa.

Christ is the ultimate example of a leader who led through authority, not power. Not only did Christ not seek power; He rejected it. He carried no weapon; He had no army; He had no money, not even a spare coin. He was so committed to our freedom that He wanted us to follow Him solely on the basis of His authority or not at all.

What gave Jesus authority? And what can we as leaders learn from His example?

First, Jesus set lofty standards. His moral teaching took the biblical ethic to an altogether higher level. This is vividly seen in the Sermon on the Mount (Matthew 5-7), and it is interesting to note that the challenge of Jesus' teaching, rather than driving people away, caused them to be "astonished" at Christ's "authority" (Matthew 5:28). Likewise, Jesus constantly challenged his disciples and followers (See Matthew 10:34-39; 19:16 ff.).

Leaders with authority, whether they be first-grade teachers, pro football coaches or CEOs, take their groups to a new and higher plateau. Most of us want to be challenged and we want to be part of something special. Anyone who follows college football recruiting knows this. Any leader satisfied with average performance and results will not have authority.

Second, Jesus modeled incarnational leadership. He lived among the people. He walked with them. In the theological sense, "though he was in the form of God ... he made himself nothing, taking the form of a servant" (Philippians 2:6-7). The one who leads with authority is the servant leader who is comfortable on the factory floor or who wears cleats to the football practice.

This is not the only way to have success as a leader. Some who are successful stick to the corporate suite, but it is hard to lead with authority from "above."

Sam Walton was an incarnational businessman. Among his rules for running a successful company such as Wal-Mart, Walton included these:

RULE 6: CELEBRATE your successes. Find some humor in your failures. Don't take yourself so seriously. Loosen up, and everybody around you will loosen up. Have fun. Show enthusiasm—always. When all else fails, put on a costume and sing a silly song. Then make everybody else sing with you. All of this is more important, and more fun, than you think, and it really fools the competition. "Why should we take those cornballs at Wal-Mart seriously?"

RULE 7: LISTEN to everyone in your company. And figure out ways to get them talking. The folks on the front lines—the ones who actually talk to the customer—are the only ones who really know what's going on out there. You'd better find out what they know. This really is what total quality is all about. To push responsibility down in your organization, and to force good ideas to bubble up within it, you *must* listen to what your associates are trying to tell you.[3]

Third, it goes without saying that the leader must be competent if he is going to have authority. People don't want to follow the lead of someone who is not highly capable. Christ was immediately recognized as someone with authority because, as a rabbi, He understood the Word of God profoundly and taught it clearly. Though His teaching was a radical departure from that of the Pharisees, people recognized that He was exceptionally wise.

The remainder of attributes that contribute to authority in leadership relate to trustworthiness, and a full discussion of these is impossible in this short chapter. Sufficient it is to note that a trustworthy leader has integrity—he walks his talk. He practices self-denial and is reliable, consistent, and loyal. He cares, and he carries more than his fair share of the load.

Of course, even the leader whose virtues qualify him to lead with authority must sometimes exercise power. In all organizations where we fallen humans are involved, the leader employs a variety of rewards and, from time to time, uses discipline to bring out the best in the people. A coach must discipline a player for breaking the rules; a manager must fire an employee who refuses to abide by company rules. Nevertheless, the Christian who seeks to lead in Christ's image will minimize the use of coercive power and maximize freedom within the organization. Wherever possible, he will liberate, empower, and equip those he leads to fulfill both their personal potential and that of the organization.

Leading with Humility

As we saw in an earlier chapter, Jesus Christ personified humility, which is the second essential character trait for Christian leaders. Instead of grasping the equality with God He could rightly claim, Christ emptied Himself. His is a perfect model of self-denial and submission to the Father's will (Philippians 2:1-11).

We need to understand that humility is consistent with effective leadership. That was certainly true in the case of the father of our country.

Before the American Colonial army disbanded in 1783, some of the officers encamped at Newburg, New York, grew frustrated about Congress's failure to pay them. It occurred to them that, while they remained an armed body, they should threaten Congress to get what was owed them. The situation was dangerous. The new nation's peace and even its democracy were at risk. Remarkably, George Washington's spectacles turned the situation around.

Washington called a meeting with the officers and gave them an impassioned speech about how the revolt they were planning would betray all the sacrifices they had made for freedom in the previous eight-and-a-half years. When he had finished, he drew from his pocket a letter from a congressman showing that Congress was doing its best to come up with the salaries that were in arrears. Dramatically, the general held the paper and paused. Then he reached in his coat and took out a pair of reading glasses.

Washington was fifty-one at this time, having been forty-three when he first took command of the American forces. In a moment of personal vulnerability, he put the reading glasses on and said, "Gentlemen, will you forgive me? I find I have grown gray in your service and am growing blind as well."

This was the end of the meeting. The officers were in tears. There would be no revolt, due to Washington's humility and meekness, not the power of his position.[4]

What Washington demonstrated more than two centuries ago is still true. While popular stereotypes would have us believe that the humble leader is doomed to failure in our fast-paced, win-lose world, business research shows the opposite.

In the best-selling book *Good to Great*, author Jim Collins and a team of researchers studied the leadership and corporate cultures of eleven successful companies, including such giants as Abbott Laboratories, Kroger, and Wells Fargo Bank. Collins chose these particular companies because they had made successful turnarounds, which he defined as fifteen years of exceptionally profitable growth after years of average performance.

What Collins discovered about the leaders of these companies, whom he dubbed "Level 5" executives, shocked him. "Compared to high-profile leaders with big personalities who make headlines and become celebrities," Collins wrote, "the good-to-great leaders seem to have come from Mars. Self-effacing, quiet, reserved, even shy—these leaders are a paradoxical blend of personal humility and professional will. They are more like Lincoln and Socrates than Patton or Caesar."[5]

Collins noted that the Level 5 executives were ambitious— "but their ambition is first and foremost for the institution, not themselves."[6] These humble leaders led the good-to-great companies to stock returns that were nearly five times higher than those of the general market over the fifteen years following their transition.

Good to Great refutes the prevailing notion that humility is inconsistent with effective business leadership. True, America has its share of arrogant CEOs, some of whom have succeeded. But those who humbly walk the road less traveled can be just as successful, even stunningly so.

In his four-volume biography of General Robert E. Lee, author Douglas Southall Freeman's description of this great leader is remarkably similar to Collins's findings about Level 5 executives. "His ambition was in his labor, whatever its nature," Freeman said. "He did not covet praise."[7]

For Lee, Freeman wrote, "There was but one question ever: What was his duty as a Christian and a gentleman?"[8] A diary entry Lee wrote during the war provides a clear picture of his approach to leadership.

The manner in which an individual enjoys certain advantages over others is a test of a true gentleman. The power which the strong have over the weak, the employer over the employed, the educated over the unlettered, the experienced over the confiding, even the clever over the silly—the forbearing or inoffensive use of all this power or authority, or a total abstinence from it when the case admits it, will show the gentleman in a plain light.... A true man of honor feels humbled himself when he cannot help humbling others.[9]

Yet another sterling example of a humble leader is John Wooden, the UCLA basketball coach whose teams won seven straight NCAA championships from 1967 to 1973 and once possessed an eighty-eight-game winning streak. A longtime student of character, Wooden developed a "pyramid of success" involving some twenty-five virtues he sought to instill in each of his players.

With a record like Wooden's, a lesser man might have become a prima donna. But Wooden stayed true to his humble nature. Throughout his career, he constantly sought to serve, even down to such actions as joining his players in helping janitorial staff when they played a road game. "We picked up all the tape, never threw soap on the shower floor for someone to slip on, made sure all showers were turned off and all towels were accounted for," Wooden recalled in *They Call Me Coach*. "The towels were always deposited in a receptacle, if there was one, or stacked neatly near the door."[10]

Those who lead in Christ's image will be humble. They will also express love.

Leading in Love

Let us return to the major attributes of love listed by Paul in 1 Corinthians 13:

> Love is patient and kind; love does not envy or boast; it is not arrogant or rude. It does not insist on its own

way; it is not irritable or resentful; it does not rejoice at wrongdoing, but rejoices with the truth. Love bears all things, believes all things, hopes all things, endures all things. Love never ends (vv. 4-8).

These words describe Jesus' love ethic. Some will say that no one can love like this and remain an effective leader. But the reality is that love and leadership are compatible and that, in its truest sense, leadership can and should be an expression of 1 Corinthians love.

Colman Mockler, former CEO of Gillette, had a life that revolved around three great loves: his family, Harvard University, and Gillette. Even during the dark times when his company was faced with the threat of hostile takeovers, Mockler found time to care for the people who mattered to him.

His wife said, "When Colman died and we all went to the funeral, I looked around and realized how much love was in the room. This was a man who spent nearly all his waking hours with people who loved him, who loved what they were doing, and who loved one another—at work, at home, in his charitable work, wherever."[11]

We saw in chapter eleven that love is, among other things, a matter of desiring the good of another and acting to obtain it. Seen in this light, humble leadership is a form of love. The best leaders have a genuine inner readiness to serve others and a willingness to sacrifice on their behalf. Since business leaders are paid for their work, their labors may not be selfless in the strictest sense, but nevertheless their work can be closely aligned with what love is all about.

Thus, the character of the effective leader can and should reflect the 1 Corinthians 13 virtues. As we have seen, leaders such as Robert E. Lee and John Wooden weren't envious, boastful, arrogant, rude, irritable, or resentful. Instead, they were patient and kind. They were intolerant of evil. They carried great burdens on behalf of those they led and yet remained faithful, hopeful, and persistent all the while.

When the group's mission faces challenges, loving leaders insist not on their own way but on the organization's way, as defined by the group's purpose, reflected by its values, and incorporated in its systems. Jesus responded the same way when the Pharisees got in the way of His teachings on freedom and love. To quote G. K. Chesterton, they were "men whom Christ himself could not forbear to strike."[12]

Is love inconsistent with tough decisions, such as firing a nonperformer or downsizing? Not when these actions are required for the good of others, such as customers, workers, and owners who depend on the economic and competitive health of the enterprise. Such gut-wrenching decisions need to be entered into prayerfully and after much deliberation and with processes to make the transition as painless and fair as feasible, keeping in mind that an unprofitable enterprise cannot bear fruit, nor can an inefficient one create value for a customer.

Having seen that a Christlike leader is one who operates in authority, humility, and love, we must look at one more key quality. One who leads in Christ's image is also a steward.

Leading as a Steward

Christ was the ultimate steward, because His Father invested Him with "all authority in heaven and on earth" (Matthew 28:18). On earth Christ was entrusted with the most important assignment ever given, and pleasing the One who had entrusted that assignment to Him was Christ's only concern. "My food is to do the will of him who sent me and to accomplish his work" (John 4:34). As steward leaders, we should seek God's grace to lead with such a disposition.

God has made us stewards in several ways.

For one thing, each of us is a steward of the gifts God has provided to us personally. Thus, we should follow the instruction of Peter: "As each has received a gift, use it to serve one another, as good stewards of God's varied grace ... whoever serves, as one who serves by the strength that God supplies—in order that in everything God may be glorified through Jesus Christ" (1 Peter 4:10-11).

Because we are all leaders in one context or another, we are to use the gifts God has given us for His glory as we lead, whether we are called to raise a child, make a profit for the owners of a business, win a lawsuit for a client, or serve as a missionary in answering the call of the Great Commission.

In addition, we are all called to carry out the commission in Genesis to exercise dominion over the earth and to make it fruitful, both materially and spiritually (Genesis 1:28). In a sense, it's fair to say that the sole reason for any business organization is to make its members more productive in exercising dominion over the earth's resources than they could by acting alone.

Finally, we are stewards of the human, moral, financial, and other resources of the organizations or work groups we lead. This means we are to use whatever gifts God has entrusted to our organization as efficiently and productively as possible. Paul exhorted all of us to "aim for perfection" (2 Corinthians 13:11 NIV). This means that excellence in everything should be every leader's goal.

In striving for excellence in stewardship, servant leaders in business will seek an outstanding return for investors. After all, those investors are stewards of the money God has provided to them, which they have chosen to invest. They have every right to insist on attractive financial returns given the risks involved in the business.[13]

Leadership and the Character Framework

We have seen that in a free society the leader's character is key and that there is much we can learn from Jesus' example about the sort of character that will help us to be effective leaders. We now return to the three P's of the character triangle because, just as they are key to individual character, so they are beneficial in molding the character of an organization, even a family.

The important responsibilities of leaders correspond directly to the points on the character triangle. For example, leaders must define the organization's *purpose*. They are also guardians of the *principles*, or values, that guide the organization. In addition, leaders are charged with responsibility for infusing in the organization the inspiration and motivation to empower the organization. That is the *power* part of the triangle. Finally, just as individuals must have internal systems—virtues—so that we live into our purpose in accordance with moral principles, so must our organizations have such systems, financial, human, and physical. This is *character*.

Let's begin considering the first of these aspects: the role of leadership in a business' purpose. Discerning and defining the organization's purpose is the first task of any leader. As Yogi Berra has said, "If you don't know where you are going, you will wind up somewhere else."

From Vision to Destiny

Leadership begins with vision, which in a good organization is an understanding of purpose in its loftiest and noblest dimension. As Peter Drucker says, "Leadership is the lifting of a person's or organization's vision to a higher standard." The skillful leader shapes how the group sees its destiny and sustains that vision at a high level.

Authors Warren Bennis and Bert Nanus studied some ninety leaders who excelled in fields ranging from business and government to sports and the arts. In their classic book, *Leaders*, Bennis and Nanus report that no matter what the field, the defining characteristic of the leaders they studied was a sense of purpose for the organization and a clarity and intensity about that purpose.[14]

Almost all great organizations owe their success to the vision of an inspired leader. Henry Ford broke all the rules of business in mass-producing the Model T. He paid workers twice the prevailing wage. In eight years, to increase the number of cars sold (not to maximize profits), he drove the price of an automobile down by 58 percent, making the Model T available to some fifteen million Americans. The *Wall Street Journal* rebuked Ford for injecting "spiritual principles into a field where they did not belong." Captains of industry condemned his practices as "the most foolish thing ever attempted in the industrial world."[15]

Sam Walton's vision was to take a discount store to hundreds of towns that had been considered too small by Sears and other department stores. Vince Lombardi's vision was that an NFL team could win the championship, as his Green Bay Packers did, with discipline, a good defense, and one signature play—the power sweep—practiced to perfection. And we could go on multiplying examples.

The leader of any organization has vision and keeps a sense of noble purpose before those he leads. The leader is also the guardian of the organization's values or moral principles.

Trustees of Values

Lord Griffiths calls business leaders the "ultimate trustees" of a company's values. Too often, we confine our understanding of fiduciary responsibility to life's financial aspects. But if leaders are focused on helping those in their organization attain their ultimate purpose, they must be fiduciaries of the organization's moral capital as well.

The leader who makes the building and protection of his organization's moral capital a top priority reaps substantial benefits. We saw in the previous chapter that research has confirmed a nexus between strong moral values and outstanding companies that lead their industries. This nexus is found in other contexts, such as sports, families, and government. Conversely, we need only look at the latest front page, financial page, or sports page of our newspaper to learn of leaders whose failure to protect the values of their organization has led to ruin.

Leaders protect moral capital in at least two ways. One is by repeatedly emphasizing the importance of the organization's values and principles. The second, and perhaps more important, is by being a model of those values and principles themselves. The mother and father who want their children to be responsible with alcohol not only repeatedly tell their children not to drink and drive; they also don't drink and drive themselves.

The third aspect of the character framework—power—is needed as much in strong organizations as in individuals.

The Power of Motivation

In organizational terms, there is no exact analog to God's enabling grace. Nevertheless, in much the same way that God's grace empowers us as individuals to follow His eternal principles as we live into our ultimate purpose, so good leadership must inspire and motivate an organization to align its values and systems so that it can achieve its goals.

Lord Griffiths calls this source of power "inspiration." Edwards Deming speaks of "the joy of workmanship." Whatever the name, in its secular expression, this fundamental quality of good leadership instills a spirit, energy, and drive in the organization's members that motivates them to achieve the group's vision. Without such inspiration from their leader, the members of a group will never experience the internal satisfaction and peace that enable them to accomplish the organization's mission. The result will eventually be failure.

Ronald Reagan was sworn into the highest office in our land at a time when we were suffering from malaise, a lack of vigor, and a vague sense that we had gotten off the track somewhere. We were no longer proud of ourselves. Yet, with his sunny optimism, Reagan convinced us that it was morning in America and that our best days lay ahead of us. For many, he was an inspiration to believe we could recover our ideals, reboot our economy, and return to a position of moral leadership in the world—and we did. Power was released in our nation that was felt around the world and eventually caused the fall of the Iron Curtain.

Along with such secular forms of inspiration, leaders can also provide power by invoking God's grace through prayer in the life of the organization. Some will find this idea inappropriate; after all, there has long been a tendency in our society to view secular activity as outside God's orbit. But it is not. John Beckett describes the situation: "Sundays were Sundays with the rest of the world largely detached, operating by a different set of rules. Can these two worlds that seem so separate ever merge?"[16]

The truth is that for every Christian these two worlds must merge. In reality, there is but one world: God's kingdom, in which we all live and serve the King in everything we think and say and do. An executive vice president, a foreman, a mother or father, or a head coach is first of all God's steward and servant and thus should invoke God's grace in every endeavor, not just the spiritual, "Sunday" ones.

Character in an Organization's Internal Systems

Just as we as individuals need virtues to lead an effective life, so organizations must have internal systems to drive them. Leaders ensure that there are adequate systems to allow the organization and its members to achieve their purpose in accordance with the group's values. This can be a daunting task. The more complex the organization, the greater the number of systems that must function effectively and remain aligned with the organization's purpose and values.

These issues need prayer as well. Yet in our pluralistic society, issues inevitably arise about how the Christian leader can invite God into the day-to-day operations of secular organizations. Particularly in the business world, many will be bothered by such open expressions of Christianity as prayer groups.

Some of those who are bothered may be our superiors; others may report to us. In the latter case, there will be concerns about discrimination in assignments and promotions if we are ostentatious about professions of faith.

Leaven and Love

What is the leader as a Christian believer to do? When called to lead in a secular setting, two principles are particularly helpful.

The first is Jesus' teaching in Matthew 13:33 that "the kingdom of heaven is like leaven." Most of what is really important in the kingdom is not seen. That means that God's grace can have enormous impact on an organization without public displays of faith.

How? Believers who are leaders pray about the purpose and values and systems of their organization—sometimes alone in private, sometimes with others in the organization in private before the day or week begins. They invoke God's power and wisdom for their every word and deed. They commit all the affairs of their work unit to God.

Everyone who knows me will confirm that whatever success I have had in work is way over my head, and I can confirm that any success I have had has been the result of prayer. Such is the privilege and blessing of leaders who are fallible but who are striving to serve God. By our committing ourselves to glorify God as we lead—through prayer, through work, through faith, and in every other way—in God's grace others are empowered to glorify God in their work. Thus they and we grow in character together.

Christian leaders dedicate themselves to aligning the organization's activities with God's Word. But for the most part, I have found, they do not wear their faith on their sleeves. In their lives and the life of the organization they lead, God's grace and power strengthen virtue and provide wisdom, and then—where it is His will—God gives blessing and favor to results. In other words, the kingdom of God is as leaven, ever present but seldom seen.

The second principle also comes from Scripture. John 13:35 teaches, "By this all people will know that you are my disciples, if you have love for one another." The example of a leader who acts from sacrificial love in all he thinks, says, and does for his organization is a far more powerful tool than any label or public pronouncement. As the old song says, "They will know we are Christians by our love."

In conclusion, effective leadership in a free society depends on strong character, and the character that will glorify God in leadership requires the full panoply of virtues, cardinal and theological. They do not oppose but actually strengthen one another. The biblical virtues of humility and love by no means compromise strong leadership. In fact, in faith and with hope, they are wind beneath our wings that allow us to soar far higher than we otherwise could.

Character Questions

1. Do you agree that character is more important than competence for leaders? Why or why not?

2. Are you a Level 5 leader, as Jim Collins has defined it? If not, what is keeping you from being one?

3. Have you ever thought of yourself as a source of power for your business or other group in the sense that you provide motivation? How can you improve your leadership skills to provide more power to help others achieve their purposes?

Conclusion: One by One, from the Inside Out

When Robert Bartley, who for thirty years was in charge of the editorial page of the *Wall Street Journal*, retired in 2002, he wrote in his last column, "What I have learned in over thirty years is that in this society ... progress happens and problems have solutions." The solutions in Bartley's era were many, including the triumph of democracy over totalitarianism, and of free markets over planned economies, and the virtual elimination of hunger in the developed world.

When it comes to character, however, problems live on. We have no public policy solutions for the challenges that plague our nation. The reason is that the crisis of character cannot be approached in a top-down way. Whatever solution we fashion must come one by one, from the inside out, and it is a process that takes time. As for the role of government, the best we can hope for is that it will keep its hands off and do no harm.[1]

We cannot impose or control character in a direct sense, not even when it comes to our own character. We can exercise will to have knowledge but not wisdom. We can will a meek demeanor but not humility. We can will lust but not love, religiosity but not faith, self-assertion but not courage, scrupulosity but not self-control.[2]

At best, all we can do is engender a desire to grow into virtue, and this by God's grace. Something must first happen inside us so that we are willing to receive what God gives and work in cooperation with Him and others to grow in virtue. No command, pill, or bribe will create this willingness. It is a matter of grace and we enter it through repentance.

We all know many outside the faith who have this willingness to grow in virtue and who have strong characters. "What about them?" we might ask. They, too, by virtue of God's common grace, have had something in their hearts stirred to desire growth in virtue.

The main point, however, is that no one, most especially the government, can by some kind of program order this. It must be desired from within. Creating this desire is the primary task of character development.

In this conclusion we will briefly review the challenges we have in character development, beginning with the individual and then moving in circles outside to the family, church, schools, and community.

The Core of a Strong Nation

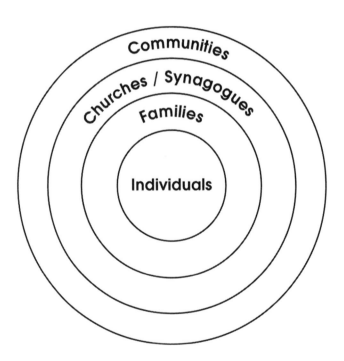

Character for the Individual

We all need to admit that the character problem begins with us. And because God is the source of all virtue, the solution to the problem begins with the means of grace—acknowledging our deficiencies, confessing them, praying about them, seeking understanding and grace through "abiding" in God's Word (see John 8:31). As I hope our discussion in the preceding chapters has made clear, our role then, in cooperation with grace, is to "make every effort" to grow in virtue through faith (see 2 Peter 1:5-8).

To illustrate how far I (and perhaps you) have to go, work with me through this exercise.

Our productivity in the United States grows at a rate of about 4 percent a year. So does our gross domestic product. The result is amazing economic prosperity, the envy of the world. Is it asking too much that virtue grow by a like amount? At 4 percent growth annually, a sum doubles every seventeen years. Having been married for forty years, I should be about five times more loving today than when I married Fairfax. Am I? Ask her.

I expect that some may bristle at any such a calculation, but my point is that we all have immense room for growth in virtue. Our progress is ever so meager. If we were growing in virtue as one would expect we might, given the sources of God's grace available to us, believers would be observably different from others of similar position. Yet we all know that too often we are not. We need to repeat the refrain with which we opened this book: "It's me, it's me, O Lord, standing in the need of prayer."

Character in the Family

The family is the fundamental unit within which character develops. Either our biological or an adoptive family is essential if we are to grow into strong character.

261

Everyone who has studied character agrees that character engravings are inscribed early in life. Character is formed in our childhood. Thankfully, in grace it can be altered for the better thereafter, but the early years are crucial.[3]

Working in God's grace to cultivate good character in our children is certainly one of life's most critical responsibilities.

Parenting as it relates to character is not a science; it is an art. It is not a matter of law but of grace. Many godly parents have been disappointed in their children. A notable biblical example is that of Eli, a godly priest. The Bible records, "The sons of Eli were worthless men. They did not know the LORD" (1 Samuel 2:12). Similarly, Pericles, one of the greatest generals and statesmen of all time, a man of great character, had sons who disappointed him.

Within families, children's characters develop in different ways, even though parents give them similar love and attention. No one expresses surprise at the totally different characters of the two sons in the parable of the prodigal son. We see these differences among siblings all the time.

A familiar adage has it that virtue is "caught, not taught." Better still, it is "bought." The first objective of parenting, as it relates to character, is to awaken in our children a desire to live the morally good life—to buy into it, so to speak. Without this desire, teaching and disciplining to moral rules, necessary as they are, will fall short.

How do we awaken such a desire? There are two keys. The first is (not surprisingly) parental love. Here the adage is "no rules without relationship." In other words, if we are to seek to influence the character of another person, we must first love him. I do not think it is too much of a generalization to say that every time the appetite for virtue has been awakened in another, it has been through love.

My prayer partner Kirby Sevier knows a lot about parenting, having six biological children and eight "godchildren" who live in the urban core. Shaun is the oldest of the kids Kirby and his wife, Becky, "adopted" to express to them the love of God. Shaun was sullen, uncommunicative, and failing in grammar school when Kirby and Becky resolved to take him to church and then to lunch every Sunday for a year. At the end of the year Shaun was bright-eyed and attentive, and his relationships and grades were improving and Kirby and Becky extended their commitment indefinitely. Shaun graduated from high school with a baseball scholarship, which led him to a college diploma. Shaun saw in Kirby and Becky the love of God, and that love awakened in him an appetite for the morally good life that he now has.

The second thing good parents must do to engender in their children a desire for a morally good life is to provide a worthy example. Edmund Burke said, "Example is the school of mankind. It will learn at no other." When we speak of character, Burke is correct. It is example and not platitudes that leads to the morally good life. Children are continuously learning character from either good or bad examples, not just in the family but also in childhood peer groups, in school, on television, and in the movies. For an example to have a positive effect, it must be of a fruit that grows naturally from a good tree; it cannot be faked.

Of course, the supreme example is Jesus Christ. First of all, He taught in parables, giving plain, everyday examples to illustrate what He meant. But more than that, Jesus Himself was an example. He washed His disciples feet as an "example" of what they and we should do. (John 13:15). If we want to know what courage or love or faith or wisdom is, we need only look to the life of Jesus. It is His example that we need to continuously hold up to our children.

Where love and good example are combined to create what we might call loving interaction, we have the most potent force for the development of strong character in children. By far the greatest potential for loving interaction is in the family between parent and child, and it can be found between grandparent and child and older siblings and their younger brothers and sisters. Beyond the family we see it in teachers, coaches, ministers, and a host of other mentors and role models. Loving interaction does its work in character development almost always, one-on-one over time.

My mother was a smart and wise lady. Yet, while she was full of do's and don'ts, such as "Brush your teeth" or "Don't chew with your mouth open," I do not remember receiving a single word of moral advice from her. But her loving interaction shaped my character far more than did any other influence on earth.

Mother embodied the virtues discussed in this book. She was humble, a faithful woman, full of patient hope, and these virtues were carried into a deep love for her husband and her children: myself and my two sisters. The two keys to virtue—self-denial and perseverance—were modeled in her life in spades, especially as related to her family. On top of this, she was a praying woman, so she exemplified the virtues as she cared for us by day and prayed the grace of God into us when we were asleep.

There is another way she provided an example to us. She read to us, and enlisted Dad to read to us, every night. We heard stories about virtuous people from the Bible and from classic children's stories and fables. These, too, modeled and engendered a desire for a morally good life.

The result was that, strictly by God's grace (certainly it was nothing my sisters and I could claim one iota of responsibility for), we cared about being "good." That is not to say that I did not consistently fall short of the do's and don'ts or rebel against some of them. But it is to say that, by and large, I grew up as someone who respected authority and who wanted to please my mother and God.

Once a child is in such a position, a virtuous cycle ensues. Virtue spawns its own rewards. We feel internally rewarded when we do good and therefore we repeat the good, forming virtuous habits. From virtuous habits there grows good character.

Virtue creates rewards in other ways. The tree planted by the water "prospers" in the natural order of things. If a child is well behaved and tries at school, the teacher pays the child compliments and gives him special attention. The child who practices harder is more likely to make the sports team, and on the basis of virtuous habits gets accolades and special attention from coaches. These things propel the child to greater effort and higher levels. Though these benefits may be seen at school or in extracurricular pursuits, their foundation is at home and their source is grace.

Character in the Church

The church is the ultimate custodian of the truths that lie at the foundation of biblical character. It is up to the churches to be sure members understand that life has an ultimate purpose and that each of our lives needs to be organized so as to live into that purpose. Likewise, the moral commandments of God and the teachings of Jesus are the special province of the church, and a love for these moral principles needs to be engendered within the membership. The source of power to live a life of biblical character—namely, the grace of God—is a truth that needs to be protected and proclaimed in the church. The virtues of the biblical life, and most especially the theological virtues of humility, faith, hope, and love, are the peculiar province of the church.

But beyond these overarching principles, the specific task of the church is to teach us how to live into our purpose, in accordance with the principles, empowered by the Holy Spirit. The church is the realm where we should be taught not simply "to" but "how to" put the teachings of Jesus into practice and to become disciples of Jesus.

Because the development of character takes place one by one, from the inside out, the most effective structures in the church for the development of character are likely to be small groups. In such groups we may more easily discuss the virtues as they relate to our daily lives and share our failings and successes as tangible examples for our brothers and sisters. Churches are ideal for providing such groups as well as prayer and accountability partnerships.

As we have discussed, evangelical churches have a strong emphasis upon evangelism, as well they should. But the great need all of us have once we come into the kingdom is for discipleship to the end that we become good trees that produce much fruit to the glory of God.

On this front there is much room for improvement. Dr. George Barna, who annually reports on the state of the church, reported in the 2005 edition that "nothing is more numbing to the church than the fact that it is mired in ... [an] unfathomable depth. The various creative approaches attempted over the course of this decade have drawn much attention but produced little, if any, transformational impact."[4]

I do not look at polls and statistics for a living as Dr. Barna does, and I am more optimistic than he. Nevertheless, I think we would all agree that the church has miles to go in improving our discipleship. I agree with Dr. Dallas Willard, who says, "How to combine faith with obedience is surely the essential task of the church as it enters the twenty-first century."[5]

Character in Schools

Most of our teachers in public education care deeply about their students and the students' character. They want to make a positive difference. But over the years, the directives that have come down from educational psychologists and the professionals in the educational bureaucracy have made it very difficult for public school teachers to influence students' character for the better.

The first schools in America were intended to teach a biblical morality and to train and discipline students in biblical character. The old *McGuffey Reader* (1836), which was used in virtually all the common schools, reflected an orthodox Puritan worldview. Though the sectarian aspects of Puritanism were later diluted to appeal more broadly to all evangelical Protestants, a basic evangelical Protestant worldview characterized moral education in the United States until the end of the nineteenth century.

At that time the philosophy of Horace Mann gained great influence in public education. The view of Mann was that the sectarian aspects of Protestantism should be scratched from public education and replaced by a progressive Unitarianism. This was an effort to impart moral values to children in a nonsectarian way that presumably would not be offensive to non-Christians.

As we moved into the twentieth century, the influence of Mann gave way to secularism with the result that the principles of revealed religion were removed from the moral education of children and replaced with the philosophy that children should determine their own values. This contributed heavily to the moral autonomy we discussed in the introduction to part three. This philosophy held sway for generations until its bankruptcy was revealed by sound thinkers such as C. S. Lewis.

Today there is an acceptance in the public schools of most states that the traditional virtues of Western civilization are a part of good character. But there is no recognition that there is a divine source behind either virtue or traditional morality. A good example of this appears in the State of Alabama, where the legislature in 1995 passed the following resolution:

NOW, THEREFORE, BE IT RESOLVED, that the members of the Alabama State Board of Education do hereby direct local boards of education to develop and implement, at the beginning of the 1995-96 school year, a comprehensive K-12 program for character education to consist of at least ten minutes of instructions per day; and

BE IT FURTHER RESOLVED, that this program of character education will focus on students' development of the following character traits: courage, patriotism, citizenship, honesty, fairness, respect for others, kindness, cooperation, self-respect, self-control, courtesy, compassion, tolerance, diligence, generosity, punctuality, cleanliness, cheerfulness, school pride, respect for the environment, patience, creativity, sportsmanship, loyalty, and perseverance.[6]

To be sure, the motivation behind the legislature's effort was sincere. But the resolution illustrates the weakness of any kind of moral instruction today in our public schools. Not only is the instruction designated for as little as ten minutes per day, but also its virtues are unconnected with any overarching purpose of life.

In our public schools, we do not refer to an ultimate purpose in life, especially if it has a biblical foundation, much less one from the Puritan tradition. Likewise, the teaching of eternal moral principles is absent as is any reference to God as a potential source of strength for a moral life. None of the theological virtues are among the twenty-five that are listed in the resolution. Thus, apparently, humility, faith, hope, and love do not get into the game.

The elimination of any theological base for the development of character in public education may be attributed to the decisions of the United States Supreme Court under the Establishment Clause of the U.S. Constitution. But there is a second problem in a pluralistic society. Where there is religious diversity, there is a strong political impulse to reach the lowest common denominator so as not to offend any group. The result is a resolution such as that previously quoted.

In addition to the fact that moral instruction in our public schools is anemic, our laws have essentially stripped the teacher of the ability to discipline within the classroom, with the result that in many classes there is a lot of disruption. More importantly, the teacher has little ability to demonstrate the difference between right and wrong, obedience and disobedience, within classroom discipline.[7] Also detracting from the development of character in city schools are grade inflation and social promotion, which reward lazy behavior and therefore penalize the conscientious student.

These are among the reasons why Christian schools are thriving and homeschooling continues to grow rapidly despite the enormous sacrifices families must make for private or home schools. Parents make those sacrifices because, in addition to a quality education, they desire for the educational system—be it in private schools or homeschooling—to supplement the work of the family in engendering strong character in children.

Because only the more affluent families can afford private education, the poorest children in our society—who need as much as anyone a good character education—are left to public schools mostly in desperately poor rural counties or under-performing systems in the big cities. As a result, we have all too many children growing up in the inner city without effective moral development in the home, who are unchurched, and who are attending public schools that default in moral education.

For a long time now, some have called for a voucher system in education, allowing parents to send their children to public or private schools where they think the kids can get the best education (including the best religious or moral guidance). Milton Friedman, a proponent of vouchers for public education, has based his argument on the benefits of competition. He asserts that the public school monopoly is giving us the inferior results we see, especially in our larger cities, because there is ineffective competition between schools.[8]

For those of us who are concerned with the diminishing reservoir of virtue in this country, a strong case can be made for vouchers that would open up educational opportunities, especially for the poor in private schools. The U.S. Supreme Court has approved the use of vouchers in religious schools, and such programs exist to a limited extent in Michigan, Wisconsin, and Florida.

For more than a hundred years, there was a fierce debate as to whether a managed or free marketplace produced the most productive and fairest economy. That debate is over. Virtually everyone now agrees that the free market system works better and is fairer.

We are at the beginning of the same kind of debate with respect to public education, and the outcome is likely to be equally as decisive. Over time we will find that not only the most effective but also the fairest educational system in our pluralistic society, especially for the poor, is one that allows parents through vouchers to choose the best school for their children, public or private, based on the educational curriculum and moral training offered by the school.

Character in the Community

The role of the community in strengthening character was noted by President Reagan when he said:

> I am calling for an end to giantism, for a return to the human scale—the scale that human beings can understand and cope with; the scale of the local fraternal lodge, the church congregation, the block club, the farm bureau. It is the locally owned factory, the small businessman who personally deals with his customers and stands behind his products, the farm and consumer cooperative, the town or neighborhood.... It is this activity on a small, human scale that creates the fabric of community, a framework for the creation of abundance and liberty. The human scale nurtures standards of right behavior, a prevailing ethic of what is right and what is wrong, acceptable and unacceptable.[9]

As it relates to our children, the community can only build on what is done in the family, because what is done in the community is voluntary. The Boy Scouts and the high school football team both develop character, but the desire to grow in virtue must be in a boy to give the necessary time to the Boy Scouts or football, to submit to the discipline of the programs, and to persevere in carrying them out.

In the United States enormous efforts go into community programs that have the direct or indirect effect of strengthening character. We see these programs in prisons, missions, alcohol and drug rehabilitation, job training, hospitals, Boys' and Girls' Clubs, YMCAs and YWCAs, summer camps, and a host of other activities.

Mama Lois has devoted her life to inner-city girls through a ministry called Grace House. Mary was one of her "girls" living in foster care with Mama Lois for years. Mary was at our church with Mama Lois weekly; she learned the Bible and was taught biblical virtues and moral laws. But most of all, Mama Lois loved Mary and her other girls as a mother in a sacrificial way and modeled a Christlike character for them.

Mary made good grades in a private Christian high school (Mama Lois raised the money for the tuition), then went to college. But after a while, she dropped out, got pregnant, and went back to her old world. We thought we had lost her. But good habits are engraved in us, and the love of God through Mama Lois was alive in Mary's heart. She bounced back and now has a full-time job, is back in church, and will undoubtedly "make it." Certainly she would not have done as well as she has but for Mama Lois. Most importantly, she will do it in a way that glorifies God.

Such is the work—one-on-one, from the inside out—that goes on in our community.

Freedom's Holy Light

In the preface we noted that the subject of character has been seen by some to be in tension with the doctrine of grace, self-development to be in conflict with self-denial. It is my hope that this book has demonstrated a unity between grace and character, with grace being the fundamental source of power and character the expression of a life lived in accordance with our ultimate purpose.

Therefore, when we confront the character challenges of our nation we need to think first in terms of grace. We must always begin with ourselves, believing

That through grace we will know that our ultimate purpose in life is bringing glory to God;

That we will accept biblical principles as moral guidelines as we live toward our purpose;

That we will rely upon the Holy Spirit as the source of power for our growth in character;

That we will through faith grow into good trees, using the virtues of wisdom, courage, and self-control to enable the virtues of humility, faith, and hope to express themselves in the fruits of justice and love; and

That we will use and preserve our God-given freedom by putting these virtues into practice.

For us to grow into good, fruit-bearing trees, we need strong families, churches, and communities. Then we will have a just government and vibrant economy. And as we put our trust in God, the nation will indeed be the "city upon a hill" that John Winthrop envisioned. May we ever pray together:

Long may our land be bright
With Freedom's holy light.
Protect us by thy might
Great God, our King.[10]

Notes

Preface

[1] Stephen Covey, *The 7 Habits of Highly Effective People* (New York: Simon and Schuster, 1990), 18 ff.

[2] See, e.g. Gilbert Meilaender, *The Theory and Practice of Virtue* (Notre Dame: University of Notre Dame Press, 1984), 36. "Acquiring an excellence, be it a skill or a virtue, is not only acquiring a capacity or tendency to act in a certain way; it is also a matter of acquiring merit." These words suggest a difficulty for anyone wishing to write about the virtues within a framework of Christian belief. Concentration upon the gradual development of one's character and an effort to cultivate the virtues within one's life may, from a Christian perspective, appear suspect. The entire effort may seem too self-centered, a failure to focus one's attention upon God and the neighbor. And the very fact that virtues are habits of behavior engrained in one's character may suggest that they become our possession and that the moral life is not continually in need of grace."

[3] I have used the masculine gender throughout my writing. I realize this, too, is not politically correct, but it is the traditional way our language has been employed and is the way I learned to write and to speak. Certainly I mean no disrespect to women.

Introduction to Part I

[1] Russell Kirk, *The Conservative Mind: From Burke to Eliot*, 7th ed. (Washington, D.C.: Regenery, 1995), 472. This book was originally published in 1953.

[2] Alasdair MacIntyre, *After Virtue* (Notre Dame: University of Notre Dame Press, 1984), 1 ff.

Chapter One: Why Character Counts

[1] Dietrich Bonhoeffer, *Dietrich Bonhoeffer: Eine Biographie*, trans. Eberhard Bethge (Munich: Christian Kaiser Verlag), 736.

[2] Ibid., 1037-8.

[3] Dietrich Bonhoeffer, "After Ten Years," in *Letters and Papers from Prison,* ed. Eberhard Bethge (New York: Macmillan, 1971), 16.

[4] Quoted in Os Guinness, *When No One Sees: The Importance of Character in an Age of Image* (Colorado Springs, NavPress, 2000), 17.

[5] Quoted in Norman R. Augustine, *Augustine's Travels: A World-Class Leader Looks at Life, Business, and What It Takes to Succeed at Both* (New York: AMACOM, 1998), 45-46, emphasis added.

[6] C. S. Lewis, *Mere Christianity,* rev. ed. (New York: Macmillan, 1952), 76-77.

[7] We should note that the bad habits that form in us also appear to be internally rewarding. People do drugs, view pornography, and have extramarital affairs because such actions feel good. Of course, the feeling is perversely good and ultimately destructive.

[8] J. C. Ryle, *Holiness* (England: Evangelical Press, 1979), 42.

[9] Oswald Chambers, *My Utmost for His Highest* (Uhrichsville, OH: Barbour, 1963), 206 (July 24).

[10] Lewis, 70-71.

[11] This may seem a harsh assessment. At least it does to me. Jesus delivers such an assessment, however, on the one who forfeits God's gifts by not utilizing his talents: "You wicked and slothful servant! ... For to everyone who has will more be given, and he will have an abundance. But from the one who has not, even what he has will be taken away. And cast the worthless servant into the outer darkness" (Matthew 25:26,29-30).

Chapter Two: Our Ultimate Purpose

[1] David Maraniss, *When Pride Still Mattered: A Life of Vince Lombardi* (New York: Simon & Schuster, 1999), 217.

[2] Stephen R. Covey, *The 7 Habits of the Highly Effective People* (New York: Simon & Schuster, 1990), 96-97.

[3] By speaking of glorifying God, I am not implying that we can do anything to add to His glory. God's glory is already infinite. We glorify God in the sense that we praise Him and we please Him by reflecting His glory in our conduct.

[4] 1 Peter 4:10-11 NIV:

10 – Each one should use whatever gift he has received to serve others, faithfully administering God's grace in its various forms.

11 – If anyone speaks, he should do it as one speaking the very words of God. If anyone serves, he should do it with the strength God provides, so that in all things God may be praised through Jesus Christ. To him be the glory and the power for ever and ever. Amen.

Hebrews 13:20-21 NIV:

20 – May the God of peace, who through the blood of the eternal covenant brought back from the dead our Lord Jesus, that great Shepherd of the sheep,

21 – equip you with everything good for doing his will, and may he work in us what is pleasing to him, through Jesus Christ, to whom be glory for ever and ever. Amen.

Ephesians 3:14-21 NIV:

14 – For this reason I kneel before the Father,

15 – from whom his whole family in heaven and on earth derives its name.

16 – I pray that out of his glorious riches he may strengthen you with power through his Spirit in your inner being,

17 – so that Christ may dwell in your hearts through faith. And I pray that you, being rooted and established in love,

18 – may have power, together with all the saints, to grasp how wide and long and high and deep is the love of Christ,

19 – and to know this love that surpasses knowledge – that you may be filled to the measure of all the fullness of God.

20 – Now to him who is able to do immeasurably more than all we ask or imagine, according to his power that is at work within us,

21 – to him be glory in the church and in Christ Jesus throughout all generations, for ever and ever! Amen.

[5] Bruce Wilkinson, *Secrets of the Vine: Breaking Through to Abundance* (Sisters, OR: Multnomah, 2001), 20-21, emphasis added.

[6] Ibid., 18.

[7] Letter of Benjamin Franklin to Joseph Huey, June 6, 1753, quoted in William J. Bennett, ed., *Our Sacred Honor: Words of Advice from the Founders in Stories, Letters, Poems, and Speeches* (New York: Simon & Schuster, 1997), 404.

[8] Jonathan Edwards, *The Religious Affections* (Carlisle, PA: The Banner of Truth Press, 1961), 320-321. The exact text reads: "Regeneration, which is that work of God in which grace is infused, has a direct relation to practice; for it is the very end of it, with a view to which the whole work is wrought. All is calculated and framed, in this mighty and manifold change wrought in the soul, so as directly to tend to this end. Yea, it is the very end of the redemption of Christ: Tit. ii, 14 KJV, 'Who gave himself for us that he might redeem us from all iniquity, and purify unto himself a peculiar people, zealous of good works.' "

[9] Wilkinson, 22.

[10] Grantland Rice, "Alumnus Football," in *Only the Brave, and Other Poems* (New York: Barnes, 1941), 144.

[11] John Piper, *Desiring God* (Sisters, Oregon: Multnomah Publishers, Inc., 1986).

[12] Randy Alcorn, *Heaven* (Carol Stream, Illinois: Tyndal House Publishers, Inc., 2004).

Chapter Three: Principles and Power for Character

[1] Oswald Chambers, *My Utmost for His Highest* (Uhrichsville, OH: Barbour, 1963), 131 (May 10).

[2] Jonathan Edwards, *A Jonathan Edwards Reader,* ed. John E. Smith (New Haven, Yale University Press, 2003), 274–81.

[3] Dallas Willard, *Renovation of the Heart* (Colorado Springs: Nav Pres, 2002), 245.

[4] When the church opposed scientific fact, as it did in the trial of Galileo, it was wrong. On the other hand, Christians are right to oppose a scientific theory such as Darwinism, which holds that human beings result from some mindless and

Godless process that brought forth life from the primordial sludge. We are right to oppose such a theory for the simple reason that the more we learn about the complexity of biological systems, of which Darwin knew very little, the more it becomes irrational to assert that from the purposeless physical laws of the universe, complex systems like the human nervous system, or even a single virus containing life and the ability to pass on a genetic code in reproduction itself could have emerged without intelligent design from the God of the universe. Atheists are on their heels in this debate.

[5] David Maraniss, *When Pride Still Mattered: A Life of Vince Lombardi* (New York: Simon & Schuster, 1999), 214.

[6] Attributed to John Bunyan, author of *The Pilgrim's Progress*.

[7] C. S. Lewis, *Mere Christianity, rev. ed.* (New York: MacMillan 1952), 155.

[8] J. I. Packer, preface to J. C. Ryle, *Holiness*, (Great Britain: Evangelical Press, 1979), vii, xi-xii, emphasis added.

[9] Lewis, 86.

[10] Richard J. Foster, *Celebration of Discipline: The Path to Spiritual Growth*, rev. ed. (San Francisco: Harper & Row, 1988), 7.

[11] Ibid., 5.

[12] Ibid., 1.

[13] Ibid., 2.

[14] Why it took me two steps—conversion plus surrender and filling—I do not know. Perhaps anyone as crusty as I needs a double dose.

[15] Judson W. VanDeVenter, "All to Jesus I Surrender."

Introduction to Part 2

[1] Traditionally, in the schema of the cardinal virtues, wisdom is called *prudence,* courage is called *fortitude,* and self-control is called *temperance.* I have chosen to use "wisdom," "courage," and "self-control" since they are more familiar terms today.

[2] Whatever core group of virtues one might choose, others can be placed in subgroups under the principal ones—patience under hope, mercy under love, meekness under humility, and so on.

[3] Of course, the question arises as to whether only Christian believers can develop the strong character that is the subject of this book. I answer this question simply by saying that I have known many who are not of the Christian faith but who nevertheless have characters that are stronger and purer than mine. I attribute their character to what theologians call *common grace*—the grace of God that in His love He apportions even to those who do not know Him through Jesus Christ.

Chapter Four: Humility: Understanding Reality
[1] Quoted in Susan Cheever, *My Name Is Bill: Bill Wilson—His Life and the Creation of Alcoholics Anonymous* (New York: Simon & Schuster, 2004), 188.

[2] Ibid., 190–91.

[3] Josef Pieper, *The Four Cardinal Virtues* (Notre Dame, IN: University of Notre Dame Press, 1966), 189.

[4] I simply cannot ascertain where I picked up this quotation up. I do think it is properly attributed to Augustine.

[5] Jonathan Edwards, *Religious Affections* (Carlisle, PA: The Banner of Truth Press, 1961), 239

[6] The Greek word is *metanoia*. Interestingly, I first learned the definition of *metanoia* from *The Fifth Dimension,* a secular book about how businesses, in order to succeed, must first become learning organizations. Only in that way are they equipped for a radical shift of mind when the competitive dynamics of an industry change, as they all too often do in today's economy.

[7] Oswald Chambers, *My Utmost for His Highest* (Uhrichsville, OH: Barbour, 1963), 12 (January 12).

[8] Augustus Toplady, "Rock of Ages, Cleft for Me"; Charlotte Elliott, "Just As I Am Without One Plea."

[9] "Number of Visible Stars Put at 70 Sextillion," ABC Science Online, www.abc.net.au/science/news/stories/s910295.htm.

[10] Blaise Pascal, *Pensees*, (England: Penguin Books, 1966) # 199, 92.

[11] Paul said the same thing in 1 Corinthians 6:19-20. Referring to the mercies of God revealed to us in Christ's sacrificial death, Paul stated: "You are not your own, for you were bought with a

price. So glorify God in your body." Again, the clear message is that, in light of Jesus' atoning death, our whole life, most especially including what we do in our bodies, is to be in submission to God, giving Him glory.

[12] Cited in Jim McGuiggan, *Jesus, Hero of Thy Soul: Impressions Left by the Savior's Touch* (West Monroe, LA: Howard, 1998), 15.

[13] Douglas Southall Freeman, *Lee: An Abridgement in One Volume by Richard Harwell of the Four-Volume R. E. Lee* (New York: Scribner's, 1961), 588.

Chapter Five: Faith: Trusting God, No Matter What

[1] "Ex-hostage: 'I Wanted to Gain His Trust,' " March 14, 2005, CNN, http://www.cnn.com/2005/LAW/03/14/smith.transcript/index.html.

[2] Karl Barth, *Church Dogmatics,* Bromiley, trans. (Edinburgh: T&T Clark, (1985) vol. 4, 618.

[3] Later books by Peck have revealed the author's Christian orientation.

[4] Rick Warren, *The Purpose Driven Life: What on Earth Am I Here For?* (Grand Rapids, MI: Zondervan, 2002), 193.

[5] George Müller, *Autobiography of Geroge* Müller, ed. H. Lincoln Wayland (1861; reprint, Grand Rapids, MI: Baker, 1981), 237.

[6] Ibid.

[7] Ibid., 231.

[8] Jerry Bridges, *Trusting God* (Colorado Springs, CO: NavPress, 1988), 52.

[9] Ibid.

[10] Martin Luther, *Commentary on the Epistle to the Romans,* trans. J. Theodore Mueller (Grand Rapids, MI: Kregel, 1976) ,xvii.

[11] John Paul II, *"Veritatis Splendor,"* August 6, 1993, 88, http://www.vatican.va/holy_father/john_paul_ii/encyclicals/documents/hf_jp-ii_enc_06081993_veritatis-splendor_en.html. Emphasis in the original.

Chapter Six: Hope: Waiting on the Lord

[1] Viktor E. Frankl, *Man's Search for Meaning: An Introduction to Logotherapy,* 4th ed. (Boston: Beacon, 1992), 83.

[2] Quoted in the previous chapter on faith.

[3] John Calvin, *Institutes of the Christian Religion,* vol. 2, ed. John T. McNeill, trans. Ford Lewis Battles (Philadelphia: Westminster, 1960), 590.

[4] Quoted in James C. Collins, *Good to Great: Why Some Companies Make the Leap—and Others Don't* (New York: HarperCollins, 2001), 85.

[5] C. S. Lewis, *The Screwtape Letters* with *Screwtape Proposes a Toast,* rev. ed. (New York: Macmillan, 1982), 39.

[6] "In His Time" (Nashville, TN: Maranatha! Music, 1978).

[7] Castle Rock Entertainment, *Shawshank Redemption,* dir. Frank Darabont, 1994.

[8] John R. Claypool, *The Hopeful Heart* (Harrisburg, PA: Morehouse, 2003), 16,20.

[9] See Kenneth Osbeele, *Amazing Grace* (Grand Rapids: Kaegel Publications, 1990), 202.

[10] George Weigel's wonderful biography of the Pope is entitled *Witness to Hope* (New York: Harper Collins, 2001).

[11] Speech to United Nations General Assembly, October 5, 1995.

Chapter Seven: Wisdom: Making the Right Choices

[1] Mother Teresa, "Whatsoever You Do ..." speech to the National Prayer Breakfast, Washington, D.C., February 3, 1994, reproduced at Orthodoxy Today, http://www.orthodoxyto-day.org/articles4/MotherTeresaAbortion.shtml.

[2] The best general discussion of the cardinal virtues, from a biblical perspective, of which I am aware is found in Josef Pieper, *The Four Cardinal Virtues* (Notre Dame, IN: University of Notre Dame Press, 1966). I am indebted to Pieper throughout this discussion of the four cardinal virtues. Michael Novak has written a great book on virtue in practical living, *Business as a Calling* (New York: Free Press, 1996), and many ideas in that book are picked up in this discussion.

[3] The same sentiment is found at Proverbs 1:7 and 15:33. See also Job 28:28 and Psalm 111:10. Clearly, it was standard practice in Hebrew thinking to link fear of the Lord with wisdom.

[4] "Only Half of Protestant Pastors Have a Biblical Worldview," January 12, 2004, Barna Research Group, http://www. barna. org/FlexPage.aspx?Page=BarnaUpdate&BarnaUpdate ID=156. Barna defines having a biblical worldview as believing that absolute moral truth exists and having a biblical view on six core beliefs: the accuracy of biblical teaching, the sinless nature of Jesus, the literal existence of Satan, the omnipotence and omniscience of God, salvation by grace alone, and the personal responsibility to evangelize.

[5] Malcolm Muggeridge *Jesus Rediscovered* (Doubleday, 1969), 216.

[6] Walter Wangerin Jr., *As for Me and My House: Crafting Your Marriage to Last* (Nashville: Thomas Nelson, 1987), 166.

Chapter Eight: Courage: Engaging in the Struggle

[1] David J. Garrow, *Bearing the Cross: Martin Luther King Jr., and the Southern Christian Leadership Conference* (New York: William Morrow, 1986), 58.

[2] Ibid., 60.

[3] Some say courage should be considered a subset of faith, not an independent virtue. I have no problem with that position. The example of Martin Luther King Jr. shows the tight inter-connection of the two. In faith, King looked to God, and from that action, courage followed. Chapter 11 of Hebrews—that great chapter on the faith of God's people—is a story of their courage, the outgrowth of their faith. When faith turns to action as we discussed in chapter five, courage is there as its offspring. Faith and courage are always found together as parent and child.

[4] C. S. Lewis, *The Screwtape Letters* with *Screwtape Proposes a Toast*, rev. ed. (New York: Macmillan, 1982), 137-8.

[5] Oswald Chambers, *My Utmost for His Highest* (Uhrichsville, OH: Barbour, 1963), 339 (December 4).

[6] Roland Bainton, *Early Christianity* (Princeton: D. Van Nostrand Co., 1960), 91 ff.

[7] Scott Peck, *The Road Less Traveled* (New York: Simon Schuster, 1978), 17.

[8] Winston Churchill, *The Unrelenting Struggle* (London: Cassell, 1942), 276.

[9] Quoted in Warren Bennis and Burt Nanus, *Leaders* (New York: Harper Perennial, 1985), 45.

[10] Chambers, 167 (June 15), 295 (October 21).

[11] George Herbert, "The Elixir," quoted in Gilbert Meilaender, *Working* (Notre Dame, University of Notre Dame Press, 2000), 115.

Chapter Nine: Self-control: Denying Self for Christ's Sake

[1] Robert Andrescik, "America's Pastor Speaks to Men," New Man, January/February 2002, http://www.newmanmag.com/a.php?ArticleID=1582.

[2] See, C. S. Lewis, *Mere Christianity,* supra., 80,94 ff.

[3] See Michael Novak, *Business as a* Calling (New York: Free Press, 1996), Chapter 5.

[4] Paraphrase. The actual words, "Quarry the granite rock with razors, or moor the vessel with a thread of silk, then may you hope with such keen and delicate instruments as human knowledge and human reason to contend against these giants, the passion and the pride of man." Quoted in J. Budziszewski, *Written on the Heart*, (Downes Grove, Ill: Intervarsity Press, 1977), 182.

[5] C. S. Lewis, *The Abolition of Man, or Reflections on Education with Special Reference to the Teaching of English in the Upper Forms of Schools* (New York: Macmillan, 1947), 33-34.

[6] Ibid., 34-35.

[7] The idea of self-control acting as a wall to free us to make wise decisions comes from Michael Novak, *Business as a Calling.*

[8] Many of the ideas in this section are taken from Watchman Nee, *The Spiritual Man,* (New York: Christian Fellowship Publishers, 1977), vol. 2, 106 ff.

[9] Chambers, *My Utmost For His Highest,* 167 (June 15.)

Chapter Ten: Justice: Being Fair to All

[1] Quoted in Josef Pieper, *The Four Cardinal Virtues* (Notre Dame, IN: University of Notre Dame Press, 1966), 64.

² Paraphrase. The actual quotation read "charity" rather than "love." "Love" in 1 Corinthians 13, *King James Version*, is translated "charity." The quotation is found in William Bennett, *Our Sacred Honor* (New York: Simon and Schuster, 1997), 313. It is taken from a letter from Rush to John Adams in 1811.

³ John Piper, *Desiring God* (Sisters, Oregon: Multnomah Books, 1996), 29.

⁴ Ambrose Bierce, *The Unabridged Devil's Dictionary* (Athens, Georgia: University of Georgia Press, 2000), 184.

⁵ Deuteronomy 15:1-3 explains that debts were to be canceled every seven years. Thus if someone lent money to another person near the "year of release" (v. 9), he had little chance of getting the money back.

⁶ "Dred Scott v. Sandford, Mr. Justice McLean Dissenting," Touro Law Center, http://www.tourolaw.edu/patch/Scott/McLean.asp.

⁷ This idea came from Richard John Neuhaus.

Chapter 11: Love: Seeking the Best for Others

¹ Robertson McQuilkin, *A Promise Kept: The Story of an Unforgettable Love* (Wheaton, IL: Tyndale, 1998), 21-23. Muriel died September 19, 2003.

² The Twelve Steps are as follows: (1) We admitted we were powerless over alcohol—that our lives had become unmanageable. (2) Came to believe that a Power greater than ourselves could restore us to sanity. (3) Made a decision to turn our will and our lives over to the care of God as we understood Him. (4) Made a searching and fearless moral inventory of ourselves. (5) Admitted to God, to ourselves and to another human being the exact nature of our wrongs. (6) Were entirely ready to have God remove all these defects of character. (7) Humbly asked Him to remove our shortcomings. (8) Made a list of all persons we had harmed, and became willing to make amends to them all. (9) Made direct amends to such people wherever possible, except when to do so would injure them or others. (10) Continued to take personal inventory and when we were wrong promptly admitted it. (11) Sought through prayer and meditation to improve our conscious contact with God as we understood Him, praying only for knowledge of His will for us and the power to

carry that out. (12) Having had a spiritual awakening as the result of these steps, we tried to carry this message to alcoholics and to practice these principles in all our affairs.

[3] Brennan Manning, *The Ragamuffin Gospel* (Sisters, OR: Multnomah, 2005), 51.

[4] John Feinstein, *The Punch: One Night, Two Lives, and the Fight That Changed Basketball Forever* (Boston: Little, Brown, 2002), 342,346.

[5] Augustine, *Confessions* (England: Penguin Paperbacks, 1986), 99.

[6] Jeffrey Marx, "He Turns Boys into Men," *Parade,* August 29, 2004, http://archive.parade.com/2004/0829/0829_coach.html. Marx has written a book about the same subject, entitled *Season of Life: A Football Star, a Ballboy, a Journey to Manhood* (New York: Simon & Schuster, 2004).

[7] This quotation appears on a wall mounting in the Auburn Sports Museum.

[8] Anthony Campolo, *Seven Deadly Sins* (Wheaton, IL: Victor, 1987), 18, emphasis in original.

[9] C. S. Lewis, *Mere Christianity,* rev. ed. (New York: Macmillan, 1952), 116.

[10] Oswald Chambers, *My Utmost for His Highest* (Uhrichsville, OH: Barbour, 1963), 132 (May 11).

[11] G. K. Chesterton, *What's Wrong with the World* (San Francisco: Ignetius Press, 1994), 37.

Introduction to Part 3

[1] Douglas Southall Freeman, *R. E. Lee: A Biography,* vol. 4 (New York: Scribner's, 1935), 278.

[2] Edmund Burke, "A Letter from Mr. Burke to a Member of the National Assembly in Answer to Some Objections to His Book on French Affairs," 1791.

[3] Charles Colson, *Against the Night: Living in the New Dark Ages* (Ann Arbor, MI: Servant, 1989), 67.

[4] "Planned Parenthood of Southeastern Pa. v. Casey, 505 U.S. 833," 1992, II, FindLaw, http://caselaw.lp.findlaw.com/scripts/getcase.pl?court=US&navby=case&vol=505&invol=833&friend=oyez.

[5] Walter Lippman, *A Preface to Morals* (New Brunswick: Transaction Publishers, 1999), 326.

Chapter 12: Character in Government

[1] John Winthrop, "A Model of Christian Charity," Hanover Historical Texts Project, http://history.hanover.edu/texts/winth-mod.html. The spelling of the quotes has been modernized.

[2] *To Bigotry No Sanction: George Washington and Religious Liberty* (excerpts from *George Washington and Religion* by Paul F. Boller, Jr., Southern Methodist University Press 1963) (Burke, Va.: The Trinity Forum, 1997), 12.

[3] For the discussion in this chapter, I am indebted to several sources: Os Guinness, *The Great Experiment* (Colorado Springs, CO: NavPress, 2001); James W. Hutson, *Religion and the Founding of the American Republic* (Washington, D.C.: Library of Congress, 1998); Mark Noll, "Evangelicals in the Founding," in James W. Hutson, ed., *Religion and the New Republic* (Lanham, MD: Rowman & Littlefield, 2000); and Paul Johnson, "God and the Americas," *Commentary*, January 1995.

[4] On the proposition that the Founders believed religion was necessary for free government, see Hutson, *Religion and Founding,* 62,81.

[5] Guinness, *The Great Experiment,* 140.

[6] Ibid., 141.

[7] Ibid., 146.

[8] Ibid., 148.

[9] Ibid., 144.

[10] Ibid., 152. At another time, Madison stated, "The belief in a God All Powerful, wise and good, is so essential to the moral order of the world and to the happiness of men, that arguments which enforce it cannot be drawn from too many sources" (Hutson, *Religion and Founding*, 96).

[11] Guinness, 151.

[12] Hutson, 148.

[13] Ibid.

[14] Alexis de Tocqueville, *Democracy in America,* quoted from Guinness, *Great Experiment*, 164-7.

[15] Ibid., 167.

[16] Cited in John C. LaRue, "Myths We Tell Ourselves," Your Church, May/June 2001, http://www.christianitytoday.com/yc/2001/003/15.88.html.

[17] At http://www.bartleby.com/124/ pres 13.html in the second paragraph of the Address.

[18] Quoted in Hutson, 80-81.

[19] Ibid., 76.

[20] Abraham Lincoln, "Meditation on the Divine Will," September 1862, in *Abraham Lincoln: Speeches and Writings, 1859–1865* (New York: Library of America, 1989), 359.

[21] Abraham Lincoln, "Second Inaugural Address," March 4, 1865, in Ibid., 687.

[22] Arthur Taff, "Unspeakable Ethics, Unnatural Law," Duke Law Journal, Vol. 1979: 1229-1230.

[23] In a speech made at the University of Notre Dame, 2000. Quoted in the *Wall Street Journal,* date unknown.

[24] Dissenting in Santa Fe Independent School District v. Doe (2000).

[25] Johnson, *Commentary,* 30.

[26] Ibid., 30-31.

[27] Russell Kirk, *The Conservative Mind: From Burke to Eliot,* 7th ed. (Washington, D.C.: Regnery, 1995), 472. This book was originally published in 1953.

[28] Richard John Neuhaus has emphasized this point repeatedly.

Chapter Thirteen: Character in Business

[1] *The Wealth of Nations* was published in 1776, the year of American independence. It's interesting to note that our economic liberties and our political liberties were born at about the same time.

[2] Michael Novak, *This Hemisphere of Liberty* (Washington D.C.: The AEI Press, 1990), 70.

[3] Peter F. Drucker, *The Practice of Management* (New York: Harper & Row, 1954), 37.

[4] Thomas Watson, Jr., *A Business and Its Beliefs* (New York: McGraw-Hill Book Co.), 4-6.

[5] Ibid.

[6] Quoted in James C. Collins and Jerry I. Porras, *Built to Last: Successful Habits of Visionary Companies* (New York: HarperBusiness, 1994), 59.

[7] The Company's Mission and Values Statement reads:

Protective Life Corporation

Mission and Values

Protective Life Corporation provides financial security through insurance and investment products. Our purpose is to enhance the quality of life of our customers, our share owners, and our people. We hold to three preeminent values—quality, serving people, and growth—which by tradition and choice transcend all others. They are the foundation and growth—which by tradition and choice transcend all others. They are the foundation of our aspirations, our plans, our best energies, and our life together in this Company.

Quality

The heart of quality is integrity. Quality is the cornerstone on which all our activity rests—quality products, services, people, and investments. We strive for superior quality and continuous quality improvement in everything we do.

Serving People

Serving people begins with being worthy of their trust. We believe we are at our best when we value and build upon the diverse talents, backgrounds, and insights of all people. We find our ultimate reward in serving these three groups:

- **Customers:** Our customers come first. Our success as a Company depends upon our ability to respond to the needs of the many different types of people we serve as customers. We prosper only to the extent that we create long-term relationships with satisfied customers. We do so in discerning their needs and responding to them; in providing high value, distinctive products; in prudent investment of policyholder funds; in systems, information, and counsel which help our customers solve problems; and in prompt, accurate, innovative, and courteous service which is the best in the business.

- ·**Share owners:** Our share owners provide the equity essential for our success. We are stewards of their investment and must return a profit to them. Profit is essential for implementing our commitment to quality, serving people, and growth. It is a critical measurement of our performance. Our objective is to rank at the top of the industry in long-range earnings growth and return on equity.

- **Protective people**: The accomplishment of our mission depends on valuing and leveraging our many differences and on building a community based on trust and teamwork. We want our people to enjoy their work and take pride in Protective, its mission and values. We are committed to opportunity and development for all to help us fulfill our potential; open, candid communication; the input, initiative, and empowerment of all people; the recognition and encouragement of one another; and creating a place where a zeal to serve our customers, share owners, and each other permeates the Company.

Growth

The keys to growth are resourcefulness, passion, and persistence. We are dedicated to long-term growth in sales, revenues, and profit, not only for our share owners, but also because it contributes to personal growth and development of Protective people. We achieve growth through innovative marketing, superior service, and acquisitions. Growth is critical for improving quality and serving people. It is essential to maintaining a position of strength in our marketplace and attracting and retaining high-caliber people.

Our mission and values can be summed up by our belief that, Doing the right thing is smart business.

[8] Five Cardinal Principles for Building Quality:

Focus on the customer.

Continuously improve.

Equip, empower, and liberate people and trust their capability and willingness to improve quality.

Concentrate on the long term, the whole process, and the team. Use statistical analysis to understand and continuously improve the process.

[9] Lord Griffiths, "The Business of Values," Speech at the Peter F. Drucker Graduate Management Center of The Claremont Graduate School, 1996, 8.

[10] Ibid., 26.

[11] Ibid., 25-26.

[12] Ibid., 48.

[13] For a general discussion of Deming's contribution to the Japanese management philosophy see David Halbertstone, *The Reckoning* (New York: William Morrow, 1986), chapter 17.

Chapter Fourteen: Character in Leadership

[1] John C. Maxwell, *The 21 Irrefutable Laws of Leadership* (Nashville: Thomas Nelson, 1998), 17.

[2] The distinction between authority and power is discussed in Anthony Campolo Jr., *The Power Delusion* (Wheaton, IL: Victor, 1986), 11-12. As Dr. Campolo points out, this idea in turn comes from sociologist Max Weber.

[3] Sam Walton, *Made in America* (New York: Banton Books (1993), 316.

[4] This story is recounted in Os Guinness, *When No One Sees* (Colorado Springs: NavPress, 2000), 41-43.

[5] Jim Collins, *Good to Great: Why Some Companies Make the Leap ... and Others Don't* (New York: HarperBusiness, 2001), 12-13. As part of his study, Collins also contrasted each of the eleven companies with a company from the same industry that possessed comparable opportunities and resources but failed to make the shift from good to great. The study found a consistent lack of Level 5 leadership in the comparison companies.

[6] Ibid., 21.

[7] Douglas Southall Freeman, *Lee*, 584. <u>supra</u>.

[8] Ibid., 586.

[9] Ibid., 585.

[10] John Wooden with Jack Tobin, *They Call Me Coach* (Chicago: Contemporary, 2004), 104.

[11] Quoted in Collins, 61.

[12] G. K. Chesterton, *Heretics* (Ripon, Yorkshire, UK: House of Stratus, 2001), 100.

[13] For steward leaders of nonprofit organizations, the goal should be to provide excellent, measurable results in attaining the group's purpose. Often there is a resistance in nonprofits to being measured. This attitude represents a default of responsibility toward those from whom the group seeks donations. After all, the donor is one of the groups for whom the nonprofit exists. Further, like an investor in a business, the donor is accountable to God for the resources he invests in the nonprofit.

[14] Warren G. Bennis and Burt Nanus, *Leaders: The Strategies for Taking Charge* (New York: Harper & Row, 1985). It's interesting to note that, in comparing the external qualities of the leaders they studied, Bennis and Nanus found their subjects shared only one characteristic: Almost all were still married to their first spouse. "And not only that: They were also indefatigably enthusiastic about marriage as an institution" (25). Bennis and Nanus wrote *Leaders* in 1985. I seriously doubt a similar study would reach the same finding today. The deterioration of the family ethic in this nation may be the most disturbing negative trend of our generation.

[15] Jim Collins and Jerry Porros, *Built to Last* (Harper Business 2002), 53.

[16] John D. Beckett, *Loving Monday: Succeeding in Business without Selling Your Soul* (Downers Grove, IL: InterVarsity, 1998), 52.

Conclusion: One by One, from the Inside Out

[1] This does not apply to such entities as the military and law enforcement agencies, which do play a role in character formation.

[2] This thought is from a *First Things* article. (I have not identified it.) I think it is in Number 113.

[3] I recognize, with sadness, that not all children are fortunate enough to have parents who are prepared to instill good character in them. Sometimes extended family members or other adults (such as Sunday school teachers) can help. And thus sometimes children have stronger character than did their parents.

Notes

[4] George Barna, *State of the Church: 2005,* 51.

[5] Dallas Willard, *Renovation of the Heart* (Colorado Springs: NavPress, 2002), 23-252; See also Dallas Willard, *The Divine Conspiracy* (New York: HarperCollins, 1998), 140.

[6] Act 95-313, 1995.

[7] Philip K. Howard, "Class War," *Wall Street Journal,* May 24, 2005.

[8] Milton Friedman, "Free to Choose," *Wall Street Journal*, June 9, 2005.

[9] Ronald Reagan from a speech entitled *Let the People Rule* delivered to the Executive Club of Chicago, September 1975.

[10] Samuel F. Smith, "America."